Happy Birthday
Mummy

Joseph and Sebby

THE GOURMET GARDENER
BOB FLOWERDEW

13/7/07

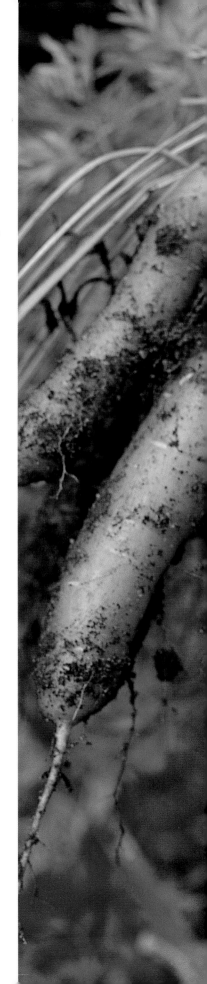

THE GOURMET GARDENER
BOB FLOWERDEW

everything you need to know
to grow and prepare the very
finest of vegetables, fruits
and flowers

KYLE CATHIE LTD

Dedicated to Vonnetta Angeleta, my dear wife who endures my writing every morning, even on our honeymoon, mind you then only the morning...

First published in Great Britain in 2005 by
Kyle Cathie Limited
122 Arlington Road
London NW1 7HP
general.enquiries@kyle-cathie.com
www.kylecathie.com

Published in paperback 2007

ISBN 978 1 85626 723 6

Senior Editor Kyle Cathie
Design and art direction Geoff Hayes
Photography Pete Cassidy
Copy editor Sharon Amos
Proofreader Penny Phillips
Indexer Alex Corrin
Production Sha Huxtable and Alice Holloway

A Cataloguing In Publication record for this title is available from the British Library.

Colour reproduction by Sang Choy
Printed and bound by Tien-Wah Press, Singapore

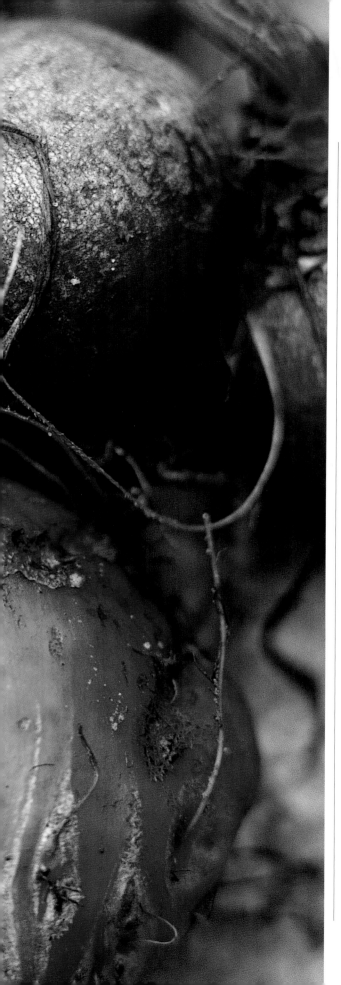

CONTENTS

introduction

Growing your favourite – superbly,
and becoming your own greengrocer
and delicatessen

This is gardening for the gourmet, for the lover of fine flowers and perfumes, fresh clean tastes and exquisite and unusual flavours, and for the gourmet who is also a gardener. It is about growing the most uniquely excellent to enjoy for yourself and not 'for show'. Not about huge for size's sake, but rather about plump and luscious. About growing the most superb fruits, divinely scented flowers and other scrumptious things to eat. Gardening as purest self-indulgence. But there is a price.

Now a certain minimum degree of effort is always required, and usually more effort means better results – especially with gardening, where if you put in more, the results magnify and expand much more than proportionately. Try it; just give one plant a large piece of ground and do nothing else and it will flourish magnificently. Or go further and prepare the site well, give it extra water, liquid feeds and foliar sprays and you will soon rival Jack and his beanstalk. But we can't, and shouldn't, give everything such lavish treatment. After all, we may not want giant beans in gross surplus too high off the ground to pick. We need to adopt different measures depending on exactly what we are after and which plants we choose to concentrate on.

I myself became consumed by gardening simply through searching for top-quality fare for my table. I just couldn't get really fine fresh ingredients without growing them. I soon realised that high quality was attainable only if you not only grew each crop but also actually grew some of them rather well. Many flowers and crops proved little effort to grow successfully, but others have long proved

more demanding. Much of the time most of us are content to get a fair return for our labours, and we often cut corners, not minding if the yields drop a bit or if everything is not quite perfect in appearance. But we can do better! I'm sure like me you have your favourites; those plants on which you dote and lavish your attention. They flourish under your care. This book is about choosing to concentrate in a similar way on the choicest crops and flowers and to produce these to a higher – a gourmet – level of perfection.

Home-grown always beats shop-bought in both freshness and variety, but some comestibles are more degraded by transit, delay and commercial culture than others and are particularly worth growing yourself if you appreciate the finest.

Opposite Peppers growing in a greenhouse – the odd hole or damaged leaf does not matter when we are after quality in another part of the plant.
Left Hard red onions lifted and spread to dry and ripen off, before storing for winter use.

Likewise you can have tasty heritage varieties and even rarities never seen for sale, as many of nature's once common delights are now ignored entirely. If you grow at home you can enjoy the finest at its best, when you wish to. You can extend the season and have your favourites available for even longer in the year. You can have them all year round by freezing, drying and turning them into conserves, sorbets, liqueurs and confections of all descriptions. And you can enjoy the pleasures of discovery, as you grow varieties never seen in the shops and trial many different ones until one day you find exactly the finest for you. Ah, but there's still another waiting that may be better yet.

You love strawberries, sweet peas or sweetcorn – then grow a garden full of your own favourite varieties to perfection, and you may not be happier but you will be more content. And why not? After all, no effort can be too great for your favourites when they reward you so lavishly. So we can use skill to grow such superb flowers, fruits and vegetables as can never be bought. Freshness and culture affect everything, and you can only really ever know for sure how old a crop is and how it has been treated if you grew and picked it yourself.

As gourmet gardeners we can grow for taste, not for sheer economic production. Most of all this enables us to choose our varieties freely, not being too concerned over yields but concentrating on matters of taste and flavour. With any plant, the variety affects the result far more than anything else. If you want yellow tomatoes or scented pink roses, you'd better sow and plant yellow tomato seed and scented pink rose bushes. True gourmets will relentlessly search till they have tried every variety of their favourite foods and, for the gardening gourmet, grown every fruit, flower and vegetable. And then they must try every related and similar contender. Only then can they be sure they are growing the best or the finest-flavoured.

But where to start? I've selected first those I think the very finest to concentrate on. Everything must be superb, but then some – such as sweetcorn, raspberries and asparagus – are so much more

As gourmet gardeners we can grow for taste not for sheer economic production.

Opposite Squeaky beans, as I like to call them.
Above Grapes from the garden are a real treat.

affected by freshness, variety and conditions than others. Some, such as bay leaves, rosemary or garlic, are little different when shop-bought, so perhaps these need no special attention – unless they are your enthusiasm. As there's no accounting for tastes, alternative choices and options have to be proffered. I can only indicate those finest and choicest varieties that I have found to grow for myself and the ways and means to improve their quality and season, and those rivals for their throne that deserve investigation. Of course you will go further – in such a book as this there is no space for the myriad details that the true aficionado will take pains with; I can only point you in the most profitable directions.

There are books by the handful covering every aspect of culture of almost every cultivated plant and, once the bug has bitten, you will be well repaid for consulting these about your favourites. And then although I am a gardening gourmet I also wear another hat once I reach the kitchen – that of gourmet chef: after all, one's interest cannot stop with the production of a fine comestible; it has to follow through to the table. So everything else on the table has to come up to the same high standard. The true gourmet needs not only to grow almost everything but also to learn to store, preserve and turn into a home delicatessen all those fine products from the garden. Let your exquisite new potatoes have fresh mint sauce, pickled beetroot and piccalilli worthy of accompanying them.

Any gourmet must grow almost all the culinary herbs, as without them no dish is complete and it's so hard to find satisfactory ones in the shops. Although so many are required, they are fortunately compact and undemanding. To follow these there are many delicious salad leaves that give us so much piquancy and zest as we start each meal; these take much more care to grow well and need a dedicated salad bed if they are to thrive. Vegetables require the most effort on the gardener's part, as they are necessarily grown on a larger scale, but they also offer a tremendous range of delights for the enthusiastic gourmet and are again all so much better when home-grown. The tree or top fruits demand some skill and space to grow really well but come in varieties numbering thousands for the gourmet to try. Then there are the currants and berries: strawberries, grapes and other soft fruits are amongst the most divine of nature's treats and few of any quality are ever in the shops, yet they're so easy to grow well. But I'm not forgetting flowers; we must always consider the pleasure we get from these. Not for their beauty – that is adequately covered in so many places. No, more for their perfume, which we may enjoy as an aperitif on an evening stroll before a meal, or for enhancing the table or room.

Well, in the following chapters I've chosen my favourites from over the years, and I'm pleased to introduce you to them and to the methods that work with them for me; I hope you'll get on famously. But remember to concentrate on that favourite or two and grow those to an even higher degree of perfection than I suggest. I've chosen mine and extolled them at length, and then suggested the numerous other gourmet delights you may find appealing and worth investigating; I hope that soon some of them will grace your eye, table and palate. *Bon appétit.*
Bob, Norfolk, IP21 4NL, UK

chapter 1 one size does not fit all

Growing only the most excellent for flavour, freshness and quality. Using different growing techniques depending on which crops we choose and what we are after

We gourmets may well wish for variety and fortunately this is easy to satisfy, as there are vast numbers of different flowers, fruits and vegetables to grow and enjoy. Garden centres sell more types of seed and plant than most of us can cope with. A few mail-order catalogues and you are overwhelmed. Of course, as the years pass and you become very keen, you'll find there are specialist catalogues devoted just to your favourites. And there are myriad traditional and heritage varieties not sold commercially but available to you if you join various clubs and societies.

The very keen gardening gourmet will also probably want crops and flowers much earlier and much later in the season. We all want enough crops for our needs. But record yields and huge sizes are not ends in themselves; though ideally each, and possibly every, crop is wanted at its very, very best.

Sadly, life is not ideal. Gardening books are necessarily written from a certain standpoint: to produce prize-winning exhibits; to grow crops as a living; to feed a family from a small plot; to fill borders with flowers; or whatever. Although a whole book could be written on almost any single plant and its culture, for brevity authors must often recommend the same general treatment for all. Of course, some gardeners employ exactly that – the same treatment for every subject. And for the bulk of plants you can probably get away with such a course; over generations we have inadvertently selected many of our garden plants simply because they're usually reliable and require little special care or effort. So we may grow a wide range of

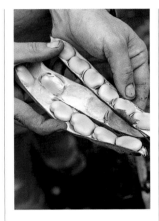

plants relatively well by some rather sloppy methods. However, some need a little more care, and others reward extra-special attention with supreme quality.

Controlling texture and taste

What we want as gourmet gardeners is not one attribute but a combination of size, texture, taste and, most of all, variety and freshness. Such variables are altered dramatically by where and how plants are grown, the soil and the climate. In hot dry places many flowers and crops grow well given sufficient water. They may grow equally well in cool, wet places but their colour, flavour and texture in the two situations will never be the same. I repeat, all plants vary tremendously in their attributes and ease of culture, depending on where and how you garden. True, you can grow almost anything anywhere with enough effort, but I doubt you will ever have a quality gourmet crop if too much effort has to be devoted to simply growing it at all.

If you examine your situation and soil, and grow well what already grows fairly easily for you in your area, then life will not become too fraught. A crop should be basically attainable before we set out on growing it to gourmet quality.

A crop should be basically attainable before we set out on growing it to gourmet quality.

Above Grapevines in pots are very productive and allow you to squeeze far more varieties in the same space.
Right Watering is probably the most crucial thing you can do to improve quality.

The gardener has many tools and methods to help boost production. We can usually improve the soil to suit any given plant – and for the gourmet, flavours and perfumes are usually best when plants are growing in the ground rather than in containers. However, the soil can be a big hurdle. Some plants do better in heavy and some in light soils; some in acid, some in alkaline. One soil type and one treatment for the vegetable bed and the flower border will not suit all. And for some crops a poor soil simply will not do, so we must use containers and a suitably balanced and enriched compost.

Containers can be very convenient, especially for small gardens with little soil space. Containers may also 'dwarf' or restrict plants to some extent, which can be helpful with fruit trees, for example, where their natural form is too large for our requirements. Containers also allow us a longer season: plants may be moved into warmer or cooler conditions, to bring on or retard their growth as wished. And we can control feeding and watering more accurately.

Seasonality is still important to gourmets: crops grown in the middle of their season nearly always taste the finest, while those forced at the extremities are often rather poor by comparison. But then half a loaf is much better than none...

Just add water
We have various ways and means of altering the soil a plant is growing in, the air, warmth and light it receives, and the way we treat it – and these all alter the qualities of the crop and when it matures. But of all these variables, water is probably most crucial. Only a few plants produce better-quality crops when running into drought. Equally, excessive moisture may raise yields fantastically while ruining eating and storing qualities. And erratic watering just spoils everything. Watering and feeding must be very carefully attended to, depending on the stage of growth and the weather, if really magnificent crops – especially melons, for example – are to be obtained.

Overdoing the feeding
Just as more water leads to lush but relatively poor-quality growth, so does over-fertilisation. Excessive

fertiliser makes crops large but ruins their quality; for example, flowers that 'blow' and mould, potatoes cooking black and cabbages smelling rank when boiled are all suffering from the results of too much unbalanced fertiliser. I advocate organic techniques, but you can just as foolishly over-stimulate plants with organic fertilisers as with artificial – and raw chicken manure can kill almost anything! Ensuring sufficient fertility is vitally important, though actually fairly easily achieved by the traditional method of adding well-made garden compost or well-rotted manure in generous but not ridiculous amounts. To get the sweetest or most succulent and tasty crops sometimes requires extra fertility of a more specific nature. Enriched composts, top dressings and natural plant feeds can be given to boost the background fertility of the most valuable nutrients at crucial stages of growth, rather than keep them constantly too high or low.

Optimum growth and the finest flavours are best enhanced by preventing stresses, checks in growth and elemental nutrient shortages. Good methods cure the first two and the easiest way to prevent the third is by regularly applying seaweed products – such as seaweed meal and calcified seaweed – to the soil, and a well-diluted seaweed solution as a foliar spray throughout the growing season. These seaweed products are rich in trace elements and act a bit as vitamins do for us.

Forcing the issue
Although we can't change the climate most of us can now easily force crops, either *in situ* with soil-warming cables (the modern hot bed) or by moving plants in containers to somewhere warmer, such as a cold frame or greenhouse. This can extend the season by months for some crops. The use of raised beds and salad beds angled to face the sun can start the season much earlier and give plants hotter, sunnier conditions – a superb way of raising earlier salad crops and strawberries. Likewise, growing successional crops in sunken and shady beds gives a succulence and prolonged season unachievable on the flat.

The microclimate of a wall can be used. The extra

The use of raised beds and salad beds angled to the sun can start the season much earlier and give plants hotter, sunnier conditions.

Above Cloches extend the season, keep plants clean and enable us to grow a whole range of crops that would be too tender otherwise.

heat and shelter making crops earlier or sweeter on the sunny side, while the shady side can be used to grow crops later than usual, or for more acid flavours. The best extension of season and the greatest improvement in conditions come about when you grow under cover. This might be with temporary cloches, an unheated greenhouse or – real luxury – a heated greenhouse or conservatory. Very enthusiastic gourmets can use extra lighting as well as heating to extend radically the range and variety of what they can grow.

For fruit, what was once called an orchard house is particularly useful – an unheated greenhouse or plastic tunnel for ripening fruits in containers. With this method the plants are grown healthily outdoors for as long as possible (and to save space) and then moved temporarily under cover to prevent damage to the crop by birds or weather. And by doing so successively we can greatly extend the season for some fruits, getting cherries, grapes and peaches to ripen months earlier. However it must be noted that the improved reliability of growing under cover is offset by reduced acidity in the fruit, which can mean potentially poorer flavour and texture unless care is taken to avoid excessive close warmth – most subjects need plenty of ventilation!

With fruits we also have the additional opportunity to improve results vastly by carefully pruning the wood and thinning the fruits. This applies not only to fruit but also to flower culture, especially when we are after fewer, bigger, better-quality blooms. Flowers respond like fruit, and many shrubs and roses can easily be made to produce fewer, bigger, choicer blooms at will.

Coming up for air

We can't prune most vegetables but we can give them space and cultivate them in various ways to ensure their quality, for example by improving the soil and watering frequently with the right water and suitable feeds. As theirs are such brief lives, extra treatment is even more essential for them than for the perennials. The most important factors for healthy plant growth are firstly air, light and water and after them nitrogen (N), phosphorus (P) and potassium (K), followed by legion trace elements and nutrients. And when flavour and texture are valued, then all these become crucial. Even though it's unseen, airflow is as important as the other factors: if insufficient air is flowing over the plants, they cannot get enough carbon dioxide to grow strongly. And in stagnant conditions they usually get moulds, rusts and mildews. Be careful as your garden ages that the relentless growth of trees and hedges does not imperceptibly reduce your sunny site to a dank shady hollow.

When and how to water

Water makes up more than four-fifths of every plant and is essential if plants are to grow succulent and sweet. Many fungal problems, especially mildews, are initiated when the plants get too dry at the roots while damp stagnant air hangs around their (probably overcrowded) heads. In this case, sprinkling or spraying on water is worse than leaving them to suffer: it increases stress and makes them even more vulnerable to disease. Wet plants are easily snapped, and touching them spreads diseases. Do not walk among wet plants and never run their leaves or flowers through your hands, nor pick flowers or fruits when they are wet. Water is the easiest essential factor to add to a crop, and in most areas much better quality and yields can be gained by one good application of

We can't prune most vegetables but we can give them space and cultivate them in various ways to ensure their quality.

water, at the right stage, than by almost any other change you can make to otherwise satisfactory growing conditions. Obviously, poor conditions like low light or compacted soil need improving first, but once the general conditions are favourable then watering is more effective than fertiliser for most crops and especially for flowers.

More plants probably do badly from under-watering than from almost all other causes put together. In times of strong growth it is almost impossible to over-water plants in the open ground. (Under cover in pots in winter, the opposite is true.) In the open ground we can improve the soil's water-holding capacity with more humus and conserve winter rains with mulches. We must learn to water well, especially before sowing, with newly emergent seedlings and transplants, and for most crops when their flowers are just setting. Never give everything a little and often, or wet large surface areas, as the water mostly evaporates. Soak water down to the roots with a funnel, buried pipe, pot or trench, inserted beside each plant to speed up watering – water can be sloshed in to percolate down slowly.

In pots and containers keeping the soil or potting compost moist but not waterlogged is difficult – and near impossible with some modern peat-substitute composts. Daily checking by feeling the weight of the pot and testing the compost with a thumb is essential. In hot drying weather you'll need to do it more frequently. Equally essential, always drain pots well afterwards. They are best watered by being stood first in trays of warm water and then drained off, wetting the compost upwards and the stem base last, if at all, to prevent undue rotting.

For large numbers of pots, drip irrigation works well as it delivers adjustable amounts, but it is fiddlesome to set up. On benches you can use simple capillary matting fed from a reservoir. However I don't trust these much, and I don't trust underground hoses that seep water to the roots at all – they are near impossible to keep an eye on. Nothing beats the personal touch with a can of, preferably pre-warmed, water. For most plants past seedling stage, use the butt not the tap.

Top Spraying foliar feeds such as seaweed makes the plants stronger without making them 'run to fat'.
Above Liquid feeds must be very well diluted to feed the plants rather than burn their roots.
Opposite Young leeks being trench irrigated as they cannot be over-watered.

The lowdown on liquid feeds

Liquid feeds may also be added with the water in weak dilutions for plants confined in pots and many others. This makes all the difference to crops that need rich conditions. But bear in mind that different plants need different feeds at different stages of their growth. In general, heavy feeding is at odds with the organic gardener's desire to avoid soluble fertilisers. Organically we foster our soil micro-organisms without using anything that may damage them, and soluble fertilisers are too strong.

Conventional fertilisers are measured by their ratio and content of soluble nitrogen (makes leaves grow), phosphorus (makes roots grow) and potassium (makes fruits grow). These used to be thought of as plant foods replacing the elements taken away by the crop. And while these elements do exist as similar chemicals in the soil solution, it is not natural to have them in very high concentrations as in conventional fertiliser granules. This simplistic chemical idea is a bit like feeding your kids cooking oil, sugar and flour; they'd do better with it cooked and mixed with other things. Well, we can make feeds from natural ingredients that provide a proper feast for our plants rather than just a few elements.

Even so, these feeds must be exceedingly well diluted with water until they are close to the natural soil solution in strength, i.e. the weaker, the better. Such feed is best given a little and often, and never if the plants are not growing strongly or are under any stress, for example from cold or low light. Liquid feeds are most important for plants with restricted root runs confined in containers and unable to reach further afield for nutrients after they have used those in the compost. They may be used in moderation to enrich the soil of hungry plants in open ground, such as leeks, celery, tomatoes and sweetcorn, and for encouraging spring greens and salad leaves to grow more vigorously, especially in slow springs.

Most sources of liquid fertility can be grouped under N, P and K in the same way as chemical fertilisers, though they work better when blended together to provide an even wider range of micronutrients. Mix several of a similar type together, and dilute further.

> Growth and root feeds are higher in phosphates, promote root growth and have an important role in creating full flavours and good textures.

Growth and leaf feeds

Growth and leaf feeds contain proportionately more nitrogen and are the most generally useful. They are used most in spring, for almost everything; in summer they are used for salad crops, spinach and greens; but they are rarely applied, and only very moderately, late in the year to avoid plants making soft growth that won't survive the winter. Growth and leaf feeds with initially high nitrogen levels soon break down and lose their value; they need making up fresh and using quickly.

Make borage tea by rotting down lush borage leaves under water, producing a highly nitrogenous concentrate that smells, works (see below) and looks like urine; it is especially good for the hungriest feeders such as melons and brassicas. Soot water from fresh clean plastic-residue-free soot is rich in nitrogen and full of other mineral goodies; it is extremely good for pineapples, carnations and citrus plants.

Manure soup is made by hanging a fine net bag of raw animal manure in a barrel of water. The resultant soup is obviously variable depending on the dung used and may also contain phosphate, making it useful as a root feed. It must be very well diluted to avoid burning roots.

Human urine is rich in nitrogen, with significant amounts of potassium and other nutrients, and it's free. The first of the day is most valuable! Dilute it down at least fifty to one and it's an excellent feed, especially for citrus. If you can't bring yourself to use it on the soil, put it on the compost heap. Never apply it neat and do not use yours if you take antibiotics or hormones, and so on. Stale urine is considered superior by the 'old boys' but really whiffs too much.

Growth and root feeds

Fish emulsion is likewise a very rich source of nutrients and also very whiffy. It is an excellent liquid leaf and root feed as it is rich in phosphorus and other minerals too. Growth and root feeds are higher in phosphates, promote root growth and have an important role in creating full flavours and

good textures. They are especially valuable to crops such as strawberries, roses, turnips and sweetcorn. Fish emulsion is probably the best, with manure soup second. Datura tea is also effective, made from thorn apple plants (*Datura stramonium*) pulled well before flowering and rotted under water to make a tea rich in phosphorus.

Flower, fruit and flavour feeds

Flower, fruit and flavour feeds are high in potash (potassium compounds), which promotes flowering and fruiting and increases disease resistance. It also has the most profound effect on flavour, especially with many fruits, onions and potatoes. Comfrey tea is a good source and this is one of the commonest liquid feeds made. Comfrey leaves are solidly packed into a bucket or barrel, weighed down with a brick and covered with water with some urine (optional), added to promote their breakdown. A fortnight later the leaves have dissolved, leaving little fibrous residue and an evil brown tea. This tea is a well-balanced feed similar to commercial tomato feed, with considerable potassium and generous nitrogen and phosphate. It must be diluted at least forty or fifty to one for use and is better fresh than aged as it loses some of its goodness with time.

Wood ash or lye water is dangerously caustic when strong but easily made and very rich in potassium. Put about a spadeful of wood ashes, preferably fresh from clean wood, in a bucket and carefully mix in water. After it has stood for a day or two pour off the lye and store in plastic (well-labelled as undrinkable) bottles; it will keep. Dilute lye by one hundred to one. (The residue ash should be added to the compost heap; if watered on, the fine nature of the ash will block the pore spaces in potting composts.)

Foliar feeding

Seaweed solution is high in potassium and also rich in every other element. However, it is expensive and best reserved for foliar feeding, where its effects are profound. Foliar sprays are just feeds applied through the leaves. They must be even more dilute than liquid feeds to avoid burning the foliage. They

should be made with tap water in most cases and never applied in full hot sun or late in the evening. Most of the liquid feeds can be used for foliar sprays, though obviously some are just too unpalatable when the residue is left on edible leaves. Seaweed solution is by far the best. It acts somewhat like a vitamin or a catalyst and the effect on plants is rapid and marked; they become greener and healthier and resist both pests and diseases better. Apply it year round and frequently, but very diluted – to at least a hundred to one on the usual strength sold. It can be watered on as a liquid feed at up to twice that strength. Seaweed solution also stimulates the soil micro-life and is a very good way of improving diversity and population. It can be sprayed throughout the growing season directly on to the ground or potting compost at the liquid feeding strength. I spray everything at least once a month from early spring with seaweed solution – including my hair!

Stinging-nettle tea spray is claimed to make plants more resistant to disease and is quite high in nitrogen if freshly made from young lush nettles. Equisetum tea spray has to be made from the chopped dried plant and boiling water, just like real tea. It is high in silica and believed to make plants much more resistant to pests and diseases.

Top dressing

There is another way to feed which is a bit more organic and essential for perennials in pots (especially once repotting is no longer an option). Top dressing involves mixing relatively insoluble but rich fertility sources in with the topmost layer of soil or compost. These break down slowly, releasing fertility over time so rarely give unwelcomely high salt concentrations – unless they get cold and wet, when the ammonia so formed can poison young plants. Like liquid feeds, top dressings should be used only in warm bright conditions. Because top dressings are slowly incorporated by micro-organisms they do not leach as readily and are fairly long-lasting. They can be applied at any time but most are best put on in spring – though some may be applied when plants are brought under cover in autumn. As with liquid feeds, they are best blended

Below Lime and other rock dusts being spread and raked in so they don't blow away. Note – bad boy Bob with no health and safety measures!
Opposite Spreading a mulch. Mulches work in many ways – adding fertility, keeping the soil moist and suppressing weeds.

together to broaden the supply of nutrients and to suit the crop and time of year. Nitrogen and phosphate sources are generally more useful in spring and summer and sources of potassium in summer and autumn.

Rock dusts

Many top dressings are ground rock dusts which are very, very slow-acting sources of natural fertility. Rock dusts are most effective on poor sandy soils; heavy clays have plenty of the same nutrients in an already finely divided form. Rock dust can also be added to the compost heap to great benefit – the right conditions and microbes help incorporate it into the compost.

Most dusts can be applied at any time but a still day stops it blowing away and light rain will wash it in, saving raking. Never inhale rock dusts, as they are dangerous to health. To avoid doing so, you can mix them to a slurry and then shake from a brush. Or mix them as top dressings with other damp fertilisers and composts.

Using manure

The traditional mixed fertiliser is animal manure. Animal manures contribute tremendously to soil fertility and for some crops are almost essential. Never use them raw. They should always be well composted first to break down pathogens and harmful compounds, which cause rank growth and ruin flavours.

Commercially composted manures are available in many varieties. Also sold are animal by-product fertilisers such as bone meal. Avoid inhaling them, as these too are slightly hazardous, but they are excellent sources of many nutrients that improve quality. The most commonly applied nitrogen-rich growth and leaf dressings are the manures. In order of preference, horse comes first as it is probably the cleanest; sheep and goat are sweet to handle; cow muck is less pleasant; and pig is vile and often contains unacceptable pollutants. Rabbit and pet droppings may be included in the compost heap but cat and dog litter is best buried under ornamentals. Poultry manures are very highly nitrogenous and rich in potash and need composting with other wastes, but once processed they are excellent.

More top dressings

Hoof and horn meal is basically toe-nail clippings, hair and feathers – all are slow-release sources of nitrogen especially good for hungry plants. Soot from fires where no plastic has been burnt has some value as a fertiliser once mellowed with age, but is especially useful for darkening the soil surface and making it warmer.

Cocoa husks make an expensive mulch on their own but are useful in binding other looser mulches, such as ground bark, together. The husks smell deliciously of chocolate, but soon rot and form a soggy cardboard-like mat which is excellent at suppressing weeds and slowly adds nitrogen to the crops, while the surface discourages slugs; therefore they are good in potting composts and for mixing in top dressings. Seaweed dried and ground into meal contains all trace elements and significant nitrogen and potassium. With a bit of

added ground rock phosphate or bone meal, it makes a well-balanced general feed and is excellent for improving flavour. Blood, fish and bone meal is the traditional balanced feed. It performs well, but many people find it's not very pleasant to handle; however it's very effective and one of the fastest-acting. It must be used moderately and well mixed in immediately or it attracts vermin and cats.

High-phosphate growth and root dressings

These especially suit sweetcorn, woody plants, turnips and roses. Some of these must be included in all dressings for container-grown plants. Bone meal is an excellent source of phosphates, containing about a third by weight. The more finely ground it is, the faster-acting it is. I cook dinner bones on the barbecue then pound them with a brick to make my own. Ground rock phosphate is a rock dust that encourages healthy roots – ideal for strawberries and roses.

High-potash flower, fruit and flavour dressings

These dressings are needed all year round as potash washes out of the soil easily. They are best applied more heavily in early summer for the fruits, but apply in spring to growing vegetable crops. Wood ashes are the best source of potash, so save them from bonfires and wood-burning stoves. Mix the ashes into the soil and compost around growing crops, especially fruit and onions, for ripening and disease protection. Ground rock potash is rich in potassium but very slow to act. Especially useful on light soils and in wet areas, it is always appreciated by gooseberries and culinary apples.

Lime is another essential element in the vegetable patch and for stone fruit such as plums. It is the most important source of calcium and sweetens and improves most soils. Garden lime is just that – the native ore, more or less, as it is graded, washed and ground. Builder's or slaked lime is burnt and hydrated and more caustic; unslaked or quicklime is fierce dangerous stuff; none of these is used where garden lime or chalk is called for. Dolomitic lime has significant magnesium content and so is doubly useful. Calcified seaweed is the very best source of lime as it contains all the trace elements.

Old mortar rubble and plaster are good sources for recycling their lime content. Lime is especially beneficial for some vegetables and in a crop rotation system it is usually put on with peas and beans. These precede the brassicas which need lime in quantity.

Ground rock basalt and granite are beneficial to most soils and composts. They contain a spread of minerals that encourage micro-organisms, and their use is claimed to revitalise worn-out soils. Clay naturally consists of similarly finely divided minerals and is superb added to light soils where roses grow badly or where crops grow weakly without flavour. It can be incorporated into the compost heap or made into a slurry and flicked with a brush on to the soil or compost surface.

Compost as a top dressing

Compost, that is, sieved garden compost, is probably the best top dressing of all. Rich in nutrients and micro-life, and dark in colour, it improves soil texture and fertility, plus it boosts the water-holding capacity. It's brilliant stuff. However,

Left If compost is worth making it's worth making well. And sieving it improves it for handling and makes it quicker to break down and incorporate.
Opposite page Compost spread under the plants is probably the very best mulch you can use.

chemical fertilisers. Any freshly bought, or even home-made, compost is far better than garden soil for sowing or potting or growing in a container. The exception is freshly composted loam made from a rotted down stack of turves of grass; the fine root system and soil granules make a good top dressing or compost base once chopped and sieved. Other nutrients can be added to make it richer for more demanding plants.

Composts for sowing and potting

For actually sowing in pots it makes sense to buy the best sowing compost, such as a John Innes No 1, as so little is needed anyway. For more valuable or difficult seedlings, pot up into John Innes No 2, or other top-quality potting compost. Stronger-growing and more robust plants can be potted up into John Innes No 3 or into sieved and enriched garden compost. I use this last for almost all my plants with a little added lime or extra nutrients for those that need it.

For plants permanently in containers you need a similar well enriched compost. A John Innes No 3 formula based on soil is heavy and helps keep plants standing upright; it does not dry out so disastrously as peat or peat-substitute composts. Once again for flavour I recommend sieved garden compost, but make it drain well by adding some sharp sand. And to ensure freedom from weeds, most containers are best topped off with a sterile mixture of sharp sand and peat or similar. Or you can make up a sterile home-made potting compost using the following recipe. Start with peat or a good substitute, like coir – leaf mould is best though some composted barks can be nearly as good. Mix three buckets of it with one of sharp sand. This mix will aerate and drain freely but contains little plant food. Add one bucket of compost from a worm bin or worm casts, or three buckets of sieved garden compost, or a measure of a balanced organic fertiliser. The latter is the best option if you want a weed-seed-free mix. I have used a balanced mixture successfully for years, made as follows: for every four two-gallon buckets of peat and sand mix, I add 3oz (75g) of calcified seaweed, 4oz (100g) of blood, fish and bone meal, 4oz (100g) of hoof and

Rich in nutrients and micro-life, and dark in colour, sieved garden compost improves soil texture and fertility, plus it boosts the water-holding capacity.

it is full of weed seeds – but that's no matter. Just hoe, pull or mulch out the seedlings – they will add to the fertility as they rot.

Compost is a good top dressing on its own and the best base into which to blend all the others. Once mixed, sprinkle it on liberally and make sure it is watered or raked in. Enriched composts can be made with high levels of desired nutrients for use on particular plants and also for potting most crops. Well-made sieved garden compost can be even better than many commercial composts for potting and growing, and the crops grown in it taste superb. However, if you don't make garden compost – or your own is poor – then buy the best leading brands of sowing and potting compost and use those. But for the gourmet the taste won't usually be as good as using garden compost. Of the bought composts the John Innes formula ones based on sterilised loam are better than most others, which are based on peat substitute or peat, sand and

horn meal and 3oz (75g) of wood ash. I use it immediately and, although not perfect, it is better than many cheap brands. Those who wish to spurn animal by-products can replace those ingredients with the same amount of seaweed meal, but it is not quite as strong, so pot up generously.

Making more and better garden compost will give you potting compost for free and make your crops taste superb. Because of the range of materials we put in our compost heaps, garden compost contains an amazing spread of nutrients and micro-life and is the favourite feast for almost all plants. You can never make too much compost; and all manures and other fertilising substances used in the garden are even better after being composted together before use. Fresh manures contain soluble nutrients which overwhelm the plants and make them 'fat' and sickly. Once stacked, turned and composted, the raw ingredients meld into a rich soil-like mass full of fertility but not so strongly active and safer for plant roots.

How to make compost

The composting process can break down almost all natural materials, but lumps of meat, bone or fat should probably be disposed of elsewhere. Likewise thorny material and diseased material is better burned. Weeds in seed can be killed by putting them in the middle of a hot heap. Or drown them in a bucket of water for a few weeks first, along with weeds with roots. Otherwise almost everything that has ever lived can be composted, especially if well chopped and mixed up. Obviously it is better if the process is quick and produces a good rich material suitable for use as described.

There are many different ways to compost and almost all are rather slow. Ideally the ingredients are accumulated in bulk fairly quickly and then mixed together. It may then cook in only a week or so but will still be best after three to six months, maturing. Composting works best when there is a mixture of many different things plus plentiful air and moisture. Large amounts of dryish material need fresh green material to balance them and vice versa. Water needs adding during mixing and

should have urine in it to improve the 'cooking'. Lime and wood ashes should also be added, especially in areas with acid soils, to make a sweeter, better-balanced compost – but remember not to use this on any lime-intolerant plants. If a good mix is made, no activator other than urine in the water is needed, but any animal manure will greatly improve the speed and efficiency of the heap. Or use seaweed, or blood, fish and bone meal. Another good activator is sievings from previous compost heaps. If you are starting your first heap ever, then get a bucketful of good compost from an 'old boy' to mix in.

Keeping the heat in

It's very important to keep the heat in a compost heap, so insulate it thoroughly. Many different compost containers are on sale, but most are too small, too badly insulated and too expensive. Four old wooden pallets tied at the corners and stuffed with cardboard make a good bin. Make a roof to keep out rain and have a 'duvet' to keep the mass warm and moist – plastic bags full of shredded newspaper do well. As you start to build up the heap, mix the materials well but do not pack them down. Mix them again later to introduce more air. In every case better compost is made when the new heap is rebuilt after a week or two, with the inside material swapping places with the outside of the heap. Repeating this again is not essential but radically improves quality by mixing the ingredients with even more air which then 'cooks' the materials further. (Commercial rotary composters claim to speed this up but I've found them ineffective in cold climates with the usual mix of garden ingredients.)

Once a heap has been made, turned and cooked, leave it to ripen for six months to a year. You can use fresh compost as a mulch or dug into the ground when planting, but for use as a top dressing or for potting it is better partially dried and sieved. Remove the sides of the bin but leave a waterproof roof on; after a few months the mass will be dry enough to push through a sieve and be ready to use. This extra effort produces a cleaner, uniform potting compost and base for top dressings, and the sievings are ready to inoculate your next heap.

Above A compost heap needs to be dried out after it has cooked so keep it covered with a plastic sheet. **Opposite** A shovel full of chicken litter will make the compost heap cook.

Problems and solutions

The commonest composting problems are making the heap too wet or having too much dry material. Both are cured if you remix and add the right sort of corrective. A white mould usually means the heap is too dry and has insufficient nitrogen, so mix in more water and urine or wet manure. Stinging nettles are good for improving any heap!

Letting worms do the work

Generally bigger heaps work better: collect more waste and you will feed your garden for free. At the other extreme, if you have only a very little material to compost, then try worm composting. This system is suitable for anyone with almost no garden space and little waste. The materials need chopping up finely and are fed to red brandling worms, the sort you find under a plank or magazine laid on wet ground. Keep them in a container such as a plastic dustbin, in a warm shed or garage. The bin should have drainage holes and a drip tray to catch the liquid feed (a manure soup) that drips out – and to allow air in. The worms slowly convert waste to worm droppings, which are best added to potting composts or used as top dressings. They are exceedingly rich in all plant foods and too strong to use on their own as a potting compost.

Left Let the worms do the digging – you can't go six feet deep.

> If you have only a very little material to compost, then try worm composting.

Making a snailery

A snailery is a similar way to convert small quantities of waste. Confine snails in a moated container – a container set within a tray filled with water – so they cannot escape. Give them some old pots and pipes to live in, feed them green wastes and wash their droppings out of the bottom of the container; then use these as a liquid feed or blended with top-dressing mixtures.

You can also utilise any of the above products to make an enriched compost that gains extra nitrogen from the air, to give a very strong dressing material. Stand a perforated plastic container such as a laundry basket in a drip tray to catch the surplus liquids. Fill it with alternate thin layers of lime-rich compounds – such as coarse chalk, lime, calcified seaweed or eggshells – and nitrogenous wastes, such as raw manures, blood, fish and bone meal, hoof and horn, feathers or seaweed meal, sprinkling freshly sieved garden compost generously over each layer. Activate the pile by pouring neat urine, borage tea or fish emulsion on top and then cover to keep the rain off. Each day recycle the contents of the drip tray back on to the top of the heap, adding more urine or tea as necessary. After several months to a year the pile will become an extremely nitrogen-rich compound for use well-diluted in top dressings and potting composts.

Green manures

Another way to grow more flavour and fertility is with green manures. These are simply home-grown compost materials, mostly grown when the soil is otherwise empty over winter, or sown and dug back into the soil as seedlings after only a few weeks' growth between crops. Anything that will grow – especially through winter – could do, but most of the recommended plants are for farmers with ploughs and are too tough for gardeners to kill off. It is better to grow several short-lived batches rather than one long one, anyway.

Legumes are best as they fix nitrogen, which is always in short supply. But remember the aim is to sow, grow and dig in – or cut off and compost – not to let the flowers set, as then the nitrogen is lost. Tough growths will need several weeks of breaking down in the soil, so cutting or pulling and composting elsewhere is the most convenient method. But soft succulent green manures can be composted *in situ* under an opaque plastic sheet. Beans and peas of any variety may be used, but only the hardiest will over-winter and in the vegetable plot they will have to be fitted into the rotation. Sweet peas are less problematical. Lupins are more useful and special green-manure varieties are sold, though garden ones will do nearly as well. Red clover is good as it is effectively an annual and does not cause weed problems like other clovers. The poached egg plant (*Limnanthes douglassii*) is one of the best green manures as it's hardy over winter, very good at keeping down weeds and easy to get rid of afterwards – if some plants are left to flower they attract bees and hoverflies.

Two salad plants, miner's lettuce (*Claytonia*) and corn salad (*Valerianella*) are excellent green manures to fill beds over winter as they can be cropped as well. Afterwards they are easily composted under a plastic sheet as they are so succulent. Fenugreek is another legume to use, and as it's not a vegetable it won't cause problems with

Below Young green manure seedlings, rich in nitrogen, can be dug in at this stage and another lot sown to do the same.

crop rotation. It's good for summer green manuring as it's quick, but it's no good in winter as it's killed by frosts. Buckwheat is another quick-growing summer green manure and if some is left to flower it's a good attractant for beneficial insects. *Phacelia tanacetifolia* is also very attractive to beneficial insects and makes a good summer green manure especially, as it is very easy to clear. Mustard is very quick to grow but being related to brassicas it must be used with care in the vegetable bed and should be grown only to the seedling stage, then immediately incorporated.

Unless you want a lot of work for little return, avoid Hungarian grazing rye, winter tares and vetches, fodder radish, most clovers and trefoils as green manures. In fact, you're better off with weeds. Many weeds accumulate different minerals and trace elements even if the soil is deficient in them. Because weeds are so successful at grabbing minerals they make very bad neighbours for our plants, but in the absence of other plants weeds are good green manures. Once they have been cropped, more nutrients can slowly dissolve from mineral particles to replenish the soil solution and what the weeds have taken can then be returned by composting to boost that naturally low level.

Nitrogen is the most important nutrient for gourmets wishing for succulent growth so it is best to regularly incorporate flushes of young growing seedlings into the soil, especially those that are rich in nitrogen, like the legumes mentioned above. Phosphorus is accumulated by fat hen, corn marigold, purslane and vetches and especially by the thorn apple (*Datura stramonium*). Potassium is accumulated by chickweed, chicory, fat hen, goose grass, plantain, purslane, thorn apple, tobacco plants (*Nicotiana*) and vetches.

Calcium is accumulated by buckwheat, corn chamomile, corn marigold, dandelion, fat hen, goose grass, purslane and shepherd's purse. Sulphur accumulates in the alliums, brassicas, fat hen and purslane; silica in plantains, couch grass, stinging nettles and *Equisetum*. However, although collecting these weeds for composting enhances its

Using well-made humus-rich compost, made with seaweed and weeds full of trace elements, makes the soil throb with life.

value, most, particularly the last three, are too pernicious to deliberately encourage in the garden. Controlling weeds is one of gardeners' most important tasks as they rob our plants of nutrients. Ironically, once in the compost heap they provide the natural fertility we need for our choicest crops.

Using well-made humus-rich compost, made with seaweed and weeds full of trace elements, makes the soil throb with life. The micro-life that proliferates on this feast is not just abundant but varied too. The profusion of different forms and all their interactions creates the fertility our plants enjoy. Basically plants imbibe all the waste products of the decaying bodies and excrement of the micro-life. This enables the plants to grow healthy and strong, and shrug off many pest and disease attacks. However, if you start to apply excessive amounts of nitrogen-rich material or use too strong a liquid feed too often, especially the growth and leaf type, then you can push plants into soft lush growth. Lush growth is less able to resist attacks, so be moderate, apply feeds little and often, never heavily.

Above left Snails disposing of surplus courgettes turn them into valuable droppings.
Opposite Make the little devils work for a living – put in garden wastes, take out fertility.

Dealing with pests and diseases

The gourmet gardener need not worry unduly about the majority of problems but it's useful to know how to deal with the commonest effectively. Many books are written on eliminating pests and diseases but these are more for commercial producers. Few of the many possible problems ever really bother the home producer for one single reason. We eat and process our produce and are not under pressure to produce identical, perfect yet immature replicas to sell to shops and consumers. As the majority of damage to crops is most often superficial and affects its appearance rather than the yield or eating quality, we win. We peel and cook most of our crops and the odd hole or blemish or weird shape is not of earth-shattering importance.

A few problems face us all, and it helps to keep these under control where we can. Here they are, in order of damage done in lost potential crops and spoilt quality at the point of consumption.

The weather. Well, we can do what we can but this beats us all. We can try to improve the microclimate but we can't make the sun shine. We can, however make it rain – by adding water!

Birds are probably the biggest controllable problem. They steal seeds, seedlings, leaves, flowers, buds and fruit. Netting is the only solution – forget anything else.

Slugs and snails bother everyone. I've found they are reluctant to climb over smooth rings cut from plastic bottles or copper sheet; likewise they avoid barriers of soot, wood ashes, crushed baked eggshell, cocoa shell or sawdust. They can be lured to slug pubs, pots full of fermenting beer, in which they happily drown themselves. (Unfortunately, useful ground beetles also drown, so provide some twigs to help them climb out.)

Slugs and snails can be trapped under buttered cabbage leaves, orange skins, wet carpet and upturned saucers, collected and destroyed. You can buy parasitic nematodes which you water on to the soil or compost to kill them most effectively.

Red spider mites cover shoots with fine webbing which repels sprays, and turn leaves yellow and desiccated, sucking the sap out with thousands of tiny pinpricks. They are most of a problem under cover, but keeping the air humid discourages them. Also try spraying often with soft soap and introduce the commercially available biological control *Phytoseiulus persimilis*, a predatory mite, which works well if introduced early in the attack.

Aphids are always a bother. They not only steal sap but then waste most of it, producing a sticky sweet residue that falls on the leaves where it turns mouldy, doing more harm than their original theft. They spread viral diseases and cause leaves to curl, especially near tips. There are many different aphids. Some are specific to only one plant; others attack many. Natural controls are the best, so use attractant plants like *Limnanthes douglasii*, buckwheat and *Convolvulus tricolor* to bring in hoverflies, ladybirds and so on to feed on the aphids. Use soft soap on heavy infestations. For aphids under cover there are many commercial predatory and parasitic controls available.

Whitefly are a big problem under cover. They are unrelated to those little moths you get outdoors on brassicas – but the same methods work for both. First thin out the flying adults with a vacuum cleaner – I'm serious, this works! Spray with soft soap and, under cover, introduce the commercially available biological control *Encarsia formosa*, a parasitic wasp, or one of the other predators available.

Caterpillars of all sorts bother all sorts of plants but rarely do they cause serious problems, except the cabbage ones. Hand picking works well but is tedious; the bacterial and fungal sprays are safe for us and soft soap works on the smallest ones. Those caterpillars with large adults, such as cabbage white butterflies, can be kept off the crop most effectively with fleece, which prevents them from getting to the plants although some may lay eggs where the leaves touch the fleece.

Ants do little direct harm save undermining some plants. However, they farm aphids, move them to better feeding grounds, and over-winter them and their eggs in their nests. They also farm other pests such as scale insects, whiteflies and mealy bugs. Non-drying sticky bands on trees and stems are a very effective way of stopping ants' antics. Standing container plants on bricks or stones in saucers of water keeps ants off too. Or put out some sugar, watch where they take it, then pour boiling water down the hole.

Scale insect attacks may occur on plants, especially those grown under cover or on walls. Basically scale insects are like aphids with raincoats. Soapy washes choke them and you can squeeze off minor infestations or buy in predators such as the Australian ladybird *Cryptolaemus montrouzieri* or one of the others available.

Nematodes or eelworms are not all harmful but some sorts build up and cause damage to crops. On potatoes they even form visible cysts on the roots. Organic soils enriched with compost suffer much less than overworked badly rotated ones – the many fungi in healthy soil control eelworms. *Tagetes* marigolds give off secretions that kill nematodes and can be planted as a green manure to help clear the soil.

Wasps are a mixed blessing; in spring and summer they hunt other insects in great numbers but when late summer arrives they eat our fruit and need eliminating. Set a trap by filling a bottle half full of water and some old jam, cap it with aluminium foil with a pencil-size hole to allow the wasps to crawl in but not to get out again. Hang plenty of these near ripening fruits to get the wasp scouts before they find the fruits and bring their friends.

Vine weevils and similar are beetles with very long snouts that eat round bits out of the edges of leaves. More harm is done by their grubs, dirty white maggots with brown heads, which destroy the roots of plants. Vine weevils are very effectively controlled with a parasitic nematode available commercially which you water on the soil or compost. Stand plants in pots in saucers of water

Below A wasp trap – it's essential to catch the first scouts to stop them bringing their friends.
Opposite Red-skinned filberts, rarely sold commercially and ten times better when really, really fresh.

on stones, or bricks, to keep the adults away, as these cannot fly or swim, only crawl.

Only secure wire netting and well-fitting gates will keep rabbits out. Believe nothing else or lose everything. Moles: I'm sorry, nothing works. Kill them or drive them to the neighbours temporarily – they'll be back. Just gather the fine soil they leave for adding to potting composts or borders. Rats must be controlled with bait, and mice with traps, or they will destroy all your seeds, stores and even your clothes and wellies. Kill them before they kill you.

Two-legged rats are worse, protected by law with a permanent closed season. They have increased to plague proportions in some areas. Senseless vandalism, litter, arson and theft are more trouble than all other pests together. Big thick thorny hedges, locks and cunning are called for.

Diseases and stress

Diseases such as the mildews, both powdery and downy, and rusts mostly attack plants under stress. The commonest attacks happen when the plants are dry at the roots with damp stagnant air above, or when they are humid and get suddenly chilled, or dry and then wetted. Good growing conditions with plentiful water, air and light, seaweed sprays and high-potash flower, fruit and flavour feeds will do much to reduce mildew attacks. Sulphur and copper compounds, equisetum and nettle teas have some virtue but little really works – even modern

Below left Some may worry about the odd hole in the leaf but it won't do as much harm to the crop as a day of miserable weather.
Below Hoeing off weeds kills them off easily and quickly.
Opposite Hoeing – working forwards means you don't stand on something you didn't notice. I prefer to see where I'm going, not walk backwards as many books suggest. (Do remember to sharpen your hoe regularly.)

synthetic chemicals. Botrytis, or grey mould, is likewise very difficult to control even with chemicals, as it is nearly always caused by high humidity and poor growing conditions such as low light and cold. Improving airflow with drier conditions helps but warmth alone makes it worse.

Wilts and rots, bacterial and viral diseases are often combined together in attacks on plants though any single disease may occur alone, often starting with a cut, a bruise or frost damage. Hygiene, healthy growing conditions and prompt and ruthless action control these most effectively.

Viral diseases actually affect many, if not most, plants; fortunately plants have learned to live with most of them. Some are more virulent and can cause serious problems – be ruthless with plants that appear blotchy, mottled, streaked or sickly and dispose of them on the bonfire promptly. Always sterilise saws, secateurs and knives between working on each plant.

Dealing with weeds

Weeds are a continual problem and must be controlled because they compete with our plants so ruthlessly. They lose us more crops than many pests as the losses go unnoticed. In every case it is essential to destroy all perennial weeds before planting or sowing, and to control flushes of seedling weeds before they establish. As crops suffer most from competition when they are young and still establishing, then the sooner any weeds are removed the better. Just pulling them up is not a good idea, as this damages the roots of nearby plants and also removes too much soil to the compost heap. Far better to hoe regularly with a frequently sharpened hoe: once a week is right, once a fortnight is harder work and monthly is foolish. Among congested plants you'll have to hand weed with a knife, severing the weeds deep down or just slicing the smaller ones off at ground level. Mulches are of great aesthetic value, added to the humus content and, best of all, can save much work by suppressing small weeds so they never even get started. However, mulches are not so widely used where early gourmet produce is

required. Most permanent plantings benefit from mulches because they retain water, but bare soil throws up more heat for ripening fruit. For the gourmet, the latter argument more often holds sway. Also, mulching crops such as asparagus, sweetcorn and early potatoes delays harvest by stopping the soil from warming up quickly.

Woven or perforated plastic sheet may be used to help prevent weeds. This may be covered with a very thin layer of a dark loose material such as sieved composted bark but not so thick as to insulate the soil. Rake and level the soil really well first, tread firm, put the sheet down and then apply the mulch, sifting it to spread it evenly. Settle it down with a spray of water afterwards. A loose mulch without the sheet needs to be thicker to suppress weeds but then the insulating effect makes for later crops. Where this is no problem, the mulch has other benefits such as being cleaner than the soil – for example, mulching strawberries with straw. And of course you can use the insulating effect of a heavy mulch to extend the season – the mulched crop will ripen that much later. Most loose mulches such as straw, bark and muck break down and add to the fertility and humus of the soil and need annual topping up. Sand, gravel and pebble mulches do not break down but do suppress weeds and allow good air and water penetration. They also throw up warmth so are excellent for ripening mid- or late- season fruit which will also benefit from the cool moist root run under the stones. But they need topping up or careful cleaning to get rid of worm casts – unless a plastic sheet goes down first.

The worst problem of all

That's human fallibility. I put it last as it ought to be simple to deal with. However much we learn and no matter how hard we try, we can never get it right every time. And often when we do remember to do it, we have already missed the right time! So keep a diary throughout the years and write in it when you forget to do an important job on time. But make a note: to do that very job, in the first week you could do it. Then each following year you will have a reminder to prompt the action in good time.

chapter 2 the gourmet's most delicious vegetables

Vegetable delights and ways of improving them. The choicest perennial vegetables. The choicest annual vegetables

We gourmets can really indulge ourselves with the range and quality of vegetables that can be grown at home. Countless varieties of the familiar supermarket fare can be found, each with widely different tastes, colours and textures, as well as mini and giant versions. And there are scrumptious vegetables you can grow at home that you never see in the shops, such as salsify and scorzonera. But whereas herbs are easy to grow and saladings respond to space and water, vegetables take more skill – and some can be quite unforgiving.

Most saladings are quick to crop and are sown successively throughout the seasons, so any particular batch is not crucial. Vegetables are usually grown in larger quantities and from fewer sowings. In other words, the windows you have to hit are smaller and failure may be more of a problem. The failure of sage or parsley is a pain; the failure of sweetcorn or potatoes, a disaster.

Vegetables require the very best conditions to crop at all, let alone well. Many of them are highly bred plants being asked to perform unnatural acts. Some are biennials, such as onion, carrots, leeks, turnips, accumulating nutrients and energy one year so they can flower and set seed the next. However, we force them to grow luxuriantly and become good enough to eat before then. This makes them unstable: the slightest check to growth or bad growing conditions can cause them to bolt and come into flower prematurely.

Weirdest of all are cauliflowers and broccolis. We want a grossly distorted mass of undeveloped flower buds to stay immature and become huge and succulent, but the plant wants to turn this into a bushy display of stems, blossoms and seeds. Similarly, a cabbage is an enormous swollen terminal bud held in suspended animation. This makes these vegetables very hard to grow well – even in good conditions.

The vegetables we grow for their seeds – such as peas and beans – are easier, as they are doing exactly what they want to do, but they must still be given excellent conditions to produce a large or good-quality crop. Courgettes and sweetcorn come from hotter countries and cannot ripen in our short summers unless started off early under cover, but then they are not difficult as they too want to make fruits and seeds.

As gourmets, we do not just want a crop: we want a superb crop. For each vegetable we must regard each facet of culture separately. Freshness, the most important quality that can overrule all else, is particularly important for vegetables such as asparagus, artichokes, sweetcorn and peas and is simply had by growing your own rather than buying them. In others, such as cabbage, roots and potatoes, freshness may be slightly less important but variety and growing method can make a terrific difference.

As I said earlier, a gourmet can't grow every plant to a superb standard, only his or her favourites; the rest have to cope with adequate attention – but do not deserve neglect. I strongly recommend separate salad and perennial herb beds to especially suit

Opposite You can't buy a red cabbage like this with the protective 'farina' untouched.

these, and it also makes sense to have an improved plot for your choicest vegetables so they can be given the best treatment. And if you practise rotation in the garden, then the attention you give your favourites will also benefit other less-favoured crops when they come to use the same site later.

Choosing a site

A vegetable bed needs careful positioning and laying out if you wish for high-quality gourmet crops. It must be in full sun because few vegetables ever do well in any shade. Wet, low-lying sites should be avoided, as they may waterlog in winter and suffer frost damage in spring (you could use these spots for summer salad crops plus leeks and celery). The shape of the plot is most sensibly rectangular and it must be laid with the rows or beds running north–south so the sun can penetrate along them. If this means the plot needs to be askew to the whole garden, then surround it with triangular borders to make all 'square' and disguise it with screens of fruit and low hedges.

Keep moving

Even perennial vegetables must move every few years and all other vegetables need annual rotation around the vegetable plot. It's not necessary to divide the plot up into four quarters as shown in many books, slavishly following the potatoes, legumes, brassicas and roots example. What is crucial is not to follow year after year with the same crop or its near relations. Keep moving on to a fresh spot and don't return a vegetable to its original site for as long as possible. It also makes a difference which crop follows which. For example, potatoes do not happily follow brassicas or legumes if the soil was limed for them; onions should not follow potatoes as the 'volunteer' spuds (unwanted plants coming from tubers missed during harvesting) left behind disrupt and choke them.

Sticking roughly to the standard rotation makes sense, but it's not gospel and can be manipulated for convenience. Of course, the more elaborate your rotation and the longer the intervals before each crop returns, the better the results. This is simpler if you grow many unrelated plants in smaller amounts and if unusual crops such as flowers and strawberries join in for a few years.

Rotation is easier if you keep accurate records of what was grown where and when, and with what success. A record of the crop and position, its variety, sowing dates, treatment and performance will aid future planning. Permanently dividing the area into rows or plots makes records easy to compare.

Block and row planting are alternative ways of laying out crops. For those that need support, such as peas, rows have the advantage but are not essential. Rows waste rather a lot of growing space on the paths between each, which also get compacted and require digging. For most crops, especially those that are closely planted, such as baby carrots, block planting is more advantageous. Apart from saving space, it helps weed control: once the plants are half grown their foliage meets and excludes light from the soil, choking out weed seedlings. It also forms a favourable microclimate and prevents moisture loss.

Above Leeks enjoy the dampness of a trench while beet and swiss chard prefer the ridges.
Opposite Sweetcorn is best grown in a block to aid pollination.

Where netting or fleece is used to prevent pests from reaching the plants, rectangular block planting is obviously sensible. Raised or fixed beds make block planting easier. These are narrow beds interlaced with access paths, and rows can still be run down the middle if the beds run north–south. The ideal width is a comfortable four feet; you can reach in two feet from either side. Make the bed no longer than sixteen feet or you will be tempted to walk over it rather than around.

Raised beds

Fixed beds may become raised beds in time as mulches, compost and root residues build up. This has several advantages: as well as reducing bending, as the bed builds up the surface area increases, allowing not only some extra planting space but increasing aeration and evaporation. Crops will get an earlier start in the spring as raised beds warm up sooner; in winter, the crops atop are in slightly warmer conditions because cold air runs off like water. On the downside, raised beds dry out more quickly in summer and mulches tend to slide off or be pulled off by birds.

Shoring up the sides with planks or bricks reduces the growing area available, while the extra materials add to costs and provide hiding places for many pests. Simple humped beds do well with paths of packed soil between. A coating of sharp sand or crushed gravel on the paths makes surer standing and if later some gets mixed into the soil it does not matter.

On the whole the advantages of raised or fixed beds outweigh their problems. Their main advantage for the gourmet is the warmer, better aerated soil which really suits the tenderer vegetables such as courgettes, French beans and sweetcorn. Growing on the flat is perfectly satisfactory for the brassicas and roots and even preferable in a light soil. Some vegetables that need extra moisture will be dealt with later on with the saladings. Although almost all vegetables would love the moisture of a salad bed, some need firmer soil and most need more minerals than the saladings.

Making the bed

The vegetable bed needs to be well dug over, and as deeply as possible initially. It will do better with a heavier texture, with clay and with more long-term fertility, such as that provided by rock dusts and well-rotted muck or compost incorporated every few years. And although water is crucial it is not needed frequently once the plants are established, although it should then be applied heavily, particularly to vegetables in flower, such as peas, beans, sweetcorn, potatoes and so on.

Extending the harvest

Vegetables need extra fertility to do really well but we do not use heavy doses at any time as we want a long period of consistent growth without check and not just a flush of leaves. Many vegetable crops are started off in a seedbed, which makes it easier to look after them until they are big enough to go out. It's also a way of staggering the harvest. When a crop is transplanted it receives a slight check to

Left Rhubarb needs forcing to give succulent stems.

The golden rule is to give each and every plant a very generous amount of space if you want good results from any vegetable.

growth: the bigger the plant, the more noticeable the check. If one sowing of, say, cabbages is divided into three portions that are transplanted to their final positions ten days apart, each batch should mature successively later.

Successive crops can also be ensured by sowing in several batches over weeks or months and also by sowing different varieties that mature at different rates and at different times of the year. The fastest-maturing varieties of any vegetable are usually called 'earlies' and tend to produce less than the slower but heavier-yielding 'main crops'.

It is hard to extend the season for some vegetables much beyond their natural range, even by growing them under cover – broad beans, for example. Cloches and growing under cover always help extend the season a bit at either end but only a few crops can actually be 'grown' as such in winter – even with the aid of a hotbed and artificial lighting. But rhubarb and seakale can be forced in a warm dark place to give delightfully fresh produce in the middle of winter. And potatoes can be grown in tubs and containers under cover to complete year-round supplies. Almost all vegetables can be grown in containers but they nearly all need a big root run to perform well: in short, they give better tastier results from cultivation in open ground.

Two for one

Where space is limited you may wish to intercrop, that is, plant two crops together. You can plant both at once or add one later when a main crop has matured and left some ground spare while awaiting harvest. Take care not to overdo intercropping, as crowding can never give gourmet produce and dense crops compete even more fiercely for water and nutrients than weeds.

Some companion crops can be grown together as long as each has sufficient space and this can give exceptionally good results. For example, instead of three separate beds of peas, potatoes and sweetcorn, try three beds with all three crops in each. The same number of plants in total all give a higher yield when grown together. In each bed grow peas down the middle, flanked on either side with

Above left Surplus sweetcorn being dried for my chickens – why shouldn't they have gourmet treats too?
Above Do remember to make your access easy.

alternate sweetcorn and potato plants. The peas provide shelter for the other tender young shoots; the mulched potatoes keep the soil covered and moist, which the sweetcorn and peas enjoy, and none shades the others excessively. Combining crops also significantly reduces the damage from some pests and diseases. Brassicas surrounded by French beans suffer far fewer pest attacks and if French marigolds are grown nearby, countless pests are deterred from almost every crop.

Space is all

The golden rule is to give every plant a generous space if you want good results from any vegetable. Answering the needs, and tricks, of each vegetable then makes the difference between a good crop and an excellent one. And you have to adapt the method for each crop for yourself and your conditions. For example, in any book or on the seed packet planting distances are given for vegetables grown in rows to commercial size, but these can be varied depending on whether you want continuous production of small immature vegetables or a few large fully grown specimens. Methods also need adjusting according to soil type, fertility, watering regime, the time of year, and so on. And then the weather affects everything more than anything we do...

Whether a crop is worth growing at all is up to you, as taste is so personal. I have grown and eaten as many sorts of vegetable as I can find and I must admit a certain lack of enthusiasm for a few. Most of those were the more unusual ones; after all, they are unusual in many cases because they aren't that good! There are a few gourmet delights that are not common, perhaps because they've got a reputation for being difficult to grow – when they are actually simple if you are but patient. I've started with these first; they are all perennials and proffer the best value all round because they are all poor stuff when shop-bought, yet asparagus and artichokes are the very epitome of gourmet food. Next I highly rate sweetcorn which is noticeably less sweet but half an hour from picking! And then glorious new potatoes, including salad, chipping and boiling types. Legumes such as petits pois and flageolet beans come next, followed, in my estimation, by the gourds, pumpkins, squashes and other cucurbits, the culinary roots, brassicas in all their sorts, alliums, and others. Despite the loss of many old varieties there are still so many to choose from. I recommend a few but these may not be what you prefer. I repeat: it is always worth trying every different variety to find out what suits your soil, situation and taste.

the gourmet's choicest perennial vegetables

asparagus

Asparagus (*Asparagus officinalis*) is the greatest luxury crop of all; a gourmet such as I can barely imagine life without it. I love the fresh spears lightly cooked then coated with fine butter, or served cold wrapped with wood-smoked ham and a hint of lemon and black pepper, to say nothing of the aromatic soup. Asparagus is expensive to buy and home-grown is so much sweeter, as the spears lose freshness within hours of picking. You can enjoy a fresh home-grown spear raw, but never a shop-bought one.

Asparagus takes several years to build up a large enough root system and crown to throw good thick spears, but once it does it may crop for two decades, so it is essential to get a good variety and to start it off well.

It was traditionally grown in the vineyards of Beaujolais and seems to do well with grapes. The foliage is attractive so that asparagus can be grown in ornamental beds, but then yields are low. For the gourmet a permanent bed on its own is essential. It should be in full sun, with very well dug and enriched soil, lightened with sand and as much well-rotted organic material as you can find. The latter will help darken the soil and bring an earlier crop. The surface can also be darkened more by dusting with soot the month before the crop appears. The bed should preferably be raised and angled towards the sun or have ridges that catch the sun.

Sow asparagus seed *in situ* if possible or in pots under cover and transplant the seedlings as

Left Green asparagus (top) has more taste than white asparagus (bottom).
Opposite top Female asparagus have berries which some consider a problem but I think it just means free asparagus plants in the garden coming up everywhere.
Opposite bottom An asparagus plant with its thick brittle roots laid over a planting mound.

You can enjoy a fresh home-grown spear raw, but never a shop-bought one.

soon as they are big enough to handle. Otherwise buy one-year-old crowns and plant in early spring. Do this by draping their spaghetti-like roots carefully over a small mound in a trench. Space crowns a good stride apart each way and then cover and firm them down, avoiding the buds. Some people cram them in closer but then reap smaller spears – though more of them – and their bed is short-lived: you pays your money and takes your choice. For gourmet spears give them more space than seems plausible; you will be rewarded. I repeat: the more space you give them the bigger the spears. Water initially and weed well and be patient: do not crop for three years from planting, and then for no longer than six weeks each year.

In autumn remove the fern-like foliage once it has withered but leave ankle-high stumps. To warm the soil, darken its surface in late winter with a dusting of soot or finely-ground bark or similar, but do not mulch if you want early spears. You can force a plant or two much earlier with a cloche.

Frequent sprays of seaweed solution are a great boon to this crop, and top dressings of rich organic compost or fertiliser will be needed to maintain cropping in later years. In some soils a light watering of salty water really improves the crop and helps discourage weeds. The only problem is the pretty reddish beetle, or rather its miserable slug-like juveniles which eat up the foliage. Treat it with cunning; once cropping has started, cut all spears but leave one crown to fern

up immediately. Most beetles will then lay eggs on that one; once cutting of the other crowns ceases, cut that one back hard and burn the foliage immediately.

Ideally grow several before making up a big bed of one sort – though if you don't it doesn't matter as most are so similar it makes little difference. Plants that do not bear seeds are male, those that do are female; selected hybrid F1 seed produces all-male offspring. Most modern hybrids are all male and theoretically produce bigger yields. Personally I prefer female plants – as they give lighter crops but of the biggest, thickest, most succulent spears. As you can rarely buy just females you must sow or plant a mixture; then after the potential has been revealed cull all poor doers of any sex, ruthlessly.

Harvest all spears, leaving none to stand, especially not 'sprue' (it pays to eliminate and replace any plants that produce much sprue after the second year on). You can tell the difference between sprue and proper spears or new buds as sprue stays small and spindly, while new buds of decent crowns will be much fatter initially and grow away strongly, getting taller and fatter fast. Sprue plants remain runty even after a couple of years and need eradicating. Cut them off carefully to avoid damaging other buds nearby. Harvest spears while the dew is upon them or in the cool of the evening. And keep them cool. Do not stand them in water: this does revive flagging spears but makes them much poorer eating.

Green asparagus has more flavour than white blanched spears, which are had by heaping a really deep mulch over the crown. White spears are much preferred on the European continent and are

usually forced in dark plastic tunnels as well as being deeply earthed up. In the UK we go for the stronger flavour of the green spears which are grown in the open, exposed to the light. No special variety is required for either use though there are local selections and preferences. There are also purple-coloured asparagus varieties such as Purple Passion, though this coloration is mostly lost in cooking as the stems turn green.

There is a host of varieties but, as the flavour and texture are totally dominated by the effects of the season, soil and culture, no one variety is a better choice than any other. The best policy, as already stated, is to start off with many varieties eliminating those that don't do well for you. Most modern offerings are all-male sorts, which are still pretty good: Fantasy, Fileas, Franklim, Grolim, Jersey Knight Improved, Lucullus and Theilim. I still prefer the good, old-fashioned Connover's Colossal and Mary Washington, though Gijnlim and Limburgia are very good, and also worth trying are the newer polyploid varieties Limbras and Purple Jumbo. If asparagus is bitter it's probably not fresh or the plants are too dry – try boiling with a change of salt water. Steaming is the best method of cooking fresh home-picked asparagus. With either method the water makes an excellent soup base.

Asparagus aficionados should read A W Kidner's book *Asparagus* and search for seed derived from his Regal strain which could throw spears weighing a half-pound each!

globe artichokes

Globe artichokes (*Cynara cardunculus* Scolymus Group) are the second greatest gourmet vegetable. Their delicious succulence and meaty aromatic flavour is unique and soon lost. Those sold in shops are macabre relics compared with a sweet freshly picked head. And the gourmet can benefit from many fine varieties never offered for sale. Purple artichokes are even tastier than the green, though they may have small thorns on their bud scales; try Purple Globe and Violetto di Chioggia. The original wild form is intensely thorny with small heads that to me taste of chicken, but they are tricky to eat safely. The standard greens such as Green Globe and Vert de Laon are excellent. The best way to start off is to find someone with a choice selection growing really big tasty heads and get some offsets (thongs) from them – if you like their flavour. Otherwise procure offsets of any good stock and plant in early spring. Or sow seed in pots in spring and transplant out as soon as possible. Select the best of these after a couple of years of building up the plants to show their worth. Never leave any flower buds on to open – especially in the first year – as it seriously weakens the plants. Dig out inferior plants and propagate from the best croppers after the third year.

Give artichokes their own bed of well dug and enriched soil, preferably in full sun and kept moist. Plants need to be at least a stride or more apart to give good crowns and big heads and then may last five to ten years before needing replacing. They benefit immensely from thick mulches of loose material such as straw, bracken or coarse chopped bark and respond well to copious water.

Right One globe artichoke head going over and too tough, the other head immature.
Opposite top left Cardoon with its delicious flower for scent – but don't eat it.
Opposite centre Beautiful rhubarb stalks.
Opposite bottom right Rhubarb being forced in a wicker basket, too small, too short, too gappy - really no point. A dustbin without a bottom would do better.

Artichokes can be fitted into an ornamental bed where their flamboyant foliage and flowers are spectacular, but they crop less well there – especially if allowed to flower. Artichokes may be lost in a hard winter unless given some protection such as a pile of loose straw or a cloche. Slugs may damage the young shoots badly in spring. If aphids or earwigs infest the heads, soak them in salt water before cooking. Pick the buds when they have stopped expanding and well before they open – better early than late – and pick all heads. If you want flowers, grow an extra plant rather than risking the main stands. Any surplus heads can be boiled and the hearts can then be trimmed and frozen, pickled or marinated, or used on pizzas and in pâtés. Old shop-bought heads can be boiled in a change of salted water to remove some of their bitterness.

cardoons   rhubarb

The cardoon (*Cynara cardunculus*) is a very close relative of the globe artichoke and almost identical. The difference is it must be grown annually to produce a mass of tasty succulent stems and leaves. These are bound up and wrapped with sacking and newspaper in late summer to blanch their white hearts for winter use. Cardoons are a gourmet delight rarely found now, save in specialist French restaurants, and well worth the trouble of growing in the gourmet's garden. Sow them in early spring. You'll need all your skills to keep them growing fast and without check in very rich moist soil to make a succulent heart for blanching. Plants need to be at least a stride apart and are thorny brutes to truss up. If left to grow on, they make coarser growth in following years and cannot be cropped in the same way, though the youngest shoots can be blanched and eaten.

Rhubarb (*Rheum x hybridum*) is an eccentric British crop although some Anglo-Americans also enjoy it. Rhubarb crumble and custard is one of the all-time dishes of culinary fame (which is weird considering it was originally eaten to promote bowel movements). Rhubarb is the first 'fruit' of the year to crop and gives tasty fresh food when little else is available.

Not only is it reliable but there are an amazing number of varieties. Victoria is very good and the standard garden variety, Timperley Early is better for forcing; Glaskin's Perpetual can be grown from seed and pulled for longer before becoming too acid. Old varieties such as Cherry, Holstein Blood Red and Early Champagne are worth searching out for their different flavours and colours.

Nearly a hundred varieties exist and there are also a few edible wild species. Buy certified virus-free plants if you can, as these are much more productive. Rhubarb is happy almost anywhere and rarely suffers from pests or diseases. However, good crops of fat, sweet stems come only from new strong plants, so rework beds and plants every five to ten years and be generous with well-rotted compost each autumn.

Rhubarb plants need to be two good strides apart and kept generously watered; they also need a year or two to build up strength before cropping. Remove any flower stems before they set seed. Pull stems with a twist rather than cutting them, and stop cropping by midsummer, as by then the acidity becomes unhealthy. Do not eat the leaves, which are poisonous!

To force rhubarb, cover an old crown or two with a bottomless bucket, barrel or stack of tyres filled with loose straw or shredded newspaper. For successional cropping, start a new batch every other week or so to ensure a succession of small crops rather than one large lot. Add a lid to keep the rhubarb waterproof and dark. Piling up fermenting manure around a metal barrel brings the crop forward even sooner. In mid- to late winter you can even dig up a root, pot it up in damp sand and keep it in a warm dark place where it will produce long succulent stems. The root should be thrown away afterwards, not replanted. Rhubarb surpluses can be frozen, made into jam with ginger, or into a potent wine.

seakale

good king henry

Seakale (*Crambe maritima*) is a native seaside plant that is rarely grown. It produces a tasty and nutritious crop (similar to brassicas) in early spring. The cleaned blanched shoots are boiled and served with a hollandaise sauce or butter only in the finest restaurants and are rarely sold in shops. Seakale is attractive enough to be grown in ornamental areas but then crops relatively poorly. To get plenty of strong young shoots to blanch you must build up a good crown, which takes a couple of years. For best results, buy 'thongs' (basal side-shoots) of a good variety, such as Angers or Lily White. Alternatively sow seed in spring, growing on only the strongest plants.

Transplant the thongs or young plants early the following spring to their new bed. Set them a stride apart and grow them on for a year or two.

During dry weather in late winter place bottomless buckets or similar over a couple of crowns every fortnight or so. Fill them a foot or two deep with a mixture of peat, fine composted bark, coir or leaf mould, and sand. When the shoots appear, remove the bucket and filling. Harvest the blanched shoots and head by cutting them off back to ground level. Then allow the plant to grow and recover all spring and summer, removing any flower stems.

Seakale can also be more simply but less effectively blanched if you fill the bucket with loose straw as for rhubarb. Left to sprout again afterwards and leaf up, a crown may crop annually for many years, but you will benefit by reworking new crowns on a new bed every decade or so. As with rhubarb, a root can also be dug up and forced indoors with warmth in the dark and discarded afterwards. Use seakale quickly. Old or tough shoots may be boiled in a change of salted water to remove some of their bitterness.

Good King Henry (*Chenopodium bonus-henricus*) is also called Lincolnshire asparagus. The young leaves and shoots are delicious eaten like asparagus or spinach and in moderation in salads. They are never offered for sale but are a delicious gourmet treat you must grow for yourself. Good King Henry crops early in the year. It is a vigorous self-seeder so needs to be cut back to prevent it from becoming a weed. It is highly nutritious and thrives in damp rich soils; indeed it loves to be by ditches and ponds and will tolerate light shade. Sow *in situ* and thin to a foot or so apart, and keep the soil wringing wet.

jerusalem artichokes

Jerusalem artichoke (*Helianthus tuberosus*) tubers are tricky to scrub clean before cooking but are healthy, tasty eating – delicious as fries or in soups and savoury dishes. Despite a general disregard for them, they are an unusual delight for a gourmet. The tall, quick-growing plants reach way over your head each season and are topped with scented flowers. They make useful windbreaks in the garden – and seem to save the wind to release once you've eaten them. They are often relegated to some out-of-the-way corner where they do miserably; give them a rich moist soil in full sun and see the difference. Plant big tubers ankle deep and at least a foot apart in early spring. In windy areas stake them upright. The plants suffer no problems and need only water. The tubers wither quickly so keep best left in the ground: straw over their bed in late autumn so you can dig them unfrozen in deepest winter. Be sure to remove all tubers: any left will become weeds. A few improved varieties have smoother, larger tubers, such as Fuseau and Dwarf Sunray.

chinese artichokes

The Chinese artichoke (*Stachys affinis*) is a similar delight to the Jerusalem, only much smaller. Vaguely resembling a lemon balm plant, it produces abundant tiny spiral tubers. These are not very hardy so need either winter protection or saving under cover. Eat them like Jerusalem artichokes – they taste best when freshly dug.

earth chestnuts

The earth chestnut (*Bunium bulbocastaneum*) is a compact native umbelliferous perennial plant that produces small sweet nutty tubers on stringy roots. These must be gathered fresh, traditionally in May, thus the old saying. I grow it because the tubers make small but tasty snacks. Other than carrot root fly it suffers no problems.

Earth chestnuts are normally cooked in a broth after their skin has been scraped off; I used to eat a few of them raw whilst gathering, and baked in the ashes of a fire wrapped in buttered foil they are scrumptious.

mushrooms

Mushrooms are another perennial crop that the gourmet may show a great deal of interest in. You can buy straightforward kits for the usual shop-type mushroom. They may work out rather expensive per mushroom produced, but they are superbly fresh. Kits and spawn (sort of live 'seed') are also available for many other gastronomic fungi, such as ink caps, oyster mushrooms and shiitake mushrooms. Shiitake (pictured above) are the finest of all and are so expensive to buy that their kits look almost economical! Really fresh shiitake are fantastic, garlicky and delicious. All of these are grown on a medium such as compost, wood, straw or sawdust and work well only if you religiously follow the instructions for each type. For most, the critical thing is to get the ambient conditions perfect: a cellar or similar is ideal for constant temperature and humidity. I grew my best when I put a boxed kit in the bilges of a houseboat I lived on.

Many sorts can be grown under grass in the garden; peel back the turf by a sunny but damp hedge base and mix the spawn well into the soil, then replace the turf. If the conditions are suitable, then you will have a harvest; if not, not. Surplus mushrooms are very easily dried or frozen. As the stalks of mushrooms are tough, I save these up for making stock or soup.

Gently fry mushrooms in unsalted butter so as not to burn either; add salt, freshly ground black pepper and lemon juice immediately before serving.

The gourmet's annual delights

Quicker to crop, these offer almost instant returns for the gourmet's efforts. I rate all highly, but have put them in my order of preference. (Tender subjects – tomatoes, melons and so on – are covered in a later chapter as they just cannot give the highest quality reliably enough outdoors.)

sweetcorn

Sweetcorn (*Zea mays*) as such is uniquely Anglo-American and relatively unknown to most continental Europeans. The cereal maize is very similar but bred for the high dry-matter content of its seeds or as a green animal fodder and is never gourmet dining. However, sweetcorn, especially the new sweet, super-sweet, sugar-enhanced and other similar improved varieties, can be meltingly succulent and sweeter than most fruits. Although some new varieties do stay sweet for longer they still deteriorate rapidly. I often pick two cobs at the start of a walk round my garden with a friend and pick another pair at the end, and immediately cook all. The first pair are always slightly tougher and less sweet than those plucked less than an hour later. Real freshness is crucial, so always pick at the last minute and put into pre-boiling water instantly.

It is eminently sensible to grow several varieties of sweetcorn to spread the risk of any one sort failing or not ripening during a dull cold period. Grow each variety in several batches to give a succession of cobs. I cannot recommend any specific variety as they change so quickly – older varieties are mostly soon superseded by far superior new ones. Good old varieties like Golden Bantam are almost redundant in terms of most attributes yet have real flavour.

Native Americans grew their corn on a hill of earth covering a dead fish, indicating this plant's need

Below A cob of sweetcorn is ready when the silks have withered and dried brown like this.
Bottom Strip the leaves from the cob and press one kernel with a thumbnail – it should have the texture of clotted cream if it is in perfect condition.

for really rich conditions. The soil should not only be in good heart but have plenty of extra compost or well rotted muck mixed in beforehand. Extra bone meal, fish meal, seaweed meal and so on will all help this hungry crop perform well. Most important, though, is copious watering once the plants have established and particularly when the flowers first appear. Ideally sweetcorn should follow a legume in the vegetable bed or actually be grown with peas or beans. I often grow climbing French runner beans up and over sweetcorn. The light shade underneath the plants suits courgettes, marrows, ridge cucumbers, squashes, and even melons in warmer climates. But for the finest crops, give them a bed on their own.

Sweetcorn suffers few pest or disease problems but is difficult to grow in cold wet conditions. It is usually started off under cover in deep pots, then planted out so that the cobs ripen when the sun is still strong in summer. Successional crops mature later and can do well given a good autumn. I sow the first batch indoors in pots in early spring and grow these on in buckets under cover for a very early crop. I sow a second and third batch a fortnight apart, during mid-spring, and then I sow fourth and fifth batches another fortnight apart, with as many sown direct in the ground as in pots. Each sowing or planting hole is dug deep and wide and partly refilled with enriched soil. The seedlings are planted out deep in these holes for shelter and I refill them slowly in stages. Later as plants mature they are earthed and mounded up further above ground, to encourage rooting from the base of the stem. This helps keep them upright and promotes stronger growth.

Similarly, when I sow direct, each hole is improved and the seed sown at the bottom but initially covered with only an inch of soil again to benefit from the shelter. Whether transplanted or sown directly, the seed or seedling is covered with a clear tubular cloche cut from a plastic bottle, left on until the plant grows proud, to protect it from the cold winds. Sweetcorn needs to be grown in blocks about a couple of feet apart each way to ensure wind pollination. It is said you should not grow extra-sweet varieties near ordinary ones as they cross pollinate with poorer results. But I have never had any serious problems apart from a lack of uniformity in kernels in some cobs. I grow early croppers next to late croppers as these rarely cross, and mid-season varieties I try to grow as far apart as possible.

A well-grown plant will throw three or four cobs, but for really good cobs remove all that form after the first two, and before they start to swell. Water and liquid feed regularly with growth and leaf types and give foliar seaweed sprays every couple of weeks. Sweetcorn is bulky to store but can be stripped from the cob after blanching, then packed in bags and frozen for winter soups and stews.

A gourmet could fill the garden with only potatoes and still not be bored with the variety of textures, tastes and uses!

potatoes

Potatoes (*Solanum tuberosum*) the humble spud: when the gourmet discovers the hundreds of varieties available, he or she can never be satisfied with the few miserable sorts sold in shops. There are soft melting new potatoes; waxy yellow firm potatoes for salads; fluffy white sorts for mash; solid ones for roasting; others for chipping; and some that grow huge for baking whole. A gourmet could fill the garden with only potatoes and still not be bored with the variety of textures, tastes and uses! I grow many sorts every year and am particularly fond of Sutton's Foremost, Epicure, Sharpe's Express, Concorde, Dunluce, and Pink Duke of York for my earlies. For salads I grow the divine waxy Pink Fir Apple, Ratte, Linzer Delikatesse and Charlotte. For main crops I grow the wonderful but low-yielding King Edward; Romano and Diana for baking. The old purple-skinned Arran Victory is good for mash, and Cosmo and Remarka for chipping (use beef dripping or olive oil for the best chips – never ever use cheap frying oil).

Try as many potato sorts as you can; their flavours, textures and yields vary dramatically, depending on soil and climate. Generally potatoes are easy to grow but need care to give worthwhile yields. They need a soil enriched with organic material and for good-quality tubers this really needs to be well dug over beforehand – potatoes thrive in a loose, moist soil. Mulches help the crop immensely, as does generous watering, but excess nitrogenous fertility causes spuds to blacken and break up when cooked. On the other hand, increased potassium helps the quality, so add wood ashes generously before planting and use a high-potash and seaweed feed when watering during growth. Do not use

Opposite Now that's fresh... **Below** New potatoes are at their best if you dig, cook and eat them straight away.

rainwater for spraying seaweed solution (it may carry disease organisms such as potato blight) and apply this only in spring and not after flowers commence.

If your tubers have scabby patches when you dig them up, don't worry – they spoil only the appearance. They can be prevented by mixing in grass clippings and well-wilted comfrey leaves in the soil around the seed when planted.

As potatoes suffer many diseases spread with the 'seed' it is sensible although expensive to buy only certified virus-free stock every year. To economise it's possible to grow self-saved tubers for a while, but buy in new stock as soon as yields drop or problems appear. Save tubers for seed only from healthy-looking plants – never from those that look unhappy, die quickly or produce only small tubers. For seed hen's-egg-sized tubers are preferable; smaller will do in good seasons but not in adverse conditions as they have few reserves to re-sprout from. Huge seed tubers should be cut lengthways not crosswise: cut through from the residual stem to the rose end, where most of the 'eyes' can be seen concentrated in a spiral. Dry the cut sides with wood ashes before planting. I advise concentrating on early varieties; these give low yields but crop fairly rapidly and can be harvested before potato blight becomes a problem. This serious disease usually appears about midsummer during a warm humid period. Second earlies are nearly as quick to crop so similarly miss most blight attacks, but highly productive main crops must grow well on into autumn to give the maximum harvest.

Blight is recognised by the sudden blackening then withering of the foliage which also smells rotten.

Most plants are rapidly affected at the same time, some varieties more than others; blight-resistant varieties (unfortunately usually not gourmet varieties) may be worth growing if blight is serious in your area most years.

Do not confuse blight with the natural withering as the crop matures: in earlies it happens about the time blight often appears. You can prevent blight by frequent spraying of the permissible fungicide Bordeaux mixture but I can't recommend it. Instead, if blight appears, I cut off the haulms (plants) immediately before it 'runs' down them to the tubers, then wait a few weeks before harvesting to give the disease time to die away.

As with all gourmet crops, search out and read catalogues diligently and try many different sorts. When you have bought your 'seed', chit the earlies and second earlies. Lay the tubers in a frost-free slightly warm place with plenty of light. They should be placed rose-end up (the end with more 'eyes') and they will slowly make short green shoots which romp away when planted, resulting in an earlier crop. Maincrops may be chitted but it is not so important as we are not trying to get them to give a crop quickly.

As soon as the weeds start to grow vigorously, it is time to plant the seed. Earlier crops can be had if the soil is pre-warmed with a plastic sheet and/or cloches. Earlies need to be planted a finger or two deep and only a foot or so apart but main crops need to be deeper and twice as far apart. For new potatoes where you want to produce many small tubers, leave all the small shoots on the seed. To grow fewer, bigger tubers remove nearly all the shoots, leaving only one or two at the rose end. (All shoots rubbed off can be potted up and grown on under cover to produce extra plants for planting out later.)

The 'seed' potato is best planted in a trench with ridges left either side for shelter. The ridges are then used to earth up the haulm, supporting it as it gets taller. Earthing up is necessary and best done in stages, beginning once the shoots first appear and especially when a frosty night is likely. It helps to add extra mulches such as grass clippings or leaves to make sure the tubers are well covered: if exposed to the light they green up and become poisonous. Grass mulches are excellent but must be applied only as thin layers when the weather is dry to stop them going slimy.

Protect the foliage against frost on cold nights by covering it with

sheets supported on sticks. Once flowers appear (not all varieties produce them), give copious quantities of water plus flower, fruit and flavour feeds and especially seaweed solution, which will increase yields and quality. Do not water excessively as the crops mature. You can increase the overall yield with no loss of quality if the first new potatoes are fiddled out from the sides of the ridges, leaving the remainder to grow on – rather than digging up the whole plants there and then.

You can also increase yields significantly if you remove the poisonous seed heads before they swell and ripen – the easiest way is to remove the flowers. At exactly the same time use chips of raw potato, carrot, beetroot or apple to bait and trap slugs before they start on the new tubers. Put the bait under cabbage leaves, next to the potato stems in the shade of the foliage, and inspect regularly.

To store potatoes for as long as possible, cut the haulm off and leave the tubers for a week or two before digging – this toughens their skins; but the most important thing is to dig potatoes in dry conditions – when it's sunny and windy. Be careful not to bruise any as you dig. Sort out the smallest tubers and any damaged ones to be used first. Place the best on a cloth on the ground in the sun for an hour or two to help dry them off, then pack them gently in thick paper bags and store in a cool, dark, frost-free place. I use a 'dead' freezer body: it is also rat proof – and the constant conditions inside make an ideal store for potatoes. I keep them in plastic trays in the freezer. Check them regularly: stored potatoes that start to sprout must have the sprouts rubbed off before they make the tuber wilt. Do not let them freeze or the potatoes will go

sweet. They also pick up taints easily, such as oil or paint.

In good conditions long-keeping varieties should store until late spring. As new potatoes, even under cloches, are never ready before early summer, there is an inevitable gap. This can be bridged by forcing potatoes in warmth under cover. Early varieties planted from mid-winter in buckets of compost and kept in a warm light place yield delicious new potatoes from early spring onwards. The yields are low and the buckets take up a lot of space under cover, but the joy of having scrumptious new potatoes when everyone else is just starting to plant theirs is worth the effort.

Although yields may be low, it is worth growing special varieties in large containers, in gardens with limited space. Buckets or bigger containers should have plenty of drainage holes. Half-fill them with very rich potting compost and plant the seed. Keep filling with compost until the haulm reaches the top. With careful watering with first the growth and leaf type feeds and then the flower, fruit and flavour feeds you can get impressive crops from a small

space – and usually completely free of slug damage.

For a Christmas or New Year feast try growing a crop of earlies from a late-summer planting under cover in a container. Ideally buy special seed potatoes sold for summer planting, or use seed potatoes you have kept in a refrigerator since spring planting, or use this year's crop of earlies after cooling them in a refrigerator for a fortnight or so first. An inferior but still worthwhile trick for the same results is to replant some of the very best of your new potatoes, as soon as they are dug, in a tin or plastic drum full of damp sand in a cool shady place.

Many potatoes are better steamed than boiled. In most cases, leave the skins on and peel them after cooking to retain the tastiest layer just under the skin. A tip worth knowing is that adding potatoes to a dish helps 'remove' excess salt if you've accidentally overdone it. And, believe me or not, but chips actually vary depending on the way you cut them from the tuber. Try it yourself: lengthways-cut chips are different from crosswise-cut ones; the former vary from end to end and the latter vary from one to another!

A tip worth knowing is that adding potatoes to a dish helps 'remove' excess salt if you've accidentally overdone it.

Below left Rooting out the potato crop is like digging for buried treasure. **Opposite** An old chip basket makes washing the potatoes, before you take them in, easy and saves the dirt blocking your drains.

legumes

peas

Legumes are all closely related. As they are predominantly grown for their seed or seed pods, they are relatively easy to crop. Legumes enrich the soil for other crops by fixing nitrogen in nodules of bacteria on their roots. These bacteria may not be present in some soils, so it can help to inoculate your soil with the right bacteria. Buy them from commercial seed suppliers or add some soil from a nearby garden (but one without brassica clubroot) that grows healthy peas and beans to your first seed drill. Because legumes need little in nitrogen terms and leave the soil enriched, they go well before almost all other crops in your rotation and follow almost any happily as well. They all respond well to watering and sprayings with seaweed solution but do not require feeding, save when grown in pots – which is feasible only for small quantities.

Peas (*Pisum sativum*) are more work than most vegetables but are such a delicious gourmet dish when truly fresh that all the effort is worth it. And most of the effort is not in the growing but in the picking and preparation! Fresh shop-sold peas are not fresh and not worth considering. Commercial frozen, organic peas look cheap compared with the work needed to get the same, but these are still not FRESH. Plus there is an abundance of varieties to try, from the sweet and soft to the hard and mealy, not to mention the pods that you can eat too.

Round-seeded varieties are the hardiest and earliest, but not the sweetest. An old one, Petit Provençal (aka. Meteor), is probably the best early and a better choice than Feltham First, but Douce Provence is sweeter still and good for over-wintering. Wrinkle-seeded varieties are sweeter but sown later: Cavalier, Daybreak, Gradus and Hurst Beagle are excellent. Petits pois are small, very sweet wrinkle-seeded peas which take days of podding but varieties such as Lynx, Waverex and Cobri are what gourmets live for.

Mangetout peas have edible pods so podding as such is not necessary when they are young and tender; later they can be eaten as ordinary peas. They mostly grow rather tall. Sugar peas are very similar and much improved. They have thicker sweeter pods but not quite the flavour of mangetout – Sugar Snap is probably the best variety. As always, try many varieties – sow a bit of a row of each, then compare and select what suits your conditions and tastes. Repeat the trial with successional sowings: some peas do much better early or late.

Peas enjoy lime in their soil: it can be applied before or during their rotation. They are one of the few crops best grown in rows and need strong supports. Do not believe claims for self-supporting ones, which really work only on a field scale and are a b***** to pick. Although short varieties produce less, they need less support and do not shade out other crops as much. Do not bother with pea sticks – they waste time to put up and take down and get in the way when picking. Instead use netting hanging from a crossbar supported by strong posts; it's quicker and easier. If you use galvanised wire netting the dried haulm can be stripped off in autumn, the roll wound up and any haulm left on burnt off, destroying spores and pests. You may also need some netting to keep birds from stealing the seed or razoring off the emerging seedlings.

I sow peas neatly, almost touching and about a thumb's width deep, in a well-watered then drained slit trench made with the edge of a spade. After sowing, I firm the soil

down and cover with a thin layer of sterile compost, which helps suppress weeds among the crop. My peas even germinate through grass clippings, but in wetter areas potting compost or similar mixed with sand is safer. Pea seed is expensive to buy and luckily self-saved seed comes true. It is not even necessary to shell stored seed: the pods can be laid end to end along the bottom of the planting trench, convex side up – provided you water really well. In dry soil, peas germinate more quickly if soaked for an hour or so beforehand; adding a dash of seaweed solution helps disguise their smell from mice. But never soak early sowings for cold soil.

For succession, peas can be sown from late winter till late summer – earlier given plastic sheet or cloches. Some peas can be sown in late autumn to over-winter and, though these do not crop well, they are early and appreciated. Likewise, the earliest sown crops never do as well as the later ones. And if later ones get dry, they may get mildew and die prematurely. Keep the soil moist and they won't suffer. One good watering when the flowers are in full bloom will improve yields dramatically, as will seaweed sprays applied regularly during growing.

Left Fresh shop-sold peas are not fresh and not worth considering. **Opposite** Summer is not the same wihout sweet pea flowers to cut for the table. Sow a few either end of the garden pea rows. (Don't accidentally pick and eat their inedible seeds!)

Maggots in the peas are most of a problem with the main crops. Remove them by washing shelled peas in salty water. Pick peas early: if left, they not only 'go over' but suppress more forming! Pod, blanch and freeze them immediately or cook and eat them with butter and mint jelly. I like to steam peas in their pods and serve them whole, eating them like asparagus by placing the pod in my mouth and pulling it out through my teeth, leaving the succulent peas within. It is a superb way; they taste better and since I started doing it, I've never seen a pea maggot.

Surplus peas can be left to dry then stored in their pods on the dried haulm. Hang them up somewhere where mice can't get them – they are excellent in winter soups and stews if soaked overnight first.

After harvest clear peas by cutting off the stems at ground level – leave their root systems to enrich the soil. Just occasionally, an early crop promptly harvested, cut back and well watered will regrow to throw a second crop. A few peas for eating raw can be grown in containers though it is difficult to get much of a crop this way. A very early crop can also sometimes be had under cover but not easily or very productively.

Asparagus peas (*Psophocarpus tetragonolobus*) are more of a vetch and not a true pea. The pods are eaten steamed when very small and tender and make a delicious addition to the menu. The seeds can be roasted to make a not un-coffee-like beverage. Asparagus peas grow happily in poor conditions and have pretty flowers. They are a crop for the adventurous gourmet – or the pathetically incompetent gardener.

french beans

French beans (*Phaseolus vulgaris*) are also known as waxpod, snap, string, flageolet, haricot, green or just dwarf beans – and then there are running French beans which climb. Green squeaky beans, as I call them, are actually available in shops in an almost acceptable form, but only in few varieties. Not only do they have a lot of names, they come in many varieties, with flat, pencil-shaped, big or small pods, in different colours and flavours and with different-coloured seeds. They may be grown for the edible pod, the fresh seed or the dried seed depending on whim. Masai, Radar and Aramis are now my favourites for really slim squeaky greens, though there are many newer contenders. Fin de Bagnol and Othello are faux-filet types – very fine beans like thick wire. Mont d'Or is the best flavoured yellow bean; for colour there's Purple Queen with its superb flavour. For fresh green flageolet seeds of a fine texture grow Chevrier Vert or Lime Light.

Most home-grown dried French bean seeds can be soaked, boiled and eaten but the gourmet should choose haricots of the best creamy texture such as Brown Dutch or the red-seeded Horsehead – reliable, and wind-producing. Beans grown for drying need the warmest spot so they can ripen well; cloches may be necessary towards the end of a bad season.

There are several climbing varieties which grow much like runner beans but have the finer texture and flavour of dwarf French beans; they are much the same to grow but obviously need supports. Try Blue Lake White Seeded and Largo; for tasty seed crops, grow the Borlotto varieties. Purple King climbers are the best for growing out of season under cover, but watch out for red spider mite.

French beans are a nutritious crop overall. The green beans freeze well and the seeds are easily dried for winter use. As with peas, enrich the soil first; then they merely need moisture and an open warm soil to do well. Beans often do best on low ridges and can go either side of a celery or leek trench. The young seedlings are prone to late frosts, cold wind and slug and bird damage, so either

Green squeaky beans, as I call them, are actually available in shops in an almost acceptable form, but only in few varieties.

sow in pots and plant out or cover them with a plastic sheet or cloches.

Mulches of grass clippings or similar encourage slugs but keep the soil soft and moist and the bean crop cleaner.

Beans can be grown in containers fairly easily – the climbing sorts are then the best, as they crop more heavily, but they'll need a frame or canes to climb up. Very

early crops can be had under cover but often succumb to red spider mite once the weather warms up.

In the open, sow successionally from late spring till late summer, an inch or so deep at a foot each way. Do not overcrowd plants, and water well and often, especially when you see the flowers. Use seaweed sprays often, especially if the weather stays hot and dry, when you should spray in the

early morning or late afternoon, not in the full heat. Keep the fresh green bean sorts picked or they stop producing more. These pods taste perfect picked before the bean seed shape can be discerned from outside and the flesh snaps crisply if suddenly bent. Blanch and freeze any surplus green beans promptly before they wither. Store dried beans in their pods in a dry rodent-proof place and remember to set them soaking the night before they're wanted for cooking.

Top right French beans are best picked young and tender. If they go over, pick them anyway and give them to friends – they're still better than the shop-bought ones.
Opposite, left Running French beans need less water and don't need pollinators, unlike runner beans.
Opposite, top right Boil broad beans, skin them and use the naked seed to make a delicious pâté.

runner beans

Runner beans (*Phaseolus coccineus*) are considered gourmet eating in the north of the UK; in the south they prefer French beans. Rarely have I met a gardener who loves both. I consider runner beans to have a coarser texture and rougher flavour than French beans, but many gardeners hold the contrary view. In any case there are numerous delicious varieties in a range of different coloured flowers, pods and seeds. Among good sorts to try are Red Rum, Desiree, Kelvedon Marvel, Scarlet Emperor and the nearly stringless Butler. Dried Csar seeds are as good as butter beans. Avoid varieties grown for show, as for them sheer size is all.

Runners need full sun and a deep well-drained soil that is permanently moist and well mulched. They need supporting with netting, preferably wire netting or strong canes – string is not rigid enough. If allowed to run, they shade out other crops but can be topped to make them bush out at any stage. They are tender perennials and the roots can be protected or over-wintered under cover for an earlier, but light, crop.

Sow seed in late spring *in situ*, two to three inches deep by the same apart, in rows. Or sow in pots and plant out while still small. French beans are self-fertile and set readily, but runners must be pollinated; mixing in a few sweet peas and other flowers encourages pollinators to visit.

Flowers dropping off early is a sign of a lack of pollinators or of dryness. Water, water, water. If you grow runner beans in a (big) container then you really need a drip watering system or they'll not fare well. The beans must be picked regularly to prevent them suppressing more – they're usually best when smaller. Inevitable surpluses can be sliced and frozen, salted or pickled. The seeds can be dried for winter soups and stews.

broad beans

Broad beans (*Vicia faba*) from the shops are disappointing. You can grow so many different and tastier varieties at home, even eating the whole pods when they are first formed. Aquadulce Claudia or Bunyards Exhibition are probably best for over-wintered crops but not the finest flavoured. Express is fast but not as tasty as any of the more tender green-seeded Windsor sorts. For small gardens and containers grow dwarf The Sutton or Feligreen. But for gourmets it has to be Red Epicure.

Broad beans are very nutritious and one of the earliest crops to harvest. They need only a decent soil to do well – better results come from spacing and supporting the plants properly. Extra early crops of the hardier sorts can be had from sowings made in early winter and cloched. Several sowings can be made in early spring but they are not happy sown any time after late spring, nor will they do well in pots, though they will grow in large tubs.

I sow them singly at about three or four to the foot and finger-deep in blocks. The seed rarely fails. Mulch between the seedlings in dry years but earth up the bases of the stems first. Pinch out the tips of each stem once the beans have started to flower; this prevents black aphid attacks and makes those pods already set swell sooner and larger.

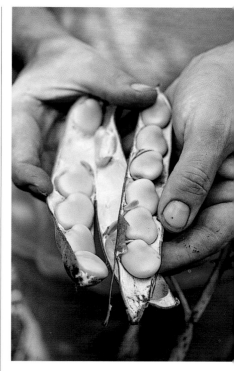

The seeds freeze well or can be dried for use in winter. They can also be used as the basis of delicious pâtés and similar dishes.

Many other peas and beans from around the world can be grown either outdoors or under cover. The soya bean, the yard long, the asparagus and the dolichos or lablab bean all make tasty changes at the table. Sufficient for a meal can be had from a few plants growing in a large tub in a greenhouse – or even outdoors in exceptional summers – and given much the same treatment as running French beans.

Broad beans from the shops are disappointing. You can grow so many different and tastier varieties at home, even eating the whole pods when they are first formed.

cucurbits

This family provides us with a wide range of culinary delights, from the commonest members such as marrows and their baby sisters the courgettes (zucchini); to the more substantial squashes and pumpkins for autumn and winter soups; to ridge cucumbers and gherkins and melons. All are very closely related – so close that some may cross-pollinate. They all need very similar conditions, especially moist rich soil, full sun and a warm start under cover. Cucurbits need copious amounts of water and frequent growth and leaf feeds to push them into vigour as soon in the season as possible. Their ideal site is a well-rotted muck or compost heap – soil enrichment cannot be overdone. (But raw muck or manure will cause rank growth and poor flavour!) Watch out for slug damage early on, but otherwise these have few treatable common pest or disease problems. Yellowed, distorted and blotchy leaves or fruit indicate an incurable viral infection and affected plants must be destroyed immediately. Do not use rainwater for making up seaweed sprays as it may carry the dreaded virus. You may water them with rainwater if you do not splash them.

Courgettes or zucchini (*Cucurbita pepa*) are highly productive plants. Picked continually they may easily crop all summer producing dozens of slim bland fruits that can be cooked in many ways. If you stop picking, they stop making more, and those left swell up to become vegetable marrows. Raven and Ambassador are excellent varieties; the yellow ones such as Golden Zucchini are poor doers but add colour. Avoid the spherical sorts unless you are prepared to gather them twice daily.

Sow courgettes singly in small pots in the warm under cover in late spring. Plant them out a stride apart once the last frosts have passed. They may also be sown *in situ* under a cloche in early summer. They need plenty of water and feeding regularly and even more so if grown in containers, preferably big ones. Early crops can be forced under cover, but with difficulty, as hot dry conditions promote male rather than female flowers and thus few fruits.

Marrows are treated similarly, except for the fact that many varieties produce long running stems, which need to be trained to keep them from invading. Like squashes, marrows can be grown in the dappled shade under sweetcorn if it is already well established. Long Green trailing is probably the best marrow; Green Bush is compact and more like a courgette plant in habit. Vegetable spaghetti is a marrow with stringy flesh worth growing if you like it.

Squashes and pumpkins need much the same treatment as marrows and courgettes, but require more space at two strides apart. Most of them keep far longer than marrows and are much better eating. When fully ripe, pick marrows and squashes leaving a short stalk. Store in a net

hung in a frost-free cool dry shed or garage roof. Golden Nugget is my favourite storing squash for winter and it has a compact habit. Uchiki Kuri is a similar Japanese form and has sweet nutty fruits which can be added to soups and stews or baked. Lady Godiva produces hull-less seed, and is grown mainly for these seeds; eat them as snacks raw or toasted – they taste really good and are good for you. Generally pumpkins such as Mammoth merely grow big, take up even more room and have little culinary virtue, unless you want pumpkin pie daily from late summer till mid-winter.

Ridge cucumbers and **Japanese cucumbers** (*Cucumis sativus*) are similar to indoor greenhouse and frame cucumbers but have small harmless prickles on their skin. They may be eaten fresh but are most often pickled, commonly with dill as a flavouring. The gourmet can choose from the allegedly Burpless Tasty Green or Marketmore, or Japanese varieties such as Kyoto. I find the latter excellent and the most easily successful – as generously productive as runner beans. Gherkin varieties such as Eureka and Vert Petit de Paris for pickling are reliable and prolific – needing frequent picking. They can be eaten as small cucumbers too. All cucumbers benefit immensely from a coldframe or cloches at the start; earlier crops may be grown in a cold greenhouse or tunnel.

Sow the seeds, standing them on edge, a finger-width deep in individual pots in warmth in late spring. Keep seedlings warm and pot up until planted out; at least a stride apart with some protection in early summer. Or sow *in situ* under cloches in early summer. Cucumbers do well in big containers. Most trail like marrows so can be grown over fences, trellis

Left A melon growing in the greenhouse.
Opposite, clockwise from top left Courgettes and nasturtiums make good companions; yellow courgettes – well they do add a touch of colour; squashes come in many shapes and sizes; a lovely young fruit.

or under sweetcorn plants. Keep them well watered and picked regularly to prevent any from 'going over'. ('Gone over', that is, bloated yellow cucumbers with well-formed seeds were in fact how they were once eaten – the preference for unripe green ones is modern.)

Melons and **watermelons** are a challenge. Too often in the UK the weather is just not warm and sunny enough and so most can only crop at all given a cloche or cold frame and really are best under full cover (see page 129).

There are many other cucurbits, also more usually grown under cover, such as kiwanos and christophenes, but these are too difficult to crop, even with a greenhouse, to make them of interest to any other than the very determined gourmet.

roots

carrots

Root vegetables are tasty and nutrient-rich as they tap levels of soil deeper down than most plants. They are soil breakers and improvers: their roots penetrate first, then die and decay, leaving paths for others to follow. Their taproots can go straight down into the hardest ground if it is moist and the seed is well covered with soil to push against. They do not need a well-dug soil. Recently dug ground, especially if full of clods or lumps of manure, causes the roots to fork and divide – making harvest and cleaning tricky. Root vegetables need a rich soil not highly fertilised with nitrogen but with added minerals. Seaweed meal and seaweed sprays benefit these crops immensely.

Spacing makes a big difference: close spacing results in baby specimens more prone to bolting; wide spacing allows bigger plants to form that are better for storing. Root vegetables are mostly natural biennials, making their reserves this year to flower the next.

Bolting into flower early is their commonest problem if they are stressed by drought or overcrowding. Remove any bolters as soon as you spot them, to prevent them encouraging others. (Bolting plants may give off hormones that encourage others nearby to flower at the same time ensuring their better pollination.)

For harvesting, I've made a two-prong fork cut from the middle of a four-prong digging fork. With this, I can lift out roots with ease: it's crucial not to damage them when digging them up. Most can be stored in damp sand for many weeks or even months if buried in a clamp or kept in trays in a dead deep-freezer body.

Carrots (*Daucus carota* subsp. *sativa*) are an essential for any gourmet's kitchen: small tender finger ones for delicious eating raw or steamed; bigger ones to grate for salads and coleslaw; and large firm ones to store for winter use. They are probably one of the most worthwhile crops in terms of kitchen value, nutrition and flavour.

Carrots need light soil rather than heavy: sandy is excellent but stony causes misshapen roots; heavy clay soils need lightening with organic material and sharp sand. Do not overfeed or use fresh manure – both will cause poor flavour and forked roots. Heavy soil may be improved the year before by sowing with a green manure of flax. I find carrots will follow onions well on a light soil. Rake a tilth into the topmost layer; sow in this and the seedling carrots will grow straight down. Regular heavy watering, especially when the crop is young, is important to improve yields. Flavour is stronger in sunny dry conditions and better with regular sprayings of seaweed solution – which also helps discourage their main pest, the carrot root fly.

Ideally grow carrots under horticultural fleece or an old net curtain to prevent the fly from laying its eggs on the roots and damaging them. Many strong-smelling herbs and remedies have been used with some success to discourage carrot root fly. Intercropping with onions, chives or leeks helps to keep it away. A high percentage of carrot root flies can be thwarted by a simple barrier around small beds. It needs to be about hip high to stop the fly, which will go round rather than fly up and over. However, the best preventative is crop rotation combined with a physical barrier to stop the fly laying its eggs.

Carrots are probably one of the most worthwhile crops in terms of kitchen value, nutrition and flavour.

Top I wash all my roots for fresh use – but not for storing.
Bottom Red carrots are a different choice.
Opposite These fresh carrots are crunchy and sweet like an apple.

Sow carrots successively and shallowly from early spring through till midsummer. Amsterdam Forcing and the Nantes types are the quickest carrots; their surpluses freeze well and they do well grown in a cold frame. Varieties like Mokum and Panther are good summer carrots with sweet crunchiness rivalling (shop-bought) apples and with far more flavour. Autumn King is a good doer, if a bit coarse, for winter storage.

Special varieties are available for much earlier and later sowings under cover. Squat ones for sowing in pots or shallow soils, such as Rondo and Parmex, are useful as they grow short and round like radish. For maximum vitamin A, Juwarot is superb, having double the average amount. Although they are interesting I would not bother sowing a lot of the yellow-, purple- or white-rooted sorts.

Station sowing at up to three per foot apart is sensible if you want large carrots for storing. For bunches of baby finger carrots, broadcast sowing is more effective. Rake the soil, water it heavily and let the water percolate away. Mix the seed with sand and sow this uniformly; cover with a thin layer of used sterile potting compost, sharp sand and fine composted bark or similar. Firm it down and cover with fleece, well-pegged down at the edges but supported in the middle on sticks.

Carrots store well in the ground over winter if covered with thick dry straw and a plastic sheet. If the ground freezes, carrots protected in this way can still be dug. Once dug, carrots store better with the dirt left on them, so only wash them immediately before use. Do not store them near apples or pears or paint as they may acquire a bitter taint.

parsnip-type roots

Parsnips, salsify, scorzonera, skirret, bulbous-rooted chervil and Hamburg parsley are all very similar roots to carrots, though larger and with differing flavours. As these are rarely available in the shop, the gourmet will certainly wish to grow them just to try.

There is a wide range of **parsnips** (*Pastinacea sativa*): big old favourites such as Imperial Crown need a foot of space each way. Modern sorts tend to be smaller: Avonresister is reliable but small; Dagger and Lancer are tasty mini-parsnips grown close together like finger carrots.

For very large top-quality roots ram a very deep ideal-parsnip-shaped hole with a crowbar. At the bottom place a spoonful of very rich compost then fill the hole with finely sifted sandy soil of low fertility and sow one seed on top. Water regularly and feed with growth and leaf feeds initially, then seaweed solution. Or just grow them in reasonable soil and well spaced. Parsnips' taste improves once the frost has got to them; try them parboiled then French fried.

Salsify (*Tragopogon porrifolium*) are like inferior parsnips being smaller and thinner with more side roots. They have a blander but superior flavour, often bizarrely and incorrectly compared to oyster – oyster mushroom more like! These do not keep at all well once lifted, so dig immediately before use, parboil without peeling, then slip the skins off and fry the roots in butter.

Scorzonera (*Scorzonera hispanica*) is slightly different from salsify; it is more cylindrical, very long and with a black skin, and even tastier. Young scorzonera shoots can be blanched and eaten in salads.

Skirret roots (*Sium sisarum*) are very small but very sweet. They are extremely prone to root fly damage and best grown under fleece. They make good eating but need improving in size!

Bulbous-rooted chervil [*Chaerophyllum bulbosum*] This is hard to germinate from bought-in seed and needs a clean soil with few weeds to give it time to emerge. Sow in autumn or as soon as seed arrives, as it does best after a winter in the soil. Keep moist and grown on at a foot's length apart, removing the lowest leaves to encourage swelling. Once swollen the root can be grated and used in moderation in salads or braised in slices in a thick stock.

Hamburg parsley produces a parsnip-like root and again is used in similar ways. It tastes of parsley and can be grated raw in moderation in salads and the leaves can be used at a push instead of parsley.

Parsnips, salsify, scorzonera, skirret, bulbous-rooted chervil and Hamburg parsley all rarely suffer from pests or diseases other than the usual soil pests and carrot root fly, from which they can be protected with cloches or fleece. They all keep well in the ground, though it is wise to dig some up to store in a shed when hard frosts are likely. Sow them in early spring, three seeds per station at about a foot apart. Protect them with a wee cloche as germination is slow. Thin to one seedling once they emerge and, other than watering and an occasional seaweed spray, you can forget about them till harvest. The seed of all of these does not keep well, and garden plants may cross with wild relatives so won't come true from seed. Buy fresh every year.

The seed of all of these does not keep well and garden plants may cross with wild relatives so won't come true from seed.

brassicas

The cabbage family or brassicas, often disdained as mere 'greens', are a far more palatable bunch when home-grown to perfection, especially compared with the overfed aged specimens usually on sale in shops. You can have fresh cabbage every week of the year, rarely repeating the same variety as there are so many to choose from. They vary so much between varieties and in their response to soil and situation that you really must try many of each sort – even more so than with other crops.

All brassicas come from a wild native that has been selected into many apparently different plants. But, just like dogs, they are all a species and so behave almost as one and cross-breed horrifically. Do not even try to save seed.

Because they are highly bred and very specialised, brassicas need an exceedingly well-enriched soil with copious free lime, and adore sprays of seaweed solution. They should be given liquid growth and leaf feeds in their water while small to get them growing away quickly. Do not feed heavily once they're heading towards maturity, though, or their flavour becomes rank.

Although brassicas perform very well sown direct, they are often started in small pots. The most reliable crops, however, are sown thinly in a seedbed, and thinned soon after emergence to a finger's length or so apart. These small plants are then lifted with a trowel and planted right back again when they are about two or three leaves high, to break their taproots and form fibrous rootballs which will later move with less check when transplated to their final site.

While small they all may suffer badly from bird damage if unprotected, and from slugs in wet

Because they are highly bred and very specialised, brassicas need an exceedingly well-enriched soil with copious free lime, and adore sprays of seaweed solution.

conditions. Brassicas benefit from strong-smelling herbs nearby, which help confuse their pests, and also do well if surrounded by French beans. Cabbage root fly may cause the young plants to purple and wither – they attack when the plants are transplanted out. To stop the fly laying its eggs in the soil by the stem, use magazine-sized pieces of thick cardboard with a slit and push these round the stem to lie flat on the ground.

The various caterpillars are best stopped by keeping out adult butterflies with fine plastic netting. Any that do hatch can be hand-picked or hosed off. Whitefly – a different species from the ones in greenhouses – are more of a problem. They can be controlled with soft soap when first spotted, as can aphid attacks. Flea beetles make little pinholes in the seedling leaves; keep the area wet to discourage them.

The worst problem brassicas suffer from is clubroot disease, and once it gets in your soil, it's ineradicable. The best 'cure' is prevention: never buy in brassica plants. If you must, then avoid any grown in soil and choose only those grown in sterile compost. Wallflowers and stocks can carry the disease and it may be introduced with muck – another reason this must always be composted before use. Clubroot can be decreased in virulence if you very heavily lime the plot before the brassicas are planted. Crops can still be had in infected soil if you start plants off in pots, then grow them in pits filled with sterile compost, so that the soil does not touch the young roots.

When planting out brassicas, mix a rich top dressing and lime or calcified seaweed in with the soil you return to the planting hole, unless you have a naturally good soil for them. Members of the brassica family are exceptionally good for our health and are reliable over-wintering crops, available in the spring when little else is, and should be in every garden. They almost all need sowing in spring and transplanting a couple of feet apart or so by early summer – read their seed packets carefully.

cabbages

Cabbages (*Brassica oleracea var. capitata*) are, technically, terminal buds and to get them to swell without opening is a marvel of controlling nature. Constant unchecked growth in rich moist conditions is required for crisp solid heads but overfeeding makes rank flavour.

Cabbages can be produced for use every day of the year but getting their best performance depends on choosing the right variety for the season, soil and available space. For early summer, grow Greyhound, any Golden Acre variant or Wheeler's Imperial under cover in pots from late winter and plant them out in early spring under cloches. Then sow the same again, along with Stonehead from early spring in a seedbed and plant these out later in spring.

For summer and autumn cabbages, sow the superb Grand Prize, Winningstadt and Red Drumhead from late spring and plant these out by early summer. For late autumn and to store for winter, sow Holland Late Winter, Christmas Drumhead and Coleslaw from late spring, plant out by early summer and store before the frosts. At the same time the Savoy types such as January King, Celtic, Savoy King and Winter King can be sown the same way but left in the ground for late-winter use.

For spring cabbages sow Early Queen, Offenham 2 Flower of Spring, Excel and Spring Hero in late summer and plant these out in early autumn. Give them cloches during the harshest weather and they should crop the following spring. Some newer varieties of summer cabbage, plus Pixie and Minicole, need to be closely planted for small heads, but generally more space equals bigger plants, so never crowd your cabbages.

Make sure the soil is firm and in good heart before planting them. They respond well to growth and leaf feeds. In early spring apply a liquid feed to get slow over-wintered greens moving again – but don't overdo it, as too much spoils their flavour and makes them prone to pests.

Don't cut a large cabbage head off in one go if you can't use it all at once. Cut a piece out and cover the rest of the head with foil – it will stay fresher in the garden than sitting in the fridge. Once the main head of a cabbage has been cut, you can get a bonus crop of smaller ones by leaving the root in the ground and cutting a cross in the top of the stem (do this only if the space is not needed for another crop).

When hard frosts are predicted, pull the storing cabbages up roots and all and hang them upside down in a cool frost-free shed or cover them in straw and a plastic bag. I store mine in a dead deep-freezer body, coated in wood ashes to slow up the slugs. Although unsightly and smelly on the surface, inside they are crisp and sweet and they keep till spring.

Couve tronchuda is the Portuguese cabbage. It is slightly more tender than many and needs growing in summer from a late spring sowing. Grow it exactly like cabbage – but it is the succulent midribs of the leaves that are prized. Try them braised in a rich stock with shallots.

cauliflowers

Cauliflowers (*Brassica oleracea* Botrytis Group) are cauliflowers only during the warm months. Winter-hardy cauliflowers are more likely to be a type of broccoli, rated as tougher than true cauliflowers. Cauliflowers are very highly bred and the most difficult of the cabbage family to grow well, and near impossible without a heavy moist soil. The perfect cauliflower is an enormous flowerhead suspended at the bud stage, so rapid luxuriant growth without check is absolutely necessary – any drought or damage will lead to 'button' heads at best.

There are pure white, pink, red, purple and green cauliflowers, and dwarf varieties that take up less space. With a spread of varieties (including caulis that may be broccolis, but who cares, provided they taste good?) and with successional sowings you can have cauliflower all year round. But it is much more difficult to get all of these to grow as well as cabbages. As these are highly specialised plants their sowing dates are critical so read the packets carefully!

All the Year Round is an old favourite and, unusually, can be sown almost any time, as can Snowball. The majority such as Dok Elgon, Lateman and Autumn Glory are sown from early spring to early summer and planted out from late spring for summer and autumn crops. Dominant is a good choice for lighter, drier conditions. More varieties such as the Walcheren series are sown in midsummer and early autumn for cropping the following spring. On light soils and in containers, grow modern mini-caulis such as Garant and Predominant; these are always sown *in situ* a hand's breadth or so apart to give small heads ideal for individual meals.

Cauliflowers resent being pot-bound so are good sown *in situ* under a mini-cloche and do well started in a seed bed if moved out early. They can be sown in pots only if planted out as soon as possible.

Caulis must have a rich moist limy soil to make good heads – do not expect superb results on light soils; space them a good stride apart in rich soil and more in lighter. Mixing in clay, regular feeding with growth and leaf feeds in the water and seaweed sprays all help immensely. When the curd has swollen, bend the side leaves over to keep the light from it and it will stay whiter. When it's fully grown and threatening to go over, pull the cauliflower up, roots and all; remove most leaves and hang it upside down in a cool frost-free shed where it will keep longer.

broccoli

One type of broccoli (*Brassica oleracea* Cymosa Group) is calabrese, which is very similar to cauliflower. Both brassicas are very highly bred and require rich moist conditions and heavy soil to form their swollen flower buds. Treat them exactly the same but you'll find that, once mature, most broccolis will give second and third crops of smaller flower buds, whereas with caulis you get just the first big one. This extended cropping from early summer through till winter makes calabrese broccolis very useful. They are very tasty and come in many varieties never seen in shops. Almost all are excellent; try Corvet, Shogun and Mercedes. Keep cutting them to get more succulent shoots – do not let them flower. Romanesco is different: it rivals asparagus as a gourmet dish and is really delicious. It has a great texture, a staggering appearance close up and a divine flavour, but it is difficult to grow well.

Sprouting broccolis are again very similar to cauliflowers but hardy enough to survive the winter and crop in spring, with many small heads instead of one big one. Grow Early Purple, Late Purple and White Sprouting broccolis for a succession through early spring.

Far left Romanesco – so good that, although this would have been at its best a week ago, it will still be delicious.
Left Calabrese purple-sprouting broccoli.
Below White-sprouting broccoli.

brussels sprouts

Keep removing any unused flower heads that threaten to open and cut back harder those that do flower to promote more. There is also a variety called Nine Star Perennial, which is like a multi-headed cauliflower that lives for several years. Although this is useful in habit, its curds are inferior to those of either caulis or sprouting broccoli and so not really worth growing.

Broccoletto is one of a series of mini-broccolis that can be sown densely and cropped very rapidly. They do best on a salad bed.

Kale (*Brassica oleracea* convar. *acephala*) is probably the hardiest of all brassicas and can feed you with tasty greens, raw or cooked, in spring when all else fails. Because it is a simple leaf, it is easy to grow well, even in demanding conditions. It's very green (especially when compared with iceberg lettuce or hard white cabbage) so very nutritious; some sorts taste really good especially if shredded and deep fried. Dwarf Green Curled and Pentland Brig are always available, but other choicer sorts can be found.

Asparagus kale is a wonderful tasty old variety that has been lost to us commercially, which is sad. Kale is partly resistant to clubroot and cabbage root fly and could possibly be used as a rootstock on which to graft more susceptible brassicas.

Brussels sprouts (*Brassica oleracea* Gemmifera Group) are another of the hardier brassicas that can be left out in the garden all winter. The range includes mini and red sorts, and these are all better than the shops' soggy yellowed fare. Brussels sprouts can be available from autumn till spring if you really want them – if several varieties are grown.

Sow successional varieties from early spring till early summer and transplant them by midsummer into a rich moist soil, but plant them deeper than for most brassicas. Try Early Half Tall (early), Bedford and Seven Hills (mid), Fortress and Rampart (late). If you adore sprouts then try Noisette, which produces tiny nutty ones. Falstaff and Rubine are red (like red cabbage) and with a good flavour. Trafalgar is reckoned the sweetest sprout and the disappearing Peer Gynt was good for small gardens.

Sprouts do not do well in containers and need really firm soil. If your sprouts are loose and 'blown', then make a note to plant extra deep and extra firm in future. Plants need to be a stride apart and in lighter soils are best grown in threes, made into a tripod tied together at the top once nearly full grown. To get the sprouts to swell more quickly, nip out the terminal mini-cabbage, which makes a tasty meal on its own. Without doubt sprouts are tastier after they have had a hard frost on them, so the later-maturing varieties are really preferable, especially as they stand for months.

The range of Brussels sprouts includes mini and red sorts, and these are all better than the shops' soggy yellowed fare.

alliums: garlic, shallots and onions

These are fairly easy to grow and store and valuable in the kitchen. To be fair, organic store-bought ones are pretty good but apart from red sorts, few varieties are available. A gourmet may wish for sweeter or stronger onions, larger or smaller – especially for pickling. Garlic is always worth growing as it is about the most expensive to buy, compared with the area and effort required to grow it. And there are many varieties of shallot to try if you like their different flavour.

Alliums all accumulate sulphur and may improve the disease resistance of plants growing near them. But they need full sun and air for optimum growth so are best on their own. All of them respond well to increased spacing and in the early stages they need regular seaweed sprays and liquid feeds. And they love wood ashes.

Garlic is essential to more than half the great cuisines of the world. There are a few varieties available in the UK, such as Germidour, Long Keeper and Pink, and these are all worth trying. Ideally plant the cloves in autumn for the biggest yields. Set them neither too shallow nor too deep: this is crucial. The holes must be between a fingertip and a finger's length deep, and at least a foot apart for good bulbs. (Bigger, fatter, outside cloves from healthy bulbs do better than small, skinny, inside ones.) Roundels like small onions sometimes occur at random in this year's crop; replant these and they split up into big bulbs the following year. Fill over the planted clove with sterile gritty sandy compost and firm well. In heavy soil make a deeper hole and partly fill with this mixture to improve drainage.

Garlic cloves can also be planted any time in spring but the earlier the better. They do not need a very rich soil. Do not feed or water unless drought conditions occur early in spring. Spray with seaweed solution regularly early on, but desist once summer starts. Always dig the crop before the leaves wither and blow away. Dry the bulbs, unwashed, in a warm dry airy place. I find they store best laid on nets stretched in roof spaces. If you fail to dig up your garlic bulbs, you'll soon spot them when they start to sprout. Dig them up, split and replant for the next year's crop.

Elephant or **giant garlic** is really a leek and about as strong tasting, with a garlic overtone – interesting for gourmets but no substitute for the real thing. Rocambole is very similar to garlic, with a smaller cloved bulb. It is different in taste and more disease resistant, and often produces an edible cluster of bulbils in place of seeds on top of the peculiarly attractive twisted neck. If you like pickled onions, try pickled garlic – it can blow your taste buds faster than chillies!

Shallots have a different flavour from onions and are often used in a subtler way. Plant healthy cloves in very shallow depressions and hold in place with a handful of sterile compost or sand. The cloves need to be at least a foot or two apart and can be planted from mid-winter on, or even during the previous autumn in mild areas. They do not need a very rich soil. Shallots are soon scattered by birds and worms and initially need replanting often, but otherwise rarely suffer any problems. Spray with seaweed solution regularly early on but stop once summer starts.

When the leaves start to wither, lift the shallots and store in a dry airy place. Immediately select the best clumps for next year's 'seed'. Some varieties such as Creation

can be grown from true seed but I've found Giant Yellow, Pikant and Sante to be superior. Hative de Niort is more of an exhibition sort but makes great gravy sauces. Shallots can be fitted in almost anywhere convenient – even in the ornamental garden if low yields per plant are acceptable. Pickled shallots are an alternative to pickled onions.

Onions are easily available in the shops all year round and in the garden they do take up a lot of space. However, they can be grown in several different ways to minimise the risks, which include fly attack, white and grey mould and a wet season, all of which have little remedy. This extends their season when they're home-grown to year round. Simplest of all are onion sets, miniature onion bulbs, which avoid many potential problems and give good results. These can be planted from autumn through winter to mid-spring; generally the earlier the better, if the ground is ready and the variety is suitable. Plant the sets on the surface at least a hand's breadth apart and fix them in place with a handful of sand or sterile compost. Keep replanting any the birds and worms pull out.

Onions need a firm rich soil which must be moist early on and allowed to dry as the crop matures. Do not feed or water once established unless drought conditions occur early on in spring. Spray with seaweed solution regularly early on but desist once summer starts.

Opposite Once the leaves start to wither it's time to lift the crop.
Top left Small ones keep better than big ones.
Bottom left More space equals bigger onions.
Left Onions must be well dried for storing.

Alliums all accumulate sulphur and may improve the disease resistance of plants growing near them.

Always lift the crop before the leaves wither and blow away. Never bend the necks down to 'help' as it reduces storage life! Onions can also be sown from seed direct *in situ*, but are more reliable sown under cover in mid- to late winter in pots or cells. They can be sown and grown at more than one plant per cell; two or three grown together produce smaller harder onions that keep longer than single big ones. Keep these seedlings growing strongly and plant them out in mid-spring. Plant them a finger apart for small long-keeping onions and give much more space for big singles or clumps. Sturon, Balstora and Turbo are excellent; Giant Zittau is good for pickling; Bedfordshire Champion a good keeper; and Southport Red Globe a change of colour.

For small pickling onions just sow thickly so that they crowd each other. Paris Silverskin are the ultimate pickling variety and especially good in piccalilli. You can sow most seed thick to grow your own sets for use the following year.

In late summer (about the middle of August in southern Britain), you can sow Japanese onions such as Senshyu Semi Globe and Imai Early Yellow *in situ* for over-wintering. These crop really early – well before midsummer, when onions are expensive to buy and the stored ones have gone. These do not store well themselves so must be used first anyway. Winter-hardy onions are prone to slugs; I mix Buffalo seed in with the Japanese varieties and sacrifice it to the slugs, leaving the other varieties thinned.

If onion fly is a problem in your area, then grow only from sets, which usually escape damage, or grow from seed under fine netting or horticultural fleece. If the leaves get a grey mould, try dusting them with wood ashes to dry up the attack. Be careful never to break or damage the leaves or bulbs – weed onions by hand and not with a hoe. Once the bulbs start to mature it helps to let the weeds grow, as they take up water and nutrients and help the ripening process. I repeat: never bend the leaves down to help ripening as this lets in disease.

Cut the onion roots well underneath with a spade or a sharp knife, then dry the bulbs off under cover in a dry airy place. They store best held on netting rather than tied up in bunches. To stop tears, try peeling onions under water. Also try slicing them both in rings and in segments as these cook differently – honest.

Spring onions are the slender sorts for salads, but thinnings of ordinary onions can be used instead (spring onions are really a salad bed item). There are also Welsh onions, which are more like chives; tree and potato onions, which are really only curiosities, though useful occasionally; and the Babbington leek, which resembles rocambole.

chapter 3 the gourmet's tastiest fruits and nuts

Divine peaches and nectarines, almonds, apples, pears, apricots, plums and cherries. Wilder fruits: hazels, cobs and filberts, figs, walnuts, mulberries and runners-up

Fresh fruits are wonderful. Full of flavour, sweetness and texture, they give pleasure to the eye an perfume to the nose, and their smooth skins ask to be caressed. How sad the offerings of the supermarket and greengrocer appear compared with the finest fully ripened specimens plucked from your own trees.

Little is easier than growing connoisseur fruits. They want to crop – it's what they do, year after year, with minimal help from us. All we need do is ensure they have the best conditions and thin the fruits so only the perfect mature. Then we have fruits fit, nay, fruits too good, for kings – let's save all for ourselves. And it is possible to grow a very wide range of fruits in even the smallest garden.

Few varieties of apple or plum are ever sold in shops but the enthusiast can find thousands of varieties to choose from to grow at home. The only problem is choosing which to grow; they're all so much better when garden-grown, but the range of varieties makes it bewildering. Tree fruits take a year or two at least to crop and even in the largest garden there is room only for so many, so it makes sense to test and taste as many as possible before you plant. Even so, it is not disastrous to have to grub a young tree up after a few years and replace it. Or it could even be reworked by grafting to a better sort.

Below The Asian pear, Kumoi

Once you know which varieties you prefer, it is not difficult or time consuming to grow a small orchard. A modern mini-orchard can be created using dwarfed trees and trained forms such as cordons. Even without a garden at all, full-size fruits can still be had from tiny trees in containers. You can even extend the season by moving these in and out of cover, using an orchard house, as it was once called. This doesn't need to be large or expensive – an ordinary greenhouse will do.

Where and how to buy fruit trees

Planting a few choice trees is not expensive, but filling an average garden with fruit trees, especially trained ones, does require an investment big enough to need careful planning and budgeting. A wider variety of better-quality plants can invariably be had by mail order, and may often be cheaper as well. I find most mail-order nurseries give excellent service. Get many different catalogues and compare them carefully before ordering, and do so early, that is during late summer as they may be dug in late autumn and you want to ensure you get your choice.

Buying trees incurs a high risk of importing weeds, pests and diseases, especially with container-grown specimens. I always investigate them carefully. I prefer bare-rooted plants to pot-grown for all but difficult subjects, as they are easier to inspect. Bare-rooted subjects are sold when dormant: without leaves they're much easier to inspect at the top as well as below. The root systems on well-grown bare-rooted trees are usually more extensive than on pot-grown, even though some is lost in the move.

Then we have fruits fit, nay, fruits too good, for kings – let's save all for ourselves.

Growing fruit trees from seed means random results and a long wait, as the new tree will not fruit until mature, which may take decades.

For the larger growing trees I believe it is risky to plant pot-grown specimens where the first yard of each root is coiled round in a ball. For smaller subjects, containerised plants are convenient and, from reputable suppliers, give good results; after all their roots can be teased out in a bucket of water.

True enthusiasts may wish to propagate their own fruit trees. All fruits can be grown in the original wild form, or as an improved form, from seed. Starting from seed means random results and a long wait, as the new tree will not fruit until mature, which may take decades. And until the fruits are produced there is no way of telling what they will be like – they may not be very good.

Almost all the best varieties of fruit are not species but clones, each of which is grown from a bit of an existing specimen grafted or budded on to specially chosen rootstocks. The rootstocks are used to restrict growth and make the trees more compact; they too affect the flavour but not significantly. Budding and grafting can be done by keen amateurs but the techniques, although apparently simple, are profoundly difficult to master, need much practice and are beyond the scope of this book (if you think otherwise, try for yourself!).

In most cases it is sensible to buy a young 'maiden' (two-year-old tree) ready to go, and train it yourself, rather than buy an older pre-formed tree. Smaller trees root quickly and after a few years make much better specimens than an initially larger (and much more expensive) tree.

Get the planting right

Remember, once the planting is over the tree's future is pretty well determined. So do a good job and do not skimp on the quality of tree or the preparation of holes. With holes, bigger is always better – that means wider and deeper. But do not mix in any muck with the soil: trees have wide-reaching roots and respond better to having any enrichment provided by mulching later. Trained trees need stakes or supports; these must be put in place before planting and must be strong enough to do the job for a good number of years. It's false economy to cheat on supports – they're hard to replace when the plants have grown and if they give way, a crop, if not the tree, is surely lost.

Do not plant trees deep. Almost all should be planted at no more than the same depth as they have grown, maybe even shallower. This is very important for choice fruits. Keep the roots near the surface in their respective layers and don't force them into a cramped hole. Gently replace the soil around roots, filling and firming as you go – you cannot over-firm! Then attach the tree to the support if needed.

I prefer to mulch heavily from the second year, making the roots go down initially by keeping the bare soil regularly hoed for the first year. Or use a plastic sheet mulch to suppress weeds. Whatever the final plan, keep a circle of soil, as wide as the tree or bush is high, totally weed-free for three years. Watering in dry spells during the first year is absolutely crucial.

Bare soil or a mulch usually gives better-quality fruits than a grass sward, though bigger and older trees may be easier to maintain if grassed under. If the sward is allowed to grow long and fall over it takes less water than when closely cut. But the quality of many fruits can be improved by keeping grass cut until late midsummer, then allowing it to grow long, when it competes for nitrogen, causing the fruits to ripen and store better.

Pruning and training

Start to prune and train early, to channel growth into superior fruit production. We often prune a plant if it becomes too large for the space available – that's just bad planning. And heavy pruning, especially at the wrong time, is counter-productive. In general, pruning moderate amounts from a tree or bush in autumn or winter stimulates regrowth, usually proportionate to the quantity removed. This is usefully employed when plants are young, to form their framework and work them to the desired

shape. But pruning in this way is not suitable for maintaining mature fruiting plants which have their structure already formed and from which we wish to obtain really good-quality fruit.

Summer pruning

Mature trees respond much better to summer pruning: cutting out three-quarters of each and every young shoot. (The exceptions are the 'leaders', the shoots that extend the framework.) This redirects growth and stimulates fruit-bud production on the short side-shoots or spurs that form. These may be further shortened and tidied in the winter, but then as only little wood is removed, vigorous regrowth is avoided. Strong sprouts need to be nipped back all the time, to maintain this clothing of short spurs clustering along an open framework of branches.

The principles of pruning

The majority of perennial woody fruiting plants can be readily trained and pruned in this way to form a permanent framework that carries these spurs, preferably uniformly, all over. Growing just one summer-pruned single stem, branch or cordon on a very weak rootstock allows us to squeeze many more varieties into the same space occupied by one full-sized plant. Although the weak rootstocks used may affect the flavour slightly, the effect of cordon and trained frameworks is to make every part of the tree accessible to air and light and open to close inspection and care. As each cordon is, in effect, but one branch, only light crops may be produced. But each fruit can be of the highest quality because of the attention given – and the yield from the small ground space occupied is very good.

Having a wide range of varieties as dwarf forms suits the gourmet, providing many different tastes and textures, and spreading the harvest and so reducing the effects of a bad year (if you grow a mixture, some varieties will do well even when others fail).

Vertical cordons are hard to maintain once they grow above head height. Sloping cordons makes them longer and increases the yield per plant,

Opposite Summer pruning MUST be done.
Below left Plum Pershore just starting to be trained as a fan.
Below Beurre Hardy pear espaliered on a south-east facing wall.
Bottom A standard gooseberry is useful if you need to plant the ground beneath.

without their becoming too high. Training two, three or more branches per tree is another way. These can be arranged as espaliers, in flat horizontal tiers, or as fans with branches that radiate from the centre, or as almost any shape you can imagine. For the vast majority of trees and bushes, the forms most commonly chosen are the expanding head, and the open bowl or goblet arrangement, on top of a single trunk.

If you give a woody plant space and freedom, it tends to make an expanding mounded hemispherical head, like an upturned bowl or vase, with dense growth over the surface and an almost empty space inside. This looks after itself but keeps getting bigger and fruits are soon produced out of reach on top, while much of the surface is in shade. To maximise the surface area of fruiting growth exposed to the sun and air, we try to invert this

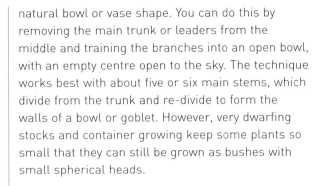

Below Cutting out the old, tying in the new.
Opposite Whitecurrant espalier, holding its fruit late into the autumn.

natural bowl or vase shape. You can do this by removing the main trunk or leaders from the middle and training the branches into an open bowl, with an empty centre open to the sky. The technique works best with about five or six main stems, which divide from the trunk and re-divide to form the walls of a bowl or goblet. However, very dwarfing stocks and container growing keep some plants so small that they can still be grown as bushes with small spherical heads.

The height at which a fruit tree's trunk divides determines how it is classified. Trees with trunks up to shoulder height are called half-standards; standards start higher still. Half-standards grow large, depending on stock, and are tall enough to mow underneath. Full standards make very big specimens usually planted only in parks and meadows. The gourmet is unlikely to be after bulk rather than quality, so should concentrate on cordons and other dwarfed and trained forms. Very dwarfing rootstocks are available for some fruits and these should almost always be selected unless huge crops are desired. Bushes and trained forms, especially those on the more dwarfing stocks, tend to be too low to mow underneath and are usually better mulched around instead.

Young unformed plants, or 'maidens', are cheaper than those with a good shape or framework ready trained by the nurseryman. It is very satisfying to develop your own espalier, goblet or gridiron from a maiden as the result reflects your skill and foresight. For speed and surety, though, buy them pre-formed.

Although most fruits crop on spurs on older wood, as explained above, some crop on new wood or on the tips. These 'tip bearers', such as most of the earliest-fruiting apples, need to be pruned on what is called a renewal principle. Whole branches or shoots are cyclically replaced as they reach a year or two in age and after they have fruited. Blackcurrants, raspberries, and peaches on walls are tip bearers and are labour-intensive as they regularly need strong young shoots tied in to replace the old fruited ones removed.

It is very satisfying to develop your own espalier, goblet or grid iron from a maiden as the result reflects your skill and foresight.

Thinning fruits

Thinning fruits is almost compulsory and always worthwhile. This is far better done in several stages rather than one. Once the fruits have set, regular visits should be made and the number reduced. First to go should be any that show imperfections or infections, then the misplaced, the overcrowded and the runts, and then some more. You cannot over-thin; those fruits left will swell even bigger in response. Two or three successive thinnings also gets rid of pests and diseases if all the chats (small, damaged and immature fruits thinned by hand or naturally) and windfalls are composted, burnt or deeply buried. Done regularly this results in huge perfect fruits at harvest.

It may seem complicated but most pruning is actually quick and simple once you've done it a few times. If you get keen on any particular fruit you will find whole books devoted to pruning regimes which claim improved results. But the simplest methods work nearly as well: let the sun and air flow freely and reduce the amount of fruiting wood the roots have to support. Providing you do not get carried away and remove unbelievable amounts of wood you are unlikely to do much harm. Use clean sharp secateurs, sterilise with alcohol, rarely use a saw and cover large wounds with a proprietary sealing compound to prevent water from getting in. Ideally do more summer pruning than winter and do it early. In the extreme case only buds not shoots are removed. Preferably summer prune in several stages so as not to shock the plant unduly, and start at the top to check the upwards growth first. If you remove a lot of fruit buds with old congested growth, you will get fewer flowers and fewer fruits but bigger better ones. Then new vigorous regrowth improves the tree's general health. Old trees often benefit from a simple thinning of excessive spurs from the remaining branches, again resulting in fewer but bigger sweeter fruits.

Stopping – nipping out the tip of a shoot a few leaves beyond a fruit – also redirects growth into the fruit and is an effective method, especially for peaches. Another way of increasing size and quality is to ring the stem below fruits. This is an old practice, and means cutting two sharp lines almost entirely around a stem or branch some way lower down the tree, then cutting across the ends of the cuts to enable the near encircling ring of bark to be peeled away. This is turned top to bottom, but still the bark side out, replaced and 'bandaged' in place with a tightly fitting plastic tape.This constriction on the downward flow of sap causes the fruits above to swell larger and earlier; however, it is detrimental to future growth. It would be rather greedy to do the same to a large branch or trunk but it can be done to bring reluctant trees into cropping – though root-pruning is probably better. Bending the branches down from the vertical is an effective, easy and safer way of improving yield. When trees are grown in containers, much less pruning is needed. The pot reduces the root run and so reduces pruning to a minimum. True, more care needs be taken with the compost and watering but then there's almost no weeding...

the choicest fruits

peaches

Peaches are probably the finest fruit for the gourmet to grow at home, especially when compared with shop-bought travesties.

Peaches (*Prunus persica*) are probably the finest fruit for the gourmet to grow at home, especially when compared with shop-bought travesties. To eat a ripe peach comfortably, you should need a bib. Such a degree of sweetly perfumed but near-liquid pleasure can be obtained only from a fresh sun-warmed fruit eaten immediately right beside the tree! The flesh varies from white through yellow; there are blood peaches like blood oranges with red-stained flesh. The skin colour may be dull green through yellow and orange to dark red. The perfume varies with variety, as does the texture, which also varies with cultivar, soil and climate.

Most peach stones are ribbed or 'perforated' with small holes in the shell. In varieties known as clingstones the flesh clings to this shell; in others, the freestones, the fruit is easier to enjoy, without the need to tease it from off the stone. Amsden June is early with greenish white flesh, is semi freestone and ripens at least a month after its name. Duke of York has better-flavoured creamy white flesh and is semi freestone. Hale's Early has pale yellow flesh and is freestone. Peregrine is the best choice for a bush tree in the UK; it has yellow-white flesh of excellent flavour, is freestone and ripens mid-season. Rochester is my second favourite for an outdoor bush; it is not quite so well flavoured with yellow flesh. Royal George comes late, has tasty, big yellow fruits flushed dark red with pale yellowish to white flesh and a small free stone. It is prone to mildew and best grown in a container moved under cover for

Opposite, **left and below** Rochester peaches, probably the best for growing outdoors in England, one looking ready for picking – do not pick unles the fruit comes away easily, then you will need a bib.

flowering and ripening. Bellegarde is a heavy freestone cropper of beautiful red fruits. These are produced so late that in cooler areas the fruits will not ripen outdoors but need to be under glass in a container. The same applies to Bonanza. Saturne is a peento or squashed peach which is very luscious if fiddly eating; it's dwarf growing and well suited to patio containers. There are many other varieties, some available only from specialists.

The most distinctive feature of peaches is the soft downy fluff covering their skin. A nectarine is a peach without this fluff. Nectarine flesh is firmer and less melting than a peach's, less prone to liquidising while you eat it. **Nectarines** (*Prunus persica*) have a definite, almost peculiar, rich aromatic vinous flavour quite distinct to that of a well-ripened peach. The colour of some nectarines also differentiates them from peaches: the older varieties have a greenish or sometimes even a purplish hue over a quite yellowish or greenish ground.

Most noticeably, nectarines just do not have any downy fuzz on their skin. They are instead very smooth and shiny, and closely resemble a very large plump plum. They need warmer conditions to fruit well but otherwise a nectarine is just a distinct and superior form of peach.

Nectarines most worth growing are Early Rivers and John Rivers, which ripen early. The best to my mind is Lord Napier, a tasty white-fleshed mid-season variety. This is followed by Elruge and Pineapple, which come late and must usually be grown in containers and ripened under cover.

Almond trees are almost indistinguishable from peach trees. *Prunus dulcis dulcis* is the sweet almond; *P. dulcis amara*, the bitter. Almonds are simply forms of peach with a tough inedible leathery 'skin' over a smooth stone containing that famous edible kernel. Named varieties of sweet almond are hard to find: Jordan, a light cropping old variety is still grown; Texas produces nuts that are especially tasty roasted and salted with the skin on. All these trees have beautiful pink blooms before the leaves appear; they are compact and somewhat resemble

willows with long lightly serrated leaves.

Peaches, nectarines and almonds can all be raised from stones but the results are somewhat haphazard and take years to fruit. (Ornamental varieties of any sort rarely ever fruit.)

Budded on to suitable stocks – St Julien A in the UK, for example – peaches will normally fruit the second or third year and may crop for twenty years but are rarely productive if longer lived. For warmer drier conditions than the UK, seedling apricot or peach rootstocks are better.

For an open site buy maidens and grow them as bushes or open goblets. The same goes for containers. On walls they do best as fans but need heavy renewal/replenishment pruning. Peaches demand a well-enriched well-aerated but moist soil with some lime. They prefer open gravelly soils to heavy and need to be at least six good strides apart. They need no supports after the first year unless being trained. Peaches need copious quantities of rich compost annually and deep mulches are obligatory to ensure the constant moisture they demand. Where they are planted against walls, water plentifully and constantly throughout the season or the fruits may split. But bear in mind they are also intolerant of waterlogging. Peaches and nectarines should not be planted near to almonds as they may hybridise, resulting in bitter nuts.

Peaches are often grown under glass, where the extra efforts of replenishment pruning and tying in are repaid by gorgeous succulent early fruits, free from the depredations of birds. The greenhouse must be unheated in winter to give peaches a rest. Red spider mite can be especially troublesome under cover unless high humidity is maintained.

Peaches are good subjects for large pots as they can take heavy pruning if well fed and watered. Pots enable them to be brought under cover during mid-winter and throughout flowering and fruiting, avoiding both peach leaf curl and frost damage. Outdoors the flowers and young fruitlets must be protected from frosts.

Peaches fruit on young shoots and it is essential to have plenty of these growths. On walls and under cover they are usually fan trained: the strongest young shoots are allowed to spring from the main frame while others are rubbed out early. These new strong shoots are then tied in to replace growths that have fruited and been cut out. Fortunately, if the pruning of peaches is temporarily neglected, healthy young bushes respond to being cut back hard by throwing plentiful growths.

More important than pruning is thinning. Peaches are very prone to overcropping, breaking their branches and exhausting themselves. Thin the fruits ruthlessly, removing those touching or anywhere near each other. Do this very early on and then again later. This is essential if you want gourmet specimens. Peaches suffer losses from birds and wasps. Small net or muslin bags can protect the crop or a big net can be draped over the whole bush. Earwigs may get inside the fruits to eat the kernel; trap them in rolls of corrugated paper wrapped around branches.

The major problem is peach leaf curl disease, which puckers the leaves and turns them red and yellow and they cease to function properly. Severe attacks cripple trees and may eventually kill them.

Above Nectarines need to be under cover.
Opposite Charles Ross – one of the best dual purpose apples.

Keeping the buds dry, either under cover or under a plastic sheet in winter, prevents the disease almost completely. Outdoors, spraying with Bordeaux mixture prevents the disease if done several times as the buds are opening in late winter. Dieback and gummosis (an oozing of a greasy or translucent sappy gum from fissures in the bark with a poor prognosis) are symptomatic of poor growth and are best treated by heavy mulching and hard pruning in very late winter.

Peaches, nectarines and almonds all benefit from alliums growing underneath, especially garlic and chives. Nettles growing nearby are reputedly helpful at preventing the fruit from moulding. If fruits start to mould remove them before they spread the infection, and use the best bits for preserves. Watch carefully for the first to ripen. A truly ripe peach is a bag of syrup waiting to burst. If picked under-ripe, the fruit never develops the full gamut of flavour or the liquidity. A good peach is a feast, drink and all. As with so many fruits, they are best straight off the tree but can be picked a few days early if handled with great care and kept cool. The slightest bruising, though, and they decompose. They keep best suspended in a fine net.

Rich in vitamin A, potassium and niacin, peaches and nectarines are healthy as well as delicious. Their jam is aromatic and a way to utilise the many fruits that get patches of rot or look unlikely to finish ripening. Fruits can be frozen after stoning and glazed in sugar – their juice is nectar. They make excellent chutneys and can even be dried for winter snacks. Almonds can be dried in their shells and packed in salt to keep for up to a year, or made into marzipan.

apples

Downing's Fruits, printed in 1866, listed just 643 varieties of apple (*Malus domestica*) . Currently more than five thousand named apple varieties – representing about two thousand distinguishable clones – exist for the gourmet to choose from. Several hundred distinct varieties are widely obtainable from nurserymen – though sadly only a half-dozen or so are grown on any commercial scale and sold in shops.

Apples vary in shape from the spheres of Gladstone and Granny Smith to the flattened buns of Bramley and Mère de Ménage, and the almost conical Spartan, Golden Delicious and Worcester Pearmain. Their colour may be white, green, yellow, orange, scarlet or dark red to almost purple. The flesh may be white, yellow or even stained blood-red as with the old Sops in Wine variety. Texture can vary from crisp to pappy and may be juicy or dry, acid or insipid, bitter, bland or aromatic. (The central core has several brown seeds, which although tasty and edible in small amounts, can cause death if eaten in quantity as they contain a natural cyanide.)

Apples are native to temperate Europe and Asia. They have been harvested from the wild since prehistory and were well known to the ancients. The Romans encouraged their cultivation and Pliny knew of three dozen sorts by the first century AD. At the time of the Norman invasion of Britain only one pomerium (orchard) at Nottingham was mentioned in the Domesday book. Costard and Pearmain varieties were noted in the twelfth and thirteenth centuries. The oldest variety known and still available is Court Pendu Plat (a mid-winter dessert apple) which may go back to Roman times but was first

Apples vary in shape from the spheres of Gladstone and Granny Smith to the flattened buns of Bramley and Mère de Ménage, and the almost conical Spartan, Golden Delicious and Worcester Pearmain.

recorded in the sixteenth century; it's still grown because it flowers very late, missing most frosts. Nonpareil and Golden Pippin also date from the same period; they may keep till the following mid-spring. Golden Reinette (a mid-winter dessert apple) pre-dates 1650, by which time about five dozen varieties were known.

Ribston Pippin (a mid-winter dessert), which is not happy on cold wet soils, has one of the highest vitamin C contents and a superb flavour; it was bred in 1707. Other early-eighteenth century varieties include Ashmead's Kernel, one of the best of the late-keeping dessert apples; Orleans Reinette (mid-winter dessert) which is juicy, very tasty with a rough skin and not very happy on wet cold soils; and the rare but choice Pitmaston Pine Apple (a mid-winter dessert) that is small-fruited but with a rich honey-like flavour.

The nineteenth century ushered in many good varieties including some from the New World such as Wagener, a mid- to late- winter, hard-fleshed keeper raised in New York State. The ubiquitous Golden Delicious was found in West Virginia; it is widely grown on the Continent commercially but actually tastes quite good grown at home – though it is prone to scab and stores badly without waxing. The Cornish Gilliflower is a very tasty late-keeping dessert. Unlike

most apples (other than Irish Peach) it is suited to a mild wet climate, but is no good for training or cordon culture. One of the best dual-purpose apples – that is, for cookers and eaters – is Blenheim Orange, a mid-winter apple with a wide, flat, golden, russeted fruit; it makes a large tree. Another classic, Cox's Orange Pippin (a late-autumn variety), is reckoned the best dessert apple, but it is not easy to grow as it is disease-prone, and hates wet cold clay soils and windy sites. Sunset and Suntan are far superior Cox offspring and well worth growing instead. James Grieve (mid-autumn dessert) is prone to canker but is the traditional pollinator for Cox's and a good cropper of refreshingly acid, perfumed fruits edible only straight off the tree.

Egremont Russet (late autumn) is one of the best russets, a group of apples with scentless roughened skin, crisp firm flesh that is sweet and tasty but never over-juicy or acid. George Cave crops in late summer and is a far better early apple than Beauty of Bath. It's better textured, and can be pruned to spurs, though is happier as a tip bearer. Discovery is the best early. It's a modern (in horticultural terms) early apple, introduced in 1962, with scarlet fruits with creamy white flesh that ripen in late summer. The flowers are fairly frost-tolerant and it is scab-resistant so rapidly dominated the early market, especially as it keeps better and for longer than most other earlies.

Other apples with excellent flavour are Charles Ross (mid-winter) which can be a huge apple and is dual-purpose and Kidd's Orange Red (mid-winter); the modern Jupiter (early winter) and Saturn (late winter) are also reliable.

It is interesting to note that, given the same conditions, some varieties contain much more vitamin C than others: Ribston Pippin typically has 31mg/100g, Orlean's Reinette 22.4mg, Bramley's Seedling 16mg, Cox's Orange Pippin 10.5mg, Golden Delicious 8mg and Rome Beauty 3.6mg. Maybe the saying should be 'A Ribston Pippin a day keeps the doctor away.'

Cooking apples are usually much larger, more acid and less sweet when raw. Fruits are often greener and generally store till mid- or late winter. Cooker trees run out of potash quickly so give them wood ashes. Bramley's Seedling (a mid-winter cooker) has one of the highest vitamin C contents of any cooker. The tree always grows too big so have it on a more dwarfing stock. Howgate Wonder grows some of the biggest fruits. Most cookers break down to a frothy purée when cooked and, unlike most desserts, few retain any texture. Bramley's, Norfolk Beauty and Reverend W Wilks are typical, turning to sweet froths or sauces when cooked. However, Lane's Prince Albert, Lord Derby and Encore stay firm and are the sorts to use in pies and tarts.

Apple pips rarely grow into fruiting trees of value, although, to be fair, many of our best varieties were chance seedlings. Apples are propagated by grafting or budding onto different rootstocks, depending on the site and size of tree required. They can be grown from cuttings on their own roots but they then get big.

For the gourmet after many varieties in a small space, the most dwarfing stock is M27. This is useful for pot culture, but if grown outdoors, trees need staking all their lives and the branches start so low you cannot

Their colour may be white, green, yellow, orange, scarlet or dark red to almost purple.

Opposite: top, left to right Discovery; Greensleeves. **Middle, left to right** Author picking apples; Charles Ross; James Grieve. **Bottom, left to right** Hamling's Seedling; Laxton's Fortune; Holstein.

mow or grow anything underneath. M9 produces a tall human-sized tree that still needs staking – this is probably the best choice for cordons. But trees on such very dwarfing stocks do badly in poor soil and during droughts. M26 is bigger though still needs a stake, but it is probably the best for garden use. Trees on this stock need to be at least three strides each way from other trees. For poor soils MM106 is better. Although compact it needs about four strides between trees and is probably more for the farm.

Apples are much neglected as trees; they prefer a rich moist and well-drained loam. Planted lackadaisically almost anywhere, and left untended, they still usually manage to do quite well for us. What they cannot stand is waterlogging, or being on the site of an old apple tree or near others that have been long established. Neither do they thrive in dank cold shady frost pockets.

On very dwarfing stocks apples are easily grown in large pots. They'll need hard pruning in winter and in summer all the lengthening shoots need nipping out, so tip-bearing varieties are not really suitable for pots. Special varieties have been developed for container growing that supposedly require little pruning but do not produce the gourmet-quality fruit we are after. Apples do not like being under glass all the time as they need a winter chill, and they are more susceptible to pests and diseases in hot dry conditions. However, some foreign varieties such as the classic Calville Blanc d'Hiver can in Britain be grown to perfection only under cover. Apples are often left to grow for years with no pruning other than remedial work once the head has formed. They may be trained and hard pruned summer and winter

back to spur systems on almost any shaped framework, though rarely as fans. For beauty and productivity apples are best as espaliers; for growing the maximum number of varieties, as space-saving cordons; and for ease and quality, as open goblet-pruned small trees.Tip bearers are best only pruned remedially as hard pruning removes the fruiting wood. Instead they must be pruned on a replenishment system (as for peaches), which is much more work.

More important to the gourmet than pruning is thinning. Removing crowded and congested, damaged and diseased apples significantly improves the size and quality of those remaining and prevents biennial bearing (where a

Below Bramley Seedling.
Right Gold Parmane trained on a gate on a pot.
Below right Apples on a serpentine wall.

tree gets stuck in a cycle of bearing so heavily one year it is exhausted and misses a year before cropping again]. Thin after the midsummer June drop occurs and at least twice again after, disposing of all the rejects and windfalls to destroy any pests. Apples are most commonly grown in much of the temperate zone and have built up a whole ecosystem of pests and diseases around themselves. But natural checks and balances mean they still crop enormous quantities most years anyway. Vigorous growth is essential to help reduce many problems, especially canker. The commonplace pests require the usual remedies, but apples suffer several others.

Holes in the fruits are usually

caused by one of two pests. Codling moth larvae generally make holes in the core of the fruit pushing the frass (the detritus produced by a grub, a mixture of masticated bits and turds) out the flower end. They are controlled by corrugated cardboard band traps, pheromone traps, permitted sprays as the blossom sets, and good garden hygiene. The other hole-maker is the apple sawfly, which bores narrow tunnels that emerge anywhere – the grubs then eat into another and even a third fruit. They are best controlled by hygiene: by removing and destroying affected apples during thinning. Permitted sprays can be used just after flower set, while running poultry underneath will help to control them.

Woolly aphis can be sprayed or dabbed with soft soap. Sticky non-setting tree bands control many pests all year round, especially in late summer and autumn.

Many varieties are scab-resistant. This disease first affects the leaves, then the fruits and – like brown rot and canker – is spread by mummified apples and dead wood. It is worst in wet areas.

All of these problems, plus mildews, are best controlled by hygiene, keeping the trees growing vigorously, well watered and mulched, and open pruned, plus seaweed sprays throughout the early growing season.

Apples also get damaged by birds, wasps and occasionally earwigs; for perfect fruits protect some with paper bags. Alliums (especially chives), penstemon and nasturtiums growing nearby are thought to reduce sawfly and woolly aphis. Stinging nettles also benefit the trees; dried as hay they help preserve stored fruits.

Early apples are best eaten off the tree; they rarely keep for long and go pappy in a few days. Most mid-season apples are also best eaten off the tree as they ripen, but many will keep for weeks if picked just under-ripe and stored in the cool.

Late keepers must hang on the trees till hard frosts are imminent – or bird damage is getting too severe. Then, if they are carefully picked, they may last for six months or longer, kept cool in the dark. In this way apples can be had most months of the year, providing you grow early- and late-keeping varieties and have a rodent-proof store.

Pick apples with a cupped hand and gently lay them in a tray, traditionally padded with dry straw. (If your store is damp, straw may taint – shredded newspaper is better.) Let the store stay open on cool nights and shut it during the day for the first few weeks to chill and dry the apples. Do not store early varieties with lates and don't keep them near pears, onions, garlic or potatoes. Fruits must be free of bruises, rots and holes, and the stalk (pedicel) must remain attached. Apples individually wrapped in paper keep longer, or you can pack shredded paper around them.

Apples are excellent raw, stewed, made into tarts, pies and jellies, especially mixed with other fruits which they help set. Apples can be puréed and frozen or dried in thin rings. The juice is delicious fresh and can be frozen too or turned into cider or vinegar.

pears

To the true gourmet there is probably no finer fruit than a good ripe pear (*Pyrus communis*). The finest pear, Doyenné du Comice, is, uniquely, delicious shop-bought. I know of no other fruit where the best can be bought. Of course, they are better still when home-grown and lovingly ripened. And there are hundreds more varieties awaiting the gourmet.

Although pears very closely resemble, and are related to, apples, there are no known natural hybrids between them. Pears are native to Europe and Asia and were known to the ancients; Pliny records 41 and Palladius 56 varieties. A list of fruits for the Grand Duke Cosmo III in late-mediaeval Italy raised the number to 209. In 1866 the American author T W Field catalogued 850 varieties. The rapid increase in numbers, and improved quality, was mainly due to breeders in France and Belgium at the end of the eighteenth century, who created most modern varieties.

As pears are now used more for dessert than as culinary fruit, and dessert pears can be cooked but not vice versa, it is worth gourmets' growing purely culinary pears only if they really take their fancy. Doyenné du Comice (a late-autumn pear) is by far the best dessert variety. None other approaches it for sweet aromatic succulence, and each pear can reach a magnificent weight. They deserve to be espaliered on your warmest wall and given the delicious Beurré Hardy (mid-autumn) as a pollinator.

Bartlett/Williams' Bon Chrétien (early/mid-autumn) is widely grown for canning but is an excellent table fruit if a bit prone to scab – and is parthenocarpic (making imperfect but edible fruits without pollination), as is

Conference (early/mid). This latter is a reliable cropper on its own, raised in 1770 in Berkshire. It's scab-resistant and very widely grown, though Beth (early) and Concorde (late) have superseded it – especially the latter which is reliably self-fertile.

Jargonelle is an old variety which crops for me in early August in East Anglia and about the same time as Souvenir de Congress – these are the earliest with good flavour. Improved Fertility (mid) is very hardy and crops heavily and regularly. Other superb pears are Clapp's Favourite and Dr Jules Guyot, (both early/mid-season); Glou Morceau and Durondeau (both late), keep into the New Year.

There are many other pear varieties, and several species, which generally have ornamental rather than esculental value. The birch-leafed pear (*P. betulifolia*), comes from fourteenth century China, where almost all parts were eaten – flowers and leaves as well as the small fruits. The Nashi or Asian pear, in varieties such as

I know of no other fruit where the best can be bought. Of course, they are better still when home grown and lovingly ripened.

Kumoi or Shinseiki, is a most apple-like pear, brown-green, russeted and crunchy; it's juicy, perfumed but a bit insipid. Some even love them over-ripe and although good fresh they make the best dried 'apple' rings I have ever tried. Asian pear trees are easy, attractive, effectively self-fertile and productive.

All dessert pears need a rich, well-drained, moist soil, preferably light and loamy. They can be cropped in the open in southern England but do better on a wall further north. Many can be cropped on a shady wall but then never achieve the same degree of excellence.

Pears are hindered by grass so this should not be allowed near them in their early years or where supreme quality is sought. You can grass under them later, especially if they're in rather too heavy, damp conditions or growing too strongly.

Blossom and fruitlets may need protection from frosts as trees flower early in spring. Pollination is best ensured by planting a mixture of varieties, but beware – old pollination tables are mostly unreliable. Some pears such as Conference will set some fruit parthenocarpically (without fertilisation), but these fruits are usually not as good as fertilised ones, being misshapen and lacking seeds.

Pears on their own roots make very big trees, too big to prune, spray or pick, and the fruit gets damaged when it drops. To control their growth they are usually grafted on quince roots, which makes them smaller and more compact trees. (For heavy damp soils and for big trees, seedling stock was used but there is little demand for this nowadays.) Pears have been grafted on to apple

stocks and even on to hawthorn. As some varieties do not bond readily with quince stock they are 'double-worked', or grafted on to a mutually compatible inter-graft on the quince. This takes more work and an extra year in the nursery. Never plant pears deep as they are prone to scion rooting where the original pear sends out roots at the point where it is grafted to the rootstock. This allows them to make bigger less fruitful trees and destroys the benefit of the rootstock.

Pears can be fruited in big tubs; they are amenable to hard pruning, responding better than most other fruits and to the cramped conditions, but need

Opposite: top, left to right
Jargonelle; Doyenne du Comice; Louis Bonne of Jersey.
Middle, left to right Beurre Hardy; Durondo; Kumoi, an Asian pear.
Bottom, left to right Conference; Williams; Kumoi.

feeding and watering religiously. While pears appreciate a warm wall they are not easy under glass as they do not like to get too hot or humid. They can be grown in containers and moved indoors for flowering and fruiting, then outdoors for summer and most of winter – they need the chill and are hardy.

Pears don't come true from seed, reverting to unproductive forms. They may root from cuttings and can occasionally be layered but always grow too big on their own roots. Grown as trees or bushes pears can be left to themselves except for remedial pruning. With summer pruning they can be trained to an endless variety of forms. As they benefit from the shelter of a wall they are commonly grown against them as espaliers, and are more rewarding for less work than a peach in the same position. There are many specialised training forms for pears. In addition to the standard cordon, espalier and fan, there are intricate and specialised pruning methods. Pitchforks and toasting forks have two or three vertical stems on short arms. The Palmette Verriers have long horizontals that turn vertical at the ends and the L'Arcure is multi-curved.

Pears will take almost any shape you choose. You will not go far wrong at keeping them in shape if you shear off almost all long growths by three-quarters in summer and then again by a bit more in winter.

Thin the fruits really hard as you would for apples. Pears suffer fewer problems than apples and, providing the flowers miss the frosts and have a warm summer, they usually produce a good crop despite any attacks, especially if well mulched and watered.

Pear midge causes the fruitlets to blacken and drop off; inspection reveals the maggots within. Hygienic removal and disposal of affected fruits is one remedy; running poultry under the trees is also effective. Fireblight causes damage resembling scorching; it usually starts from the blossoms. Prune damaged parts and burn immediately, cutting back to clean wood. Scab is a problem in stagnant sites and it affects the fruits before the leaves – the opposite to apples. Sprays are unnecessary with the more resistant varieties such as Conference. Good open pruning and healthy growth not overfed with nitrogen reduce attacks. Always remove all mummified fruits and dead wood immediately.

Leaf blistering is usually caused by minute mites; these used to be controlled with lime sulphur sprays before bud burst, but soft-soap sprays have proved effective too.

Ripening can be poor in very cool or hot weather, resulting in hard or mealy fruits. Leaving the fruits too long on the tree or in storage causes them to rot from the inside out. Early pears are best picked almost, but never fully, ripe – they should come off when lifted to the horizontal. Keep an eye on them as they finish ripening; they will ripen slowly if kept cool, faster if warm. Left on the tree they go woolly.

Leave late pears until bird damage is too great – like apples, pick them with a stalk. Kept cool and dark, late varieties keep for months, ripening up rapidly if brought into the warm. Do not wrap them with paper and do not store apples and pears near each other as they cross-taint.

apricots

A home-grown apricot (*Prunus armeniaca*) ripened on a wall or in a pot is such a different delight compared with the sad old things you get from the shops; you may not realise they are the same fruit. The superlative texture, the sharp tartness and the sweet aromatic flavour of a good apricot are unsurpassable. Apricots resemble plums but their colour is distinct and the apricot stone is more spherical. The kernel is sweet and edible and the fruit flavour unique.

I rate Bredase most highly; it's the old Roman variety's modern descendant. I rate Moorpark next best; from 1760 it is the commonest variety and it may be a plum apricot hybrid; whatever it is, it is exquisite. Gourmets will search out Alfred, New Large Early, Hemskirke and Farmingdale which are early ripeners. Later come Breda, Goldcot, Hongaarse, Luizet, Shipley's Blenheim and Tross Orange. All are delicious.

Apricot trees are budded on to rootstocks such as St Julien A, which survives longest in wet heavy soils. Budding on to seedling peach or apricot rootstocks is better for lighter drier soils and in pots. Apricots can be raised from stones and come fairly true, but take a decade to fruit. Hunza wild apricots from northern India make large bushes with ornamental rather than cropping potential in the UK.

In most cool areas apricots crop reliably only against a sunny wall or in containers on a warm patio or under cover from late winter (as with peaches and nectarines). For container culture a goblet or bush shape works fine and will need little pruning – only removing dead and diseased wood as necessary. On a wall a fan of old branches with fruiting spurs works better, just as for apple. Nip and prune back to these spurs summer and winter. Apricots need moist rich soil with plentiful lime and full sun; given such conditions they give regular crops. They need a cold winter period to rest, and warm autumns to ripen their wood, so they cannot be kept under cover permanently. The plants themselves are tough but the flowers are so early that they and the young fruitlets are always in danger from frost. Protect the blossoms and small fruitlets from frost overnight with sheets. Thin heavy crops ruthlessly or they'll all be small or drop.

Apricots suffer from dieback and gummosis – resiny gum oozing out of the branches or, fatally, the trunk. These are symptomatic of poor growth, which can hopefully be corrected by more compost, mulches and water, seaweed sprays and hard pruning. Cut out any dieback until no discoloration is seen in the middle of the stem. Apricots may benefit from alliums growing underneath, especially garlic and chives. Ants introduce, and farm, scale insects and aphids and need eliminating. Apricots ripen best on the tree but turn mealy if they go over. Check them carefully once they are nearly ripe. Unripe or green fruits removed during thinning make surprisingly good tarts. Apricot jam is superb, and the fruits can be frozen, dried or preserved in brandy or rum. Rich in vitamin A and potassium they are healthy snacks. The edible kernels are used to make wonderful ratafia biscuits.

The superlative texture, the sharp tartness and the sweet aromatic flavour of a good apricot are unsurpassable.

plums

Plums (*Prunus domestica*) come in more permutations than most other fruits, varying in season, size, shape, colour and taste. Yet in the shops we get Victoria plums and maybe one other. And not even good Victorias at that.

Our European plum has mixed native ancestors from most of the temperate zone and was known to the ancients. Pliny describes cultivated varieties that were probably spread with the Roman Empire throughout Europe. During the crusades Henry VII is recorded as importing a 'Perdrigon' plum. By 1864 over 150 varieties were offered in nurserymen's catalogues. There are still hundreds of good varieties.

Victoria is famous and rightfully so, as it's self-fertile, pollinates many others and has golden-yellow-fleshed, large yellow ovoid fruits flushed with scarlet. Victoria ripens mid- to late August in Sussex where it was found in 1840; Jubilee is a new but similar larger-fruited variety which ripens a week sooner. Coe's Golden Drop almost resembles an apricot; sweet and delicious, it's a shy cropper and needs a warm spot or a wall. Severn Cross is an improved self-fertile seedling from Coe's. Czar has frost-resistant flowers and is self-fertile but is more use as a culinary plum than for dessert. Marjorie's Seedling is dual-purpose, late cropping and self-fertile. Both Victoria and Czar will even do on a shady wall but unless on very dwarf rootstock will soon get too big.

If plums are trained they prefer a herringbone shape, but this is tedious and much work.

Greengages (*Prunus italica*) are like plums, fruiting in mid-season with sweet, greeny yellow to golden fruits with perfumed flesh. The fruits tend to be smaller, firmer, more rounded and less bloomed than plums, with a deep crease down one side and frequently with russet spotting. The trees are sturdy, not often thorny and bushier than most plums, though not quite as hardy. Old Green Gage is original but can be unreliable; Cambridge Gage is an improved seedling. Transparent Gage is another old variety from France and is honeyed in its sweetness. It has almost transparent golden-yellow flesh heavily spotted with red and it fruits in late summer. Reine-Claude de Bavais possibly has a plum as one parent, fruiting a fortnight or so after the previous varieties, in early autumn. It makes a most delicious jam, a touch more acid and tasty if picked a week or so early. Golden Transparent, another hybrid, is a large round transparent yellow; it ripens late and needs a wall in most cool areas but is self-fertile.

Denniston's Superb (aka Imperial Gage) comes from the USA and has some flavour; it is larger-fruited, hardier, regular cropping and most valuable of all, self-fertile. Jefferson is similar, later but not self-fertile. In colder areas gages need a wall: some will fruit even on a north wall to only small detriment if well thinned. Try Denniston's Superb, Early Transparent Gage and Oullins Gage.

Damsons (*P. damascena/insititia*) closely resemble plums, but the fruits are more oval, with less bloom and a spicy flavour once cooked. Their trees are compact, tough and usually self-fertile. Damsons are now found in only three varieties. Farleigh from Kent is a heavy cropper if well pollinated and a sturdy bush often used as a windbreak. Merryweather has slightly larger fruits with greenish yellow flesh earlier in autumn. The Shropshire or Prune Damson, which ripens last, has the better flavour but is a light cropper.

Above left Victoria, the most ubiquitous plum.
Above right Early Transparent Gage is delicious fresh or cooked.
Right Purple Pershore makes two delicious jams, with skin and without.
Opposite You haven't lived until you have a home-grown apricot.

Plums come in more permutations than most other fruits, varying in season, size, shape, colour and taste. Yet in the shops we get Victoria plums and maybe one other. And not even good Victorias at that.

The **cherry plum** or myrobalan (*P. cerasifera*) is often confused with the mirabelle. The latter is similar but smaller-fruited, much more flavourful – and rarely grown, save in France. Yellow myrobalan plums are often sold as mirabelles in shops to ensure they sell. Myrobalans are self-fertile. Their fruits are spherical, a little pointed at the bottom, and can be yellow, red or purple with insipid sweet juicy flesh – used under-ripe they make good jam. The growth is less brittle than most plums so can be woven into hedges, and trees are often used as a windbreak.

Japanese plums (*P. salicina* and *P. triflora*) are large plums without much flavour, such as Burbank and the similar Beauty. They are red with sweet juicy yellow flesh that clings to the stone. Blossoming early, they're vulnerable to frosts but more

tolerant of a wider range of warm conditions than ordinary plums so may be better grown under cover.

Bullaces (*P. insititia*) are the common wild plum of central Europe, but are rarely offered for sale. Also known as quetsch, they are the source of many good liqueurs; they have blue-black berries with golden yellow flesh on a compact twiggy tree. British bullaces are spherical. The Black Bullace and the improved Langley Bullace are bluey black; Shepherd's Bullace is greeny yellow. These fruits ripen later in autumn than most other plums, are small and too acid to eat raw, but make excellent preserves that the gourmet should swoon for.

The rest of the wild *Prunus* species are very much tough hardy alternatives for difficult spots or wild gardens. **Sloes** are the fruits of the blackthorn (*P. spinosa*); they are black ovoids with a bloom like plums and hard juicy green flesh. They're far too astringent to eat raw, though like many children I forever used to search for a sweeter one. Use them to make sloe gin. There are several plum/apricot hybrids known as plumcots which are hard to find but worthwhile. There are also many ornamental plums that may fruit and amongst the best is Spencer Hollywood which is pink-flowered and purple-leafed.

Plums like a heavier, moister soil than many other fruits. This means they are often grown on cold damp sites and heavy soils which they really do not like.

Because of their susceptibility to spring frost, brown rot and wasps, a few choice sorts are worth flowering and fruiting under glass in large pots in the orchard house, just as for peaches. They can go outdoors for summer as they do

> **Very heavy crops of plums must be thinned ruthlessly – even with shears. Even so, the branches may break if not propped.**

Above left Cherry plums, good for jam and for windbreaks.
Opposite, clockwise from top left Purple Pershore is a cooking plum that is both tart and sweet, if you like a sharp taste; Reine-Claude de Bavais makes the most incredible jam picked just under ripe; be careful with Victoria – some nurserymen offer inferior clones; Marjorie's Seedling, another very popular, dual purpose plum.

not relish hot conditions and should be out from after fruiting until the following spring.

Plums can be grown from stone but take years to fruit and never come true. They're best budded on the most dwarfing rootstocks such as Pixy unless you want immense quantities. Grow them as a short standard or bush; leave them well alone once the head is formed except to cut out dead and diseased wood. Any pruning is best done in midsummer. Plums on dwarfing stock such as Pixy can be trained on walls.

Very heavy crops must be thinned ruthlessly – even with shears. Even so, the branches may break if not propped. Plums get several pests, but provided the flowers survive the late frosts they are so productive there is usually a surplus. Plum moth maggots can be trapped with pheromone bait. Avoid planting anemones nearby as they are alternative hosts for plum rust. Wasps and birds can be excluded by nets.

Picked under-ripe for cooking, plums keep for days but then have poorer flavours. Many plums can be peeled which avoids the worst side effects of excessive indulgence. It also means you can make two epicurean preserves from the one fruit: without skin and with. Plums are easy to jam, juice and make into cheese; they freeze well if stoned first and are wonderful preserved in plum brandy syrup. They can be stoned and dried – California became infamous for sending us prunes, which are no more than dried dark-skinned plums. Although special sorts of plums for prunes are available, such as Fellemberg and Pruneau d'Agen, prunes dry on the trees better in California than the UK, so use an oven if you need to (see chapter 8).

sweet cherries

Sweet cherries (*Prunus avium*) are sold in shops but they are never truly ripe nor of the choicest varieties. Gourmets must grow their own. As they are so irresistible to birds, they must be grown under netting or protected under cover. The delicious fruits come in pairs on long pedicels or stalks all along the fruiting branches. The flesh is creamy white or yellow, sweet or bitter, but once ripe is rarely acid. Years of continuous selection and cross breeding has given us sweet cherries of very mixed parentage. The Duke or Royal cherries have some sour cherry or Morello ancestry which makes them tastier with more acidity – as well as making the trees hardier. There are countless old varieties of cherry such as May Duke which is very early, often ripening before the longest day, and may fruit successionally on a shady wall. Governor Wood and Bigarreau Napoléon are my favourite old ones and they are also mutually compatible so they can pollinate each other. The former has red fruits a week or so before the yellow of the latter which makes the bigger tree. The white Merton Glory is another superb fruit.

Pollination is crucial for cherries and finding compatible varieties is difficult, so the most useful modern cherries are self-fertile and thus better bets to grow. Stella, Celeste, Cherokee, Sunburst and Summer Sun are fully self-fertile, with sweet dark red fruits in midsummer.

If you have an unknown sweet cherry that does not fruit, plant a Morello to pollinate it.

Cherry trees grown from stones take years to fruit and get too big. Normally, sweet cherries are budded on to dwarfing stocks such as Gisela and Tabel, which makes them smaller and easier to constrain. Prune them as little as possible after the initial head formation; any pruning must be done early during the growing season.

Sweet cherries are very particular to soil and site. They need plentiful moisture at the roots but loathe waterlogging and need a very rich but well-aerated soil with some lime. Poor soil conditions can be helped by growing trees on grass-covered mounds with clover and alfalfa to give back fertility.

Pot cultivation is the most effective way to get cherries, though they somewhat resent it. Growing in tubs and moving them temporarily into an orchard house, as for peaches, enables them to avoid flower damage from frost or rain and protects the fruits from birds. The trees need to go out after fruiting for a cool dormant period in winter. Unprotected cherries suffer terribly from bird damage but often escape the wasps by fruiting early. Rain during flowering can cause unprotected flowers to mould, and sudden heavy rain during ripening invariably splits the fruits.

Once ripe, cherries can be picked and kept for several days if absolutely dry and left on the sprigs – do not pack them deeply. Cut the cherries off the tree rather than risk damaging next year's buds by pulling off the stalks. They can be frozen, but this is fiddly as they need stoning first. Sweet cherries lack acidity and often do not make as good preserves as sour cherries. Combine them with redcurrant or whitecurrant juice for added acidity.

Morello cherries (*P. cerasus*) are very similar to sweet cherries, but are not so sweet – though very palatable if left to ripen fully. Their

Above Don't even consider cherries unless you've got a cage or good netting.

Poor soil conditions can be helped by growing trees on grass-covered mounds with clover and alfalfa to give back fertility.

trees are smaller than sweet varieties with slightly lax, more twiggy branches. They can be pruned much harder. The fruits have shorter stalks, tend to be darker colours and are more acid. More than fifty varieties of Morello and sour cherry were in cultivation before the Second World War – now only the generic Morello is offered by most suppliers. This last favourite, representative of all its missing brethren, is deep crimson to black in colour, with a richly bitter, slightly sweet flavour.

Sour cherries are late-flowering, so avoid the frosts more often than sweet cherries, making them more reliable. They ripen in mid- to late summer, towards the end of August in southern England. Morello is self-fertile and will pollinate almost any other cherry of any type if their flowering periods coincide.

Morellos fruit on younger wood than do sweet cherries and thus can be pruned harder. However, it is usually more convenient to stick to removing dead, diseased and congested growths in spring or summer. They are best grown as low bushes for picking and bird protection, but they can also be trained as fans. They will even crop well on north-facing walls. Morellos were one of the first fruits to be stored frozen and are still one of the best. They can be frozen without sugaring and retain their flavour superbly. Red Morellos, Amarelles or Griottes are closely related, slightly more stubby trees with red fruits. The Kentish Red and the similar Flemish have endured since at least 1700; they're self-fertile with a scarlet skin, soft flesh and are slightly bitter. The wild cherries (*P. padus*) native to Europe, known as bird cherry, gean or mazzard, have richly flavoured bitter black fruits of little value except for liqueurs.

hazels, cobs and filberts

Chocolate is much enhanced by hazelnuts – and they're only the dry old commercial ones. Creamy fresh hazels are sweet and delicious and come in several forms unseen in the shops. Hazels and cobs have a husk around the base of the nut; filberts (full-beards) have a husk that totally envelops the nut.

Hazels are shrubby trees with the well-known yellow catkins (male flowers) in early spring. The even more gorgeous carmine-red female flowers are minute, with sea-urchin-like tentacles that come out only on warm days. Wild hazels were originally *Corylus avellana* but, being wind pollinated, have crossed with cobs or Turkish or Barcelona nuts (*C. colurna*), and the filbert (*C. maxima*).

Hazels were known to the ancients; Pliny claims filberts were introduced by the Romans from Damascus. Best of all are red-skinned filberts (pictured on page 28), with tight russet husks – small and fiddly but, oh, so delicious. Cosford Cob is thin-shelled and a good pollinator for others. Kentish Cob (aka Lambert's Filbert) is a more prolific cropper of large nuts. Pearson's Prolific (aka Nottingham Cob) is compact, a good pollinator and has large nuts.

For the best flavour you can't beat wild hazelnuts. These can be grown from seed and crop in eight to ten years. Layering or grafting can be used to propagate the varieties but root suckers are even better. Detach them in autumn and pot up or plant *in situ* or in a nursery bed for a year before their final move. Hazels prefer stony hilly ground; a well-drained soil will do, but heavy or damp rich soils cause too much rank growth and fewer female flowers. They seem to associate naturally with bluebells and primroses, and

truffles can be inoculated and grown on their roots (that's the theory but the practice has failed me).

Hazels are best planted severally to ensure pollination. There seems no reason to grow hazels under cover and I suspect they would not like it anyway. They grow quite happily in pots but seldom crop well. For gourmet-quality nuts train the plants to spurs on open goblets – the trees must not be left to

become thickets. It is essential to keep them on a single trunk and remove suckers. Weedy growth underneath makes it hard to find nuts so keep it grassed down or well mulched. The latter is better as then you can rake up the nuts the squirrels have hidden. Hazels suffer few problems other than pigeons, pheasants, rooks, rabbits, rodents, children and especially squirrels. They all will eat the nuts unripe but they must be harvested fully ripe to store – ideally after

they have fallen off but then too many are thieved. Theoretically the nuts must be dehusked and dried to keep well, though I never dehusk mine. I store them for years, just packed in salt. The nuts of all varieties are used in savoury dishes but more often in sweet dishes and confections – hazel macaroons are really good.

The nuts are also used for liqueurs and make a light edible oil for exquisitely flavoured salads.

Right A filbert (full beard) nut (if the end was stuck out of the husk it would be a cob).

figs

Figs (*Ficus carica*) are sold in top-class greengrocers, but the gourmet gardener can grow better from an amazing range of several dozen varieties which crop over a long season.

Figs were one of the first fruits brought into cultivation and became an intrinsic part of the diet of the Mediterranean basin long before Classical times; Pliny notes no fewer than 29 varieties. Dried figs were brought to England by the Romans, though the plants were not officially introduced until the sixteenth century.

In the UK our figs are seedless and become a soft greeny yellow and pink within as they ripen from midsummer, and even earlier under glass. Brunswick produces large fruits which improve a couple of days after picking; Brown Turkey is reliably prolific and commonly available; White Marseilles has pale fruits and is a choice, but more delicate, cropper. Also available are: Angélique, Black Ischia, Bourjasotte Grise, Castle Kennedy, Negro Large, Osborn's Prolific, Rouge de Bordeaux, Saint John's, Violette Dauphine, Violette Sepor, White Ischia... more than a few!

Plants grown from seed are unlikely to fruit well. Instead, layers can be made during summer; suckers may be detached; or foot-long well-ripened or old wood cuttings taken during late autumn will root if given some bottom heat.

Figs vary in hardiness and are tougher once they get older; even if the top is lost, most will regrow from the roots, especially if these are protected from frost. For this reason, figs are often planted a little deep, to encourage stooling with multiple stems from below ground level, which are then worked as a fan. Best grown against a wall, they often crop in the open in southern Britain, their main enemy being excessive wet rather than cold.

It is traditional to confine the roots of wall-grown figs in a brick box to promote fruiting, but this appears unnecessary if heavy feeding is avoided. Nitrogen promotes too much soft growth but some seaweed and potash fruit feeds should be added to the water, especially for pot-grown specimens.

Figs fruit and ripen much more reliably in containers and more so under glass. With heat, artificial light and great care three crops a year are possible, although one summer crop usually gives better figs.

Figs need large well-drained pots and a compost with some lime and grit. They make excellent foliage plants for house or patio, though requiring careful watering and training. The most fruitful wood is well ripened, short-jointed and sturdy – long soft shoots are unproductive and better removed. Figs can be pruned any time during dormancy, preferably just before growth resumes in spring.

More important is to remove all fruits and fruitlets in late autumn, to prevent these from hanging on all winter and failing to ripen while suppressing a second crop that would otherwise succeed. In other words, don't be greedy: go for one summer crop, with several varieties to spread the season, and thin the fruits heavily.

Fig plants have few problems except birds and wasps. Under cover and sometimes on walls, figs may suffer from red spider mites. Weeding must be thorough in open ground to prevent rodents from eating the bark at the base of the trunks.

Most figs set some fruit parthenocarpically, that is, without actual fertilisation. However, varieties in hot climates have separate cropping plants and caprifig plants; the latter are cultivated to produce fig wasps, which crawl into the fruits on the female crop plants to pollinate them. Without caprifigs or wasps, our plants can never set viable seed. But this does not spoil the fruits, which are excellent, especially if grown under cover or on a warm wall. Ripe figs are delicate so do not travel or store well. They are delicious fresh; surpluses are best made into conserve and chutneys as only those grown in hotter countries to produce seeds can be dried easily.

Top Left A ripe fig. Be careful of the white rubbery sap which is very irritant to some people.
Left Immature figs.
Below left A nearly mature fig being treated with a drop of olive oil to help it ripen.

With heat, artificial light and great care three crops a year are possible.

walnuts

Walnuts (*Juglans regia*) are only ever sold, well past their prime, at Christmas, usually in a net bag with other, even older, nuts. There are few varieties of walnut but the gourmet must grow a walnut tree, for this nut is unbelievably better when really fresh, just shelled and the thin bitter skin peeled away. Try it and see. Once the nuts are old and dry the skin cannot be easily removed.

The fruits resemble peaches with a green husk around the nut, enclosing the kernel, wrinkled like a brain. The trees are very slow-growing, eventually getting massive. They have insignificant female flowers and yellow grey male catkins. All parts have the same distinct sweetish aromatic smell. The common or Persian walnut (*Juglans regia*) is native to western Asia: it reached Britain in the sixteenth century, if not in Roman times. Named varieties of common walnuts such as Franquette are hard to find. The black walnut (*J. nigra*) from north-east America is even bigger than the common and the nuts are larger and very hard to crack. Another American species, the white walnut or butternut (*J. cinerea*) has nuts half as big again as common nuts but strong tasting and oily. The heartnut from Japan (*J. sieboldiana var. cordiformis* or *J.*

ailanthifolia) has small easily-shelled nuts hung on strings.

Walnut species can be grown from seed but are very slow. Improved varieties are grafted or budded, and still take a decade to start to fruit, finally maturing around the century. They should be started in pots and transplanted to their final site while still small as they resent any move. Walnuts prefer a heavy moist soil and should not be planted where late frosts are common. As pollination is difficult they are best planted in groups – save fresh male catkins to pollinate later female flowers; hang them in a net bag on a tall cane.

The old saw 'The wife, the dog and the walnut tree, the more you beat them the better they'll be' puzzles many. Beating the tree doesn't encourage fruitfulness; it damages the bark, which then produces a more valuable distorted grain in the timber.

In the first century BC the Roman writer Varro noted the land was sterile near walnut trees; the leaves give off exudates that inhibit many plants by preventing seeds from germinating. The American species seem to have an even worse effect than the European. Minimal pruning is required but branches become massive: remove badly positioned ones early on and only in autumn as they bleed in spring.

For pickling gather the nuts small and early when a skewer can still be pushed through, before the shell forms. Later, knock the ripe nuts down before the squirrels get them. Remove the sticky staining peel and then dry the nuts, which will store for up to a year. Walnuts are delicious eaten fresh or cooked in association with coffee or chocolate, and they yield a sweet oil for salads.

mulberries

I have not often seen mulberries (*Morus nigra*) for sale. They are best gathered from a sheet laid under a tree to ensure ripeness, so I doubt the shop ones are worth comparison.

Mulberry trees become big, and can take a while to crop. The commonest, the black mulberry (*M. nigra*), has dark red fruits through purple when ripe and they stain everything that comes near them. The white mulberry (*M. alba*) is pale red or pinky white and not such good eating. The red mulberry (*M. rubra*) (with fruits that are almost black) is a native of North America and considered the best by many. I prefer the black. Named black mulberries such as Chelsea, King James I and Charlton House are not necessarily varieties but clones derived from old trees. The improved Large Black is sometimes sold. Sadly, most often you get a random, not very distinctive selection of the species.

Black mulberries have been known since Greek times but became widespread only when Emperor Justinian encouraged their planting as part of the silk-production process. Whoops, just like King James much later: black mulberry trees were planted mistakenly and not white, which the silkworms prefer. The right species was finally introduced to Britain in the sixteenth century. Cultivated mulberries have been selected for self-fertile forms, thus cropping well on their own. Species tend to be dioecious (male and female flowers on different trees) in the wild, i.e. seedlings and nondescripts may need another for pollination.

Long cuttings of well-ripened growth with a heel taken in late autumn often root; layering is a surer method – allegedly whole

branches will root, though not for me.

Mulberries need a moist, warm, well-drained soil, and the roots are brittle so they are best planted small in early spring. Mulberries do well in southern Britain in the open and are rarely bothered by frosts as they come into leaf and flower late. They are traditionally grown as specimen trees in a fine grass lawn to enable the fruit to be collected reasonably cleanly once it drops. If it's foliage you're after, mulberries can be pollarded hard and recover well. Left unpruned, they get congested, so thin the branches out early on to get a good open shape. Mulberries are tasty when fresh and ripe but go off so rapidly they are fit for gourmets only when home-grown. Any surplus can be frozen or made into jam or jelly, and the wine is unique.

quinces

Left Vranja, the Polish quince, hard as nails, but perfumed.
Below The Chaenomeles quince, just as hard but with small and more decorative flowers.

They are inedible raw though delicious and aromatic once cooked.

Classic quinces (*Cydonia oblonga*) are rock-hard fruits resembling pears. They are inedible raw though delicious and aromatic once cooked. These are way down my list as they're of so little use raw – save for perfuming a room – but quince jelly is delicious. There are several distinct forms: the Portuguese has bright yellow small fruits and the tree is lax; Vranja (aka Bereczki) has larger fruits and is more erect; Meech's Prolific is earlier to bear, fully self-fertile and keeps well with a good flavour; Champion is round, not pear-shaped, and has little flavour. Also relatively easy to track down are Ispahan, Maliformis (or apple shaped), Orange, Pineapple, Sobu and Smyrna.

Quinces were known to the ancients such as Pliny and Columella and, in the ninth century, Charlemagne encouraged the French to grow more. In Portugal and Spain they became popular served as *dulce de membrillo* or *marmelo*, a sweetened pulp that is the forerunner of our citrus marmalades.

Quinces like moist soil and love to grow well above water level near a pond. They are unhappy in cold and exposed places, though the decorative pink and white flowers come late and are rarely bothered by late frosts. Plant trees at least three strides apart. There is little to be gained by growing quinces in containers unless you are forced to by lack of space, in which case they are amenable.

Quinces do not come true from seed, and suckers removed from pear trees where quince has been used as rootstock are poor fruiters. So buy a named variety. Quinces can be trained but their contorted twisted habit makes this difficult. They need little pruning but thinning is important to improve the size of the fruits. There are no widespread problems; even the birds leave them alone. Pick the fruits before they drop and store like pears – but do not store with apples or pears or vegetables as they taint everything.

Quinces make a divine clear aromatic jelly, or a pulpy conserve-cum-cheese to accompany either sweet or savoury dishes. Pieces of quince can be added to apple and pear dishes for both their texture and their aroma. They keep their shape when cooked – hacking the raw quince into pieces requires a sharp axe.

Japonica quinces (*Chaenomeles japonica*) are a similar but smaller fruit the gourmet may prefer for their jelly. They also make a more attractive shrub more fitting for small gardens. Most japonicas have *C. speciosa* or *C.* x *superba* ancestry and are ornamental hybrids and varieties that also happen to fruit. Boule de Feu is my favourite and a heavy cropper. A related species *C. cathayensis* has larger green fruits and big thorns.

Hardier than cydonia quinces, these are easy almost anywhere, even on shady walls. However they're untrainable; a tangled thorny mass covered with red, white, orange or pink blossom in early spring. The hard round fruits vary from green to red and yellow and, like their cydonia counterparts, are even ignored by birds. They do well in containers so can be grown anywhere. Do remember to thin for bigger fruits.

medlars

I've got to include medlars (*Mespilus germanica*) as you may like them, but I don't. And you never see them in the shops. Fortunately they grow on compact small trees and resemble browny green pears or giant rose hips with a 'leafy' bottom. Medlars seldom ripen fully in cool regions, so are picked and stored like pears till at the point of decomposition or 'bletted' as this is called. The taste is somewhat like rotten pear. Pliny refers to the Romans having three sorts and that seems more than enough for us now! Dutch and Monstrous are the larger varieties, Royal and Nottingham allegedly tastier but smaller.

Medlars are obliging and will grow in most places, generally preferring a sunny spot in lawn or grass. The trees are hardy and the contorted framework and general attractiveness make them good specimens for a big tub. They can be grown from seed but are usually grafted on pear, quince or thorn stock. They must not be pruned as they bear fruit at the tips; if you must prune, remove whole branches. It's a good idea to thin the fruit.

rowan berries

Rowan jelly, from the berries of the rowan (*Sorbus aucuparia*), is piquant and sharp and goes well with savoury dishes, especially ham and game. You can buy it in discerning shops but home-made is better and there are several sorts of related conserves to try. Rowans have big heads of unpleasant smelling cream flowers followed by massive clusters of the well-known red berries.

The *Sorbus* genus is large and includes many ornamental species with edible berries. The rowan or mountain ash (*S. aucuparia*) has scarlet berries that birds love but are too sour and bitter for modern tastes until jellied with sugar. Rather than the common species, the gourmet will plant *S. aucuparia* var. *edulis*, which has larger sweeter fruits in heavy bunches. *S. aucuparia* var. *xanthocarpa* has yellow fruits, that last longer before the birds get them.

The whitebeam (*S. aria*) has similar red berries which were once eaten and used for wine. Fruit of the service tree (*S. domestica*) was also once eaten; they are brownish green, resembling small hard pears. The wild service or chequers (*S. torminalis*) has smaller, even harder, more ascerbic fruits.

Sorbus are tolerant of most soils, preferring drier to wetter sites. They can be cropped in big tubs as such a small amount of fruit is needed. Selected forms are budded in midsummer or grafted in early spring on to seedling rootstocks. Rowan fruits are thought to get larger if grafted on to service tree rootstock. Rowan berries can be used in all sorts of preserves, syrups and liqueurs, or added to spice up apple dishes. In emergencies dried berries have been ground into meal and made into bread.

sweet chestnuts

Sweet chestnuts (*Castanea sativa*) are included for completeness, as the gourmet can only grow exactly what can be bought in the shop. The trees get enormous and rarely crop in the UK. *Castanea sativa* is most often sold as the species though better forms exist, such as *C. sativa macrocarpa* or Marron de Lyon. The American sweet chestnut (*C. dentata*) had smaller richly flavoured nuts but has been wiped out by chestnut blight. New hybrids with the resistant Chinese chestnut (*C. mollissima*) may prove worth growing.

Sweet chestnuts are native to the Mediterranean region and were highly valued by the Romans. They do not like thin chalky soils but are not calcifuges and will grow on an alkaline soil if it is also light and well drained. Minimal pruning is required and best tackled in winter with care. In southern Britain sweet chestnuts generally crop after two hot summers: one to ripen the wood; the next the nuts.

Up to three nuts are found in each brown softly spined fruit, but you have to beat the squirrels to them. Rodents and birds, especially rooks and pheasants, also take them. Beat the nuts from the trees, remove the husks and dry the nuts. They will keep up to a year or much longer if oven-dried. Chestnuts are never eaten raw but roasted. They are the basis of scrumptious marrons glacés, and can be ground into flour and put into all sorts of sweet and savoury dishes.

cornelian cherries

Cornelian cherries (*Cornus mas*) resemble small waxy red cherries. They are too sour to eat raw but make excellent gourmet preserves. The variety *C. mas macrocarpa* has somewhat larger fruits. In France and Germany they were called sorbets and existed in red, white and yellow forms. Once widely consumed they were made into tarts, confectionery and sweetmeats and used as substitutes for olives.

The **red osier** (*C. stolonifera* syn. *C. serica*) and Kinnikinnik (*C. amomum*) are north-American plants with edible berries. *C. kousa var. chinensis* is a smaller tree than *C. mas* and sometimes produces juicy tasty fruits but thrives only in a moist acid soil.

C. macrophylla and the tenderer *C. capitata* fruits are eaten raw and made into preserves in India.

Bunchberry or dwarf cornel (*C. canadensis* syn. *Chamaepericlymenum canadense*), is a dwarf lime-hating plant resembling a sickly raspberry. Its interesting, if insipid, red fruits can be added to summer puddings.

Once widely consumed, cornelian cherries were made into tarts, confectionery and sweetmeats and used as substitutes for olives.

strawberry tree

Pliny did not regard the fruit of the strawberry tree (*Arbutus unedo*) as worth eating. I agree. It is planted for its beauty but not really for the fruit which has remained unimproved and is like a poor litchi. Other species include *A. canariensis* whose berries are made into sweetmeats, and the madrona (*A. menziesii*) from California, which has cherry-like fruits also said once to have been eaten. *A. unedo* prefers a mild climate and a warm soil rich in leaf mould and preferably acid. It is worth growing in a big pot as an ornamental, but be careful to use rainwater. Harvested a year after the flowers, the fruits can be made into confections and liqueurs but are rarely eaten raw.

azarole

Azarole (*Crataegus azarolus*) is a more edible relation of the well known haw or quickthorn. It is cultivated in Mediterranean countries for its yellow, orange, red or white cherry-sized fruits, which have an apple-flavoured pasty flesh with a few big seeds. The berries make excellent preserves, wines and jellies. From Armenia the tansy-leafed thorn or Syrian hawberry (*C. tanacetifolia*) is another similar berry almost palatable raw. The common hawthorn or quickthorn (*C. monogyna*) is not at all palatable. The young leaves and buds once known as bread and cheese had a nutty taste and made welcome additions to salads but are apparently slightly poisonous.

Some North American species have edible fruits. Blackthorn or pear thorn (*C. tomentosa*) has hard, orangey red pear-shaped fruits, *C. flava* has yellow and *C. douglassi* small but sweet, black ones with yellow flesh. These berries were very popular with the Native Americans who mixed them with choke cherries (*Prunus virginiana*) and service berries, then dried and pressed them into cakes.

carob

Carob (*Ceratonia siliqua*) is the locust bean or St John's bread: an edible purple-brown bean-like pod from the Mediterranean that tastes much like chocolate and is often used as a substitute. The seeds are not eaten, only the pods – some were excavated at Pompeii. They are widely used today as animal feed and I actually quite like chewing them.

yew

The foliage of the yew (*Taxus baccata*) is deadly poisonous with no cure and the seed is also poisonous, but the red flesh or aril around the seed has been eaten for centuries and is tasty and not harmful. Eat with care.

custard banana

Custard banana (*Asimina triloba*), the northern pawpaw, has a bottle-shaped fruit reaching melon size. It ripens from green to yellow bronze, with yellow pulp, big brown seeds and a sweet resinous flavour. It is not very tasty raw but better cooked. Closely related to the papaya, it is much much hardier and in its native North America is found almost up to the Canadian border. It makes a large attractive suckering bush with fragrant purple flowers in moist warm soils. Male and female plants are needed and pollination is by flies but it is slow to grow and crop. It does not do well in Britain; it should do better under cover but I've lost mine.

chapter 4 the gourmet's sweetest currants and berries

The choicest berries: strawberries, grapes, gooseberries and raspberries. The runners-up: bramble berries, currants, blueberries and wilder tastes

Some of the finest gourmet delights of nature are these soft, cane, bush, vine or fruitcage fruits – or currants and berries. It doesn't matter what you call them, these are sweet colourful gems packed full of flavour; a feast for the eye as well as the palate and rarely making us replete or uncomfortable.

In my opinion, the most exquisite of all are strawberries and grapes; nothing can surpass these freshly plucked from the garden. Admittedly, dessert gooseberries and possibly raspberries are nearly as good – and are easier in a damper climate.

There is an amazing abundance of edible currants and berries rarely offered in the shops but easy to grow – though some need blending with sugar or less acerbic fruits to bring out their exquisite flavours. All are perennials, quick to crop, easy to propagate and fairly compact, or can be kept so. Most are found growing naturally at the woodland's edge and thrive given moist root runs with a humus-rich mould and thick mulches. They will grow and even crop heavily in light shade, though produce sweeter, better-tasting fruit given more sun. A few, such as grapes, must have full sun to ripen well so give these prime positions. And always give each plant far more space than seems necessary – especially if you are after the highest-quality results.

In sunnier temperate regions most soft fruits crop well, especially where warm dry autumns help ripen their wood. Generally almost any soft fruit can be cropped anywhere; it's just that you may have to work harder. In hot dry places many become unhappy and prone to pests and diseases. But in wetter regions strawberries and grapes become prone to mould and berries generally do better than currants. Most soft fruits need a winter chill; seaside or mild regions may not induce sufficient dormancy and the plants may wither away. Severe cold may kill them; harsh winds will also ruin their chances. Waterlogging at any time is likely to be fatal for all save blueberries.

Good drainage and free air circulation are crucial but almost any soil will do as it can always be improved.

Keeping the birds out
The biggest problem with all fruit, after the weather, is the birds; everything else is irrelevant by comparison! Exclusion is the only effective solution and total exclusion best of all. Black plastic netting is ideal: to exclude blackbirds and pigeons a coarse $3/_4$ inch (2cm) mesh will do. Squirrels and rodents can be stopped by netting with galvanised chicken wire. This is always worth the extra expense at ground level where most damage occurs. Note that very fine mesh netting will exclude wasps and, unfortunately, bees.

In my opinion, the most exquisite of all are strawberries and grapes; nothing can surpass these freshly plucked from the garden.

The net or a fruit cage has other benefits. It creates a more sheltered environment because light frosts are kept off and chill winds reduced. In very hot regions denser netting provides welcome shade and cooler conditions. Fruit cages can be fitted into any site with ingenuity, using either second-hand materials or ready-to-assemble commercial cages. In areas of strong wind substantial materials have to be used; in sheltered sites you can get away with less.

Cage construction
Permanent sides of galvanised wire mesh and/or gravel boards are most practicable, with a light removable net supported on wires for the roof. The roof net needs to be easy to remove if snows are forecast, as a thick layer on top will break most cages. Masses of leaves from nearby trees also need removing promptly. For my fruit cage I use a huge recycled polytunnel frame with fine plastic mesh over the top and galvanised wire at ground level. It's vast and economical with plenty of headroom in the middle and very strong.

There are alternatives to a fruit cage such as individual paper bags, temporary netting or even bird-scarers, but nothing works half as well as a proper cage enclosing the crop on all sides. An existing shed or wall can form one side or a shallow cage can be made to fix against a wall. In every case do a thorough job: much time can be lost evicting trapped birds who find their way in. Be especially vigilant at ground level as creatures such as hedgehogs and rats make holes which others then use. (Strawberries are conveniently low-growing so can be given temporary protection with a net supported on strings on short posts and simply rolled back for access.)

Extending the season
A wall may be used for a barrier and for extending the season by planting the same crop on both sides – on the shady and the sunny side. Fruit on the sunny side will ripen first and will always taste finer; fruit on the shady side will swell bigger and be more luscious. Given the protection of a fruit cage too, most will hang on for a very long season

regardless. I often pick redcurrants and blackcurrants many months later than usual, well into late autumn when they are sweeter and much appreciated.

Going under cover
Extending the season can also be achieved by growing fruit in containers and moving these in and out of warmth or cool as necessary. By employing a greenhouse as an orchard house and with thoroughly good ventilation, you can have most soft fruits a month or more earlier simply by bringing them under cover in containers from late winter on. But protected cropping with the plants housed permanently under cover is difficult: most need a serious winter chill and free airflow. Plants in container culture also tend to be short-lived. Most like a wide-ranging root run, well mulched, moist and cool – just about the opposite of a pot! So containers need to be large, wide and deep, ideally full of moist, rich compost well-mulched with leaf

Above Tree fruits, such as apricots, rarely need nets or a cage whereas every soft fruit must be protected from the birds.
Opposite A crop of raspberries can be got from any reasonable soil as long as it is moist and well mulched.

mould, and kept shaded and cool. The constriction of a container gives the usual benefit of compacting the plants and bringing forward fruiting but it shortens the life of most, especially berries that produce runners rather than those growing more shrubbily on a single leg.

Most soft fruits are grown on their own roots: they don't need special rootstocks to help keep them small as they are compact already. Their natural form is usually bushy and, left to themselves, they crop freely.

Pruning for size and quality

We are after finer, larger fruits of gourmet quality, so we need to use pruning less to control plant size and more to improve the fruit's size and sweetness. Most soft fruits need a summer and also a winter prune. The gourmet wanting finer and choicer fruits will prune heavily in summer and thin hard. This reduces the quantity of fruit and ups its size, and saves wasting the plant's energies on unwanted shoots. In most cases disbudding or green-shoot pruning in early summer is better than hardwood pruning later in winter, apart from remedial work on the framework. Removing many fruits, particularly any that are diseased or infested, causes the rest to swell larger and keeps them cleaner.

To get a few extremely choice fruits, ringing the stems works but should be confined to one stem per plant per year and the stem should be discarded afterwards. Stopping – nipping out the tip a few leaves beyond a fruit – also redirects growth into the fruit and is especially effective for grapes. For the very best fruits, and to squeeze in the greatest number of varieties in a confined space, those that can should be grown as cordons, espaliers or other trained forms, with few branches, all open and exposed to the light and air (see chapter 3).

Soil preparation

As most fruitcage crops have very shallow root runs they prefer a richly mulched, cool, undisturbed soil, but not heavily enriched as future fertility is better added continually as mulches. The site must be exceedingly well prepared initially as later disturbance does too much damage, though it does not actually need to be dug very deeply unless the soil is badly drained or compacted. Start by establishing and sticking to paths. I use stepping stones to avoid compaction – and each is a tiny cool weed-free mulch in itself. Most soft fruits respond well to thick mulches, seaweed sprays early in the season and generous watering; combined with summer pruning and thinning, these improve the fruit quality tremendously. Generally they do not like having vegetables grown with them, especially if this involves digging or hoeing. However, some companion flowering plants such as French marigolds, *Limnanthes douglassi*, red clover and *Phacelia* are invaluable.

We are after finer, larger fruits of gourmet quality, so we need to use pruning less to control plant size and more to improve the fruit's size and sweetness.

the choicest berries

strawberries

The strawberry (*Fragaria* species), the most delicious of fruits, really needs no introduction! The gourmet will have despaired at the tasteless commercial travesties air-freighted from foreign parts to decorate his or her fruit salad. Few soft fruits improve in taste so dramatically when grown at home. The epicurean strawberry does not travel well and so only the toughest, most flavourless are shipped. To say little of the number of sprays used, to ensure that each commercial strawberry so nearly resembles a plastic replica in its pristine perfection. Shame they forgot to keep the taste!

Modern summer-fruiting strawberries are hybrids developed relatively recently (in the 1800s) from *Fragaria chiloensis*, the Chilean Pine, and *F. virginiana*, the Scarlet Virginian. The first contributed larger fruit with a pineapple tang and the latter provided the superior flavour and is still grown commercially as Little Scarlet for top-quality conserves. These wild species combined to give us hundreds of varieties during the early Victorian age, with even more intensive commercial development since. Sadly, commercially, the strawberry has become a shadow of itself but, fortunately, the home market is strong enough for more richly flavoured but frankly less productive and disease-resistant sorts to survive.

Almost every country and region in the temperate world has its favourite varieties – strawberries can be grown even in the tropics with the aid of shade. The biggest difficulty there is that strawberries are day-length dependent, making it hard to get them to fruit when the day length is constant or very short. New varieties from California breeders are now claimed to be capable of fruiting independently of day length; otherwise, chilling pot-grown ones in a fridge may help extend their season by giving them a 'winter'. There are far too many gorgeous strawberries to list and new improved ones are continually becoming available. My favourite for years was Royal Sovereign, beautifully flavoured if light cropping and originally introduced in 1892, but it has now become impossible to find good stocks. Cambridge Late Pine is simply delicious as are Gariguette, Ciflorette and Marshmello. Earlies such as Elvira and Rosie are good. Midsummer brings Darselect, Elsanta, Eros, Hapil, Korona and Tenira. Later come Florence and Alice. For sheer size try Maxim. All these are among the better-flavoured varieties though hundreds more are available.

Then there are the remontant or perpetual-fruiting strawberries, which fruit continuously through summer and autumn in flushes. They start to set early crops even before most summer sorts, but these are best removed to ensure bigger crops later, when the summer crowd have gone over. Some have extremely good flavour probably due to some woodland strawberry (*F. vesca*) ancestry. Among the finest-flavoured is Aromel; also well flavoured are Mara des Bois, La Sans Rivale, Bolero and Challenger. The wild European strawberries (*F. vesca*)

Above The yellow alpine strawberry fools the birds.

The gourmet will have despaired at the tasteless commercial travesties air-freighted from foreign parts to decorate his or her fruit salad.

and the hautbois (*F. elatior*/*F. moschata*) are like miniature versions of garden strawberries and are the fruit that Shakespeare knew. The hautbois remains more popular, especially on the Continent, as it's the most fragrant of all. The green strawberry (*F. collina*/*F. viridis*) has sadly vanished.

Alpine strawberries (*F. vesca* Semperflorens) form clumps about a foot across with lighter green leaves. They flower from last to first frost often producing their finest-flavoured fruits in moist half-shade. True alpines are little improved on the wild form though yellow- and white-fruited versions are available. Baron Solemacher is a larger-fruited selection; Alexandria is tastier and juicier.

Alpines, species and a few varieties can be grown from seed with good results, but for the usual summer strawberries seed-grown plants generally produce poor fruiters – believe me, I've tried. When buying plants choose only certified virus-free stock. Never accept any plants from someone who proffers 'my old granny's [virus-infected and disease-ridden] favourite' – 'it's not a heavy cropper but it tastes wonderful' (translates as 'it's the only one I know'). Plants are cheap! Get the best; you deserve no less. Once you have tried a wide number of varieties, propagate your favourites from then on.

Unfortunately strawberry plants become relatively unproductive after three or four years, so continual planning and replenishment are called for.

Replacing the lot every so often means years of gluts followed by shortages, as all plants are the same age. Annual replacement of a quarter or a third of your plants, preferably on a new bed, is sensible. Plants grown from runners are the obvious replacement and usually available to excess (you should remove surplus runners regularly anyway). The best runners come from quality deflowered plants reserved for propagation; half a dozen good replacements can be had from each. The first plantlets on early runners can be pinned or held to the ground or preferably rooted into a pot of compost for easier transplantation. Remove all other runners and flowers.

Starting new beds with new plants in late summer or very early autumn allows plants to establish so they can crop well next summer. Late autumn or spring plantings should be deflowered the first summer to build up the plants' strength for a massive crop the following year. It's possible to keep varieties for many years but only if healthy plants are propagated and the old eradicated ruthlessly every third year.

All preparation for a new strawberry bed is well repaid; you cannot overdo it. The richer you make the top layer of soil the better – but don't use highly nitrogenous manures, except possibly for the first few months of establishment. Strawberries need a soil full of humus and slow-release phosphates such as bone meal. Well-rotted manure, well-rotted compost, leaf mould and seaweed meal dressings will be repaid with better, tastier crops. When you're establishing a new bed, digging in a green manure crop of soya beans beforehand will help prevent root rots. Growing borage, and any beans or onions nearby also reputedly helps strawberry plants. Otherwise do not crowd or shade the plants (except for late crops).

Strawberries crop earlier and more reliably if grown on earthed-up ridges, which warm up and dry out quicker in spring. A sloped bed as made for salads is also worth the effort for the real addict. The more space you give strawberry plants the better: a stride each way is the minimum – and, believe me, further apart is worth it if you want prize crops. To prevent the foolish mistake of cropping under-established plants too early, it is safer to plant twice as many plants at half the intended spacing. Then deflower alternate plants so that you crop only half the plants; remove these immediately after, allowing the deflowered 'virgins' to grow on and crop even more magnificently next summer.

Thinning out the flower trusses on plants will increase the size of each of the eventual fruits. Once the fruits have set, remove any misshapen ones so all energy flows to the best. Spraying with seaweed solution benefits strawberry plants but should be stopped once the flowers have set. You can resume once the fruits have been picked. Liquid feeding, too, is best reduced while the fruits are swelling and ripening, to get the finest flavours. Adding more sun helps no end; try prayer. Cloches, coldframes or plastic sheet covers can bring cropping forward by many weeks, and will keep the birds and rain off –

though semi-permanent cover may promote as many problems as it prevents. Cover a few plants of early varieties every fortnight from late winter on. Earlier cropping may also be aided by planting through a specialist woven black sheet, which helps warm the soil and exclude weeds and dirt, while allowing air and water to penetrate. Traditional strawing-up is not essential but does help give really clean crops. Never straw too early as this encourages slugs: apply it when the first green fruit is seen swelling. Heavily mulched crops tend to ripen somewhat later than unmulched ones, as the warmth from the soil is lost – the blossoms also become more prone to frost damage once mulched. Special mats, cardboard, newspaper and so on can all be used to help keep the fruit clean. Grass clippings and hay may give fruit a taint, but cocoa-bean shell and rough chopped bark are usable, and pine needles are reckoned to improve the flavour. Strawberries can be grown successfully in pots or containers, but must have rich well-drained compost that is regularly fed and watered copiously. Plastic and pottery containers, sometimes tower shaped, are often sold for strawberry cultivation. While essentially a good idea, especially for a tiny garden, they are tricky to get to work well. The small amount of root run and compost, the hot above-ground position and the dryness because of low water-holding capacity make poor growing conditions for strawberries, which respond with low yields.

If you grow strawberries in containers, use a car-tyre-sized one per plant and you will be rewarded with gourmet results. Car tyres themselves make excellent containers though I have some misgivings as to their pollution status. I make tyre walls and include planting cavities: then I get extra-early crops on the sunny side and late ones on the other, with the strawberries conveniently high up trailing away from many pests.

Container growing is successful only if the watering is well attended to and the plants are replaced regularly. Its greatest advantage is that pots allow strawberries to be moved and put into the chill or full sun to slow down or accelerate growth.

For much earlier crops with total freedom from birds and rain damage, force plants under glass or plastic. They don't need heat, indeed it should not be hot, only bright; strawberries in hot dry conditions suffer from red spider mite. The best plants are early runners rooted into small pots, potted up and grown on outdoors all autumn. They can be brought indoors in batches from late winter, when they will burst into growth and crop months earlier.

The best place is high up in a greenhouse, close to the (very well cleaned) glass. It's worth constructing special shelves for the plants; preferably open to allow airflow. Or establish new plants in some heavy-duty guttering in summer and bring that in at the end of winter to suspend from the greenhouse roof (if strong enough). The plants then dangle their fruits freely in the air and rarely ever suffer from slugs or mould.

All forced plants are best discarded afterwards and new ones started for the following year – second-year-forced plants perform badly!

After plants outdoors have fruited, shear back surplus runners and dead leaves and remove these along with old straw and so on for composting. Doing this will control many pests and diseases. Most major losses with strawberries are from human thieves, birds, slugs and mould. Individual bunches of berries can be protected from most pests and many diseases with jam jars. Mould can be controlled by prompt strawing-up and removing fruits that rot, preferably before any mould goes 'fluffy'. Or try using temporary cloches or cover to keep the fruits drier – although in humid air this becomes near impossible. There are many minor pests and diseases and the usual remedies apply, but starting a new bed with clean stock is usually the simplest solution.

Strawberries must be consumed quickly as they keep for only a day or so once picked. They last longer if picked with a stalk and handled carefully. Bruising or chilling soon damages their appearance, and never pick the berries when wet! Try them still partly green: you may be surprised to find they are already sweet and tasty.

Strawberries can be juiced and made into squashes and syrups, or jammed and jellied – the addition of apple, red- or whitecurrant juice or purée will give a more pleasing acidity and help them set – they are notoriously difficult. If frozen they lose their texture but are still delicious. Ideally freeze them individually on a tray dredged with sugar, before packing into bags; then they are easier to separate later. However, as with many gourmet delights, strawberries are finest when eaten freshly sun-warmed in good company.

Container growing is only successful if the watering is well attended to and the plants are replaced regularly.

grapes

Grapes (*Vitis* species) are grown across the globe. These delicious succulent health-giving fruits are so well known, but few gardeners grow dessert grapes successfully simply because they grow the wrong (usually heirloom) varieties by the wrong method. The gourmet will not let such treasures pass by. Not only do grapes eat so well but home-made raisins can be out of this world and fresh grape juice is pure nectar. Even the flowers are sweet scented, though insignificant. The leaves can be used in many dishes and colour well in autumn, red-berrying varieties tending to go red and white sorts yellow.

The Romans spread vines all over Europe and long after their empire collapsed monasteries kept vineyards going. The Victorians raised grape cultivation to perfection almost year round in hothouses, but outdoors vines are still a bit of a gamble anywhere as temperate as the UK. But with the right choice of variety and method, fresh grapes can be had for up to three-quarters of the year.

Although most dessert grapes on sale are grown in hot areas, the very best for flavour, size and succulence are from grapes ripened in the cooler regions. Dessert varieties make bigger grapes with thinner skins than wine varieties; they are hardy but depend on protection and warmth to ripen in time, so many will not crop outside except in favourable years. On the other hand, under cover we can ripen almost any variety – but at a price. Vines growing indoors build up pests and diseases that are hard to eradicate. Secondly they need a real winter chill, making them hard to house permanently. Vines also grow rather too strongly if planted in the ground, resulting in a lot of pruning. The gourmet who

Not only do grapes eat so well but home-made raisins can be out of this world and fresh grape juice is pure nectar.

Opposite The only sensible way to grow grapes in England is in a container, brought under cover from late winter until Autumn. Note the wasp trap.

wants several choice varieties will grow them in containers, which can be moved in and out of doors. Only a few vines should ever be allowed to grow in the ground – maybe for a summer outdoor crop against a wall or for a real favourite under glass.

The hardiest and best grape I have found for outside in a cool English climate, with or without a wall, is Boskoop Glory. This is a delicious loose-berried dark purple grape which is outstanding, cropping regularly. It is sweet and very disease-resistant. Siegerrebe, which has rosé fruit with a sweet Muscat flavour, is more tricky, resenting an alkaline soil and being more prone to mildew. It ripens so early it is unfortunately prey to wasps, but it is still worth growing on a wall or in a fruit cage as it is divine. Regent is a red-black grape with a good texture and flavour that will crop well on a wall. For the gourmet these three are really worth considering outdoors – believe me, I've tried dozens!

If you have a very sheltered sunny garden and the space, you may appreciate the peppery taste of the Russian varieties such as Gagarin Blue and Tereshkova. For juicing you may try Phoenix, Seibel 13053, Triomphe d'Alsace, Léon Millot, Maréchal Joffre, or even the oddly flavoured – but you may like it – Strawberry grape, which is vigorous and productive even without a wall.

For under-cover ripening in a container, all the vines mentioned will do admirably but superior indoor sorts are as easy and much better quality – providing they are taken under cover for the growing season. Siegerrebe is so good, it's worth growing wherever you can and it does well in a tub. Muscat Hamburg is by far the best, not

self-fertile but superbly flavoured with black bunches of firm sweet perfumed grapes. Black Hamburg (aka *Vitis vinifera* Schiava Grossa) is a fine old variety with bigger grapes in larger bunches but not so fine-flavoured. Buckland Sweetwater is small, white, sweet and long keeping. Muscat of Alexandria is another fine white.

Chasselas d'Or (aka *V. vinifera* Chasselas) is early, with translucent yellow fruits; it's the most reliable grape and may even crop outdoors on a warm wall in a good summer, yet also hangs well. Hundreds more varieties await the connoisseur, especially the Muscats which carry the finest flavours. Do not bring grapevines home from holiday, not even bits.

In the UK we have no phylloxera root aphids so we can grow grapes on their own roots (any ripe cutting a foot or two long can be rooted in autumn to make a free plant). Even a single bud can be rooted and grown on. Elsewhere in the world, vines must be budded on phylloxera-resistant rootstocks. Growing vines from seed is easy but usually gives poor results, producing bunches resembling the wild forms. Vines really do not need rich conditions to crop well. Do not enrich their soil beforehand. By all means dig it over and improve aeration and drainage, but rich soil means rank unfruitful growth. Vines will crop better in a warm poor dry soil. They need a hot dry spell to ripen well; outdoors in cooler regions they are usually best grown on walls. Any improvement in sunlight and warmth, especially in aspect or ground slope, helps improve the quality. Although vines will grow magnificently in shade or moist conditions, any grapes produced will be sour. The more space, light and air each vine gets the better.

In pots or containers the compost needs be free draining, and the plants respond well to light liquid feeding with their watering, together with a little top dressing of a mixture of wood ashes, calcified seaweed and powdered bone each spring. With this treatment I have cropped the same plants in 25-litre containers for more than twenty years.

Grapes benefit from French marigolds growing nearby. They can be cropped mixed with asparagus in the same bed but the competition reduces quality. Left to themselves, vines produce rank growth and exhaust themselves with overcropping.

There are many ways to prune grapes and many sub-variations, enough to fill a library on their own. Grapes grown in the ground under glass are usually treated the same as vines trained outdoors on a wall. Indeed vines are commonly planted outside, then trained in through a hole in the greenhouse wall and up on to wires. Strong wires spaced about an arm's length apart and run up under the roof will give a vine enough space and keep it well away from the glass.

The vine's framework is formed over the first years, when it will cover the wires with permanent canes, which later produce fruiting spurs. These spurs shoot from their buds each spring and a flower truss appears between the third to fifth leaf. After another five or six leaves each shoot should be tipped, and any replacements removed as they appear.

Thinning the number of canes and the number of bunches is essential. Cut back unproductive canes and leave no more than two bunches per arm's-length run of remaining young cane. In winter

cut all shoots back to one or two buds out from each spur – unless extending or replacing the permanent framework. The more of the recent growth you keep, the more fruitful the shoots, one from every new bud. But leave too many buds and the vine can't ripen all the wood or crop.

I leave several buds but rigorously nip out the surplus shoots once enough flower trusses have set. Fewer bunches means bigger grapes. True fanatics also thin out the number of grapes in the bunches, especially round the shoulders, using a pair of special thin scissors.

In pots, vines grow much less vigorously and new canes can be grown vertically or wound as spirals around a central supporting post, from only three to five spurs, which are allowed to build up on a very short permanent leg. The plants are compact and attractive and crop well on sunny patios.

Growing in pots combined with some greenhouse space gives even better results on the old orchard-house principle. The pot-grown vine can be cropped under cover, safe from weather and birds, then moved outdoors once it's dropped its leaves and the shoots have been cut back very hard. The vine then spends all winter outside and is brought indoors again only in late winter for the earliest crops or kept in a cool shady place and brought in late for a later crop. Hard pruning and the exposure to winter weather scours most pests and diseases from the vines, which are quite happy with this treatment. When they come under cover they grow and crop quickly and reliably even in an unheated place. This method can be used to crop even hothouse varieties most summers, as the early start is all that is needed.

Grapes make good jellies; any further suplus can be made into wine.

Mould can be common in damp ripening seasons and mildews in dry ones – though rarely when grapes are grown on the orchard-house principle. There are organic sprays to combat these, based on sulphur, copper or sodium bicarbonate, but often the more resistant varieties such as Boskoop Glory crop unaided. Vine weevils may appear and are best treated with traps and by applying the parasitic nematode solution obtainable commercially. I find my hens keep the outdoor vines free from insect pests.

The earliest crops in containers are best eaten fresh, as soon as they colour, or the wasps will have them. Likewise for Siegerrebe grown on a wall. Most other outdoor sorts ripen later than the wasps usually survive, so are troubled only by birds and the wet.

Kept cool and dry, grapes hang on the vines well until the frosts start. On vines under cover, grapes may hang in usable condition till mid-winter then shrivel, but these are problematical for both pruning and the next crop. It's much better to cut bunches joined by their stalk to a piece of stem popped into bottles of water and to store these in a cool, dry place for months. Cut a piece off the end of each stem each week and renew the water – and remove any rotting grapes. The less they are handled the better they keep!

When you've eaten the best grapes as dessert fruits the rest are easily juiced and the juice can be frozen for year-round use. Grapes make good jellies; any further surplus can be made into wine. Grapes can also be dried slowly to make your own raisins from black grapes and sultanas from white. Muscat grapes make the tastiest dried fruits of all (see chapter 8).

gooseberries

Gooseberries (*Ribes uva-crispa* var. *reclinatum*) in the shops are green bullets for culinary use, with nothing like the melting sweetness of well-ripened dessert varieties you can grow at home. Gooseberries have big hairy berries and sharp thorns. Easy to grow, they're often handicapped by being grown as a stool (lots of stems at ground level), overcropped and picked too early. Given attention and good pruning, large succulent berries can be had, in almost any colour, and with delicious flavour – from clean acid sweet through vinous plumminess.

Gooseberries were once widely grown for competition; hundreds of varieties in red, green, yellow and white were bred. One variety, London, an outstandingly large, not-so-hairy red, was biggest exhibited for 37 years! I love Langley Gage (a mid-season berry), which has divine, bite-sized, syrupy sweet, translucent white globes hanging in profusion. Early Sulphur (very early fruiting) has golden yellow, almost transparent, tasty, medium-sized berries. For a substantial dark-olive-green, strongly flavoured large berry choose Gunner (mid-season), though it's not a heavy cropper. Leveller (mid) has delicious yellow-green fruits in profusion. The currant gooseberry (*R. hirtellum*) is an edible American species with small reddish fruits.

Most other American gooseberries and our own Worcesterberries are derived from *R. divaricatum*, have smaller berries and are resistant to the American mildew disease that can damage European varieties. Generally gooseberries do not pick up many serious diseases and old plants can be utilised for propagation by taking foot-long cuttings, disbudding the lower end to prevent suckers.

Gooseberries do better hard pruned from the start to form spurs on a goblet-shaped frame with a short leg. To get larger berries, or more varieties in a confined space, gooseberries are best grown as vertical cordons, double cordons, espaliers or even standards – though then they are better grafted on to a different rootstock, such as *R. odoratum*.

Gooseberries love rich moist loamy soil and do not like hot dry sandy sites or stagnant air – they prefer a breeze about them. They will not stand bad drainage. Nor are they awfully happy in pots. Their season can be extended by having some plants in sun and some in cool shade, but they do not like going under cover at all. Always add more leaf mould and other organic mulches to their soil, and be generous with wood ashes and other potash sources, as gooseberries need copious amounts. Tomatoes and broad beans nearby are reputed to aid them and I often grow *Limnanthes douglasii* as ground cover.

I leave pruning till late winter; then the thorns protect the buds from the birds, which perversely delight in disbudding gooseberries. Summer pruning is too prickly for some to practise but ideal; in winter all shoots should be trimmed back to spurs on the permanent framework. Remember, the more young wood left, the more flowers, the more fruits, and the smaller and less sweet they will be – so prune hard! And thin, thin, thin the young berries!

American mildew may wither tips and felt the fruits with a leathery coat that dries them up. Sadly, resistant varieties such as Pax and Invicta don't appeal to most gourmets. Hygiene, moist roots, hard pruning and good air

circulation reduce the damage. Sodium bicarbonate sprays and sulphur-based ones (which burn some varieties) are possible correctives.

Occasionally, often in the third or so year after planting, gooseberries suffer damage from sawfly caterpillars. First appearing as a patch of minute holes in a leaf, they will move on to strip the entire bush. Vigilance and early thumb and finger action prevent serious damage.

Gooseberries do not have as much bird appeal as many fruits; the green ones can even sometimes be grown without protection. Birds and wasps still steal them once they're ripe;

Given attention and good pruning, large succulent berries can be had, in almost any colour, and with delicious flavour.

Left Cordoned training allows you to get the most gooseberries in a small space.
Opposite Leveller, one of the more commonly available, yet actually quite decent gooseberries.

otherwise the fruits mellow and hang on till late summer if protected from damp. Picked small and green in a heavy thinning they make the most delicious acid jams and tarts – which turn red if overcooked. For true green gooseberry jam, use only unripe green gooseberries that ripen green!

As gooseberries ripen they become less acid and fuller-flavoured for dessert purposes and in most varieties their colour changes. Over-ripe fruits for cooking combine well with redcurrants, which improve the acidity and can be jellied to remove the tough skins and seeds.

Gooseberry wine can be excellent.

raspberries

Raspberries (*Rubus idaeus*) are too good to be true, so sweet and so mouth-refreshingly tart. They are one of the least durable or transportable fruits and must be processed or eaten within a matter of hours. Those sold commercially are the toughest and the least meltingly fragrant. Although many have described the strawberry as the finest fruit, others rank the raspberry as good if not better. Strangely, raspberries are also little grown as garden fruits, yet they are among the easiest to care for and cultivate and are a delight for the gourmet.

Raspberries vary considerably in size and are usually red, though black and yellow sorts exist. In good varieties the conical fruit pulls off the plug easily, leaving a hole. Some are less easy and the berries may be damaged on picking as they are very soft and thin-skinned.

The young shoots are usually green, but soon go red or brown as they grow. Eventually the canes reach way overhead; they are often bristly and occasionally thorny. Short-lived individually, the canes spring from a suckering root system one year, to die the following year after fruiting. In theory, the root system could spread perpetually, though they most often fade away from viral and root infections. Raspberries belonging to the species *Rubus idaeus* are selected from native Europeans living on the edge of woodlands, especially those with acid soils as far north as 70°.

There are many similar wild species enjoyed in other temperate countries and many hybrids closely resembling them. Others are much like brambles or blackberries. In North America they cultivate red and yellow raspberries descended from *R. strigosa*, which are similar to European raspberries, plus black raspberries or blackcaps (*R. occidentalis*), which are less hardy and with fewer stouter canes more given to branching.

Most of our raspberries can be summer or autumn cropping depending on treatment and pruning method rather than any inherent tendency. Autumn Bliss and Galante are probably the best varieties specifically for autumn fruiting and the yellow Allgold is delicious. For summer fruiting today's varieties are soon replaced by new ones at a great rate and no list can be complete.

I still like the almost obsolete but tasty Malling Jewel (early), Glen Moy (early), Glen Ample (mid), Glen Prosen (mid) and Malling Admiral (late). I also love yellow raspberries. These originated alongside the reds and are less vigorous, with paler leaves, and naturally tend towards autumn fruiting. Golden Everest is superb, with richly flavoured, soft sweet berries, lacking the sharpness of many reds. Norfolk Giant is another good old variety now almost unobtainable. The Mysore black raspberry (*R. niveus*) comes from Asia and needs to be grown under glass. Because they are prone to viral disease, do not propagate heirloom plants but buy new certified stock – which you can propagate if no problems appear. Transplant any piece of root with a bud or young cane in the autumn. Pot-grown specimens may be planted in spring. Summer fruiters should not be cropped the first year but built up first; autumn fruiters may be cropped if they were well established early the previous autumn.

I have found seed can provide very vigorous and productive – if variable – plants, but it is a safer plan to buy new named cultivars. Preferring cool, moist conditions

Strangely, raspberries are little grown as garden fruits, yet they are among the easiest to care for and cultivate and are a delight for the gourmet.

raspberries do wonderfully in Scotland. Although they can be grown elsewhere in most soils they do considerably better given plentiful moisture, a rich neutral or acidic soil or at least copious quantities of compost and very thick mulches. I have fruited raspberries in large pots, but they resent it and do not crop well or flourish – they really need a bigger, cooler root run. They are mostly very hardy and need no protection. Providing they are kept cool and airy, they can produce good crops, and grown under cover benefit immensely from the bird protection.

With hot dry summers and wetter autumns, the autumn-fruiting varieties can be much more productive – especially on drier sites. They also suffer less from maggots. Summer fruiters need a moist site, and do not mind quite heavy shade. They do not enjoy the dry conditions against walls but can be grown on cool shady ones if they have a moist root run. Raspberries reputedly benefit from tansy, garlic or marigolds growing nearby. Strawberries may be grown close by but not directly underneath them.

Too lax to be left free, raspberries are best restrained by growing them between pairs of wires or winding the tips around horizontal ones. Alternatively they can be grown as tripods, with three well-spaced stools being joined at the apex.

Pruning for summer raspberries is done in autumn. Remove all old canes that have fruited or died and fix in place the new ones, selecting only the strongest at about a foot apart. (It helps to pre-thin these when the shoots emerge in early summer.) Autumn fruiters are easier still: just cut everything to the ground in late winter (thinning

in spring is again advantageous). Weeding must be done carefully because of their shallow roots, so thick mulches are almost essential.

Birds are the major cause of lost crops – no protection, no fruit! Raspberry beetles can be controlled with hygiene and mulching – rake thick mulches aside in winter to allow birds to eat the pupae – or use permitted sprays. (Their maggots are rarely a problem with autumn fruiters.) Viral diseases may appear, mottling the leaves with yellow and making the plants unproductive. Replacing all the stock and moving the bed to a new site is the only solution once yields have dropped. Interveinal yellowing of the leaves is a chlorotic reaction to alkaline soils; seaweed-solution sprays with added magnesium sulphate help immediately; heavy mulching with compost and leaf mould is more permanent.

Pick raspberries before the birds get them. Pick gently, leaving the plug on the plant. If the berry won't come easily do not force it! By the time you reach the end of a row, more will have already ripened where you started. Try lying down underneath the rows and looking up – you'll spot even more! Raspberries do not keep for long if they're wet, and even less if warm too. If you want to keep them for longer than an hour, cut the fruiting stalks with scissors and do not touch the fruits.

Raspberries can be frozen but, like strawberries, have poor texture afterwards. Containing valuable amounts of vitamin C, riboflavin and niacin, raspberries make wonderful juices, jellies, drinks and sorbets, and are often combined with redcurrant juice to add acidity.

Above The Autumn Bliss.
Right The All Gold.
Below right Miriam the cat – one of these will keep the birds off your raspberries.

the runners-up: brambles, blackberries and dewberries

Brambles, blackberries and dewberries (*Rubus fruticosus* and *species*) have similar habits and flavours to raspberries. The gourmet with access to the wild will probably search for the finest native bramble berries but, if these do not satisfy, there are countless garden varieties and other similar species to grow at home – and many hybrids. True wild blackberries may have more flavour than some of the cultivated ones, which were bred to be thornless or large fruited. But there are many good ones to try, with a wide range of flavours.

Common brambles (*Rubus fruticosus*) have fern-like leaves, thin purple or green stems, white or light purple flowers and small hard berries, some of which are delicious and others sour. Forms of *R. ulmifolius* have stronger-growing plum-coloured stems with five-lobed leaflets that are light on the underside. The **dewberry** (*R. caesisus*) is smaller berried, with fewer drupelets which separate as you pick them.

Opposite, clockwise from top left
The loganberry is much better cooked than raw; the Bedford Giant ripens one berry on each stem ahead of all the others; the Oregon thornless blackberry is useful for confined spaces; the Japanese wineberry ripens red and fools the birds.

The gourmet with access to the wild will probably search for the finest native bramble berries.

The thornless Oregon cutleaf blackberry is not in fact American but an old English variety of the parsley-leaved blackberry (*R. laciniatus*); its bigger fruits are well flavoured and it comes almost true from seed. Bedford Giant has a rich flavour and crops early, with long pliable canes. Himalayan Giant is a heavy cropper and well flavoured, but the viciously thorny canes can be as thick as a small tree – not for the faint-hearted. For sheer size of berry grow Fantasia. The better thornless varieties such as Waldo, Loch Ness, Sylvan, Helen and Veronique are worth growing where space is tight, as is Adrienne, which has long berries.

The commonest hybrid, the **loganberry**, has raspberry-like, cylindrical dull red fruits that are firm with an acid flavour, making them sour raw but exquisite cooked. The thornless loganberry LY59 is sometimes thorny and the fruit does not pull off the plug easily, but it has a good flavour. The **boysenberry** is not as hardy as most hybrids and does better in a warmer site than the rest. The fruits are sweeter, more blackberry-like, larger and reddy purple; palatable raw, they make the celebrated jam. The laxtonberry has a round raspberry-like fruit and is not self fertile. The veitchberry is large and mulberry-like and ripens late.

Japanese wineberries have bristly red stems and delicious orange fruits and are a must for all gourmets.

When fully ripe the Medana tayberry has enormous loganberry-like fruits of dark wine red to purple, nearly three times the size of most other berries and of a rich vinous flavour. It's another must. The tummelberry is similar to a loganberry while the marionberry and the youngberry or young

dewberry are like blackberries with more flavour – a bit like the American Black raspberry (*R. occidentalis*). The blackcap (*R. leucodermis*) has purple-black sweet fruits with a plum-like bloom; rare yellow- and red-fruited forms occur in its native north-west America.

The black loganberry comes from New Zealand and resembles, well, a black loganberry. Another antipodean the Australian thimbleberry (*R. parviflorus*) has insipid red berries. The salmonberry (*R. spectabilis*) has acid orange-yellow fruits; apparently native Americans ate the cooked young shoots too, but I've not tried them. The arctic or crimson bramble (*R. arcticus*) has amber-coloured fruits said to taste of pineapple – I've not yet managed to verify that either.

There are so many species and varieties, it makes sense to grow many temporarily until you know their value. From then on be ruthless and keep only the best.

To multiply them, the tips of most shoots can be encouraged to root and form new plants in the autumn: make sure these go into pots of compost if you want extra plants. Suckers and seedlings come up everywhere, but the latter are variable; even of species.

The bramble family love rich moist soils; they will crop in light shade but are sweeter in the sun. Their cultivation and control is like a pitched battle: if you give way they'll take over your garden, but then they'll crop the best. Heavy dressings of compost and thick mulches keep up the yields. They do well grassed up and allegedly benefit from tansy or stinging nettles nearby. They make a good sacrificial crop for grapevines, ie. some of the bramble berries are

eaten instead of all the grapes. It would be foolish to try to grow brambles under cover and few varieties would like the cramped conditions pots afford. However, in tiny gardens it is worth using large containers to grow the thornless varieties.

Blackberries can fruit wood that is older than one year and the canes do not always die. New wood is better, though, and carries fewer pests and diseases. When the leaves fall cut out all old and dead wood and tie in the best of the new. The canes are long and carry heavy loads, so strong supports are necessary. Young canes need tying in during summer and, if new plants are not needed, they must be shortened in late summer to stop them rooting wherever they hit ground.

Blackberries are picked as they ripen from late summer till the first frost, when the devil supposedly spits on them and makes them sour. The berries of most black brambles are unusable red but turn soft to the touch as they blacken. The seeds of raw berries are an irritant to the stomach. Partial ripening can be due to insect damage, though Bedford Giant ripens one berry in each bunch ahead of all others.

Most bramble berries are fairly tough-skinned. They last longer than raspberries if picked when dry and loosely packed; still they are best used as soon as possible or frozen. Bramble berries once cooked are much tastier and do not have such deleterious effects on one's insides as raw berries. They make excellent preserves, though as jams are unpleasantly seedy, the jelly is more often made. Apples can be mixed in most blackberry concoctions to aid the setting – the flavours combine lusciously too.

blackcurrants

Blackcurrants (*Ribes nigrum*) have dark purple, almost black, berries with a most distinct and unforgettable aroma that echoes that of the aromatic foliage and stems. Those you can buy are nowhere near as good as those you can grow. Varieties such as Ben Sarek (mid), Ben Lomond (late) and Ben More (very late) are easily available and generally more productive, with better disease resistance than old favourites. Laxton's Giant (mid) and Ben Connan (early) are the biggest, and Seabrook's Black (mid) is supposedly resistant to big bud disease.

The josta berry is a much larger-growing hybrid, more like a thornless gooseberry. American species include the fragrant-flowered buffalo currant or golden currant (*R. odoratum*), often used as the stock for standard gooseberries, and the American blackcurrant (*R. americanum*).

Blackcurrants soon pick up diseases and degenerate so do not propagate from old or heirloom bushes. Infected stock must be replaced with new clean material – do this again after ten or fifteen years, or when yields have dropped too far.

There are no easier cuttings, though! Bushes are best grown as a stool with multiple shoots from ground level. Cuttings should have all buds left on and later the young plants should be replanted deeper still, to ensure new shoots from below ground level.

Blackcurrants revel in rich moist ground – the richer the better – and respond to heavy mulching, especially with nitrogen-rich dressings. They do not mind light shade; indeed they crop exceedingly well in shade. The bushes really prefer to be cool so they are not happy for long under cover. I imagine they could be forced, though I've never tried, but they can be grown and fruited successfully in large pots. They can stand having wetter roots than most other fruits.

In order to provide as much young fruitful wood as possible, remove all the older shoots from one-third of each bush. You can do this when picking the crop. Cut off the oldest branches, pick the fruit then discard the branches. Heavier pruning results in fewer but much bigger fruits.

Nettles nearby benefit blackcurrants and also hide unprotected ones from the birds. Mildew is aggravated by a combination of stagnant or damp air with dry roots and is cured by better air circulation, open pruning and restoring vigorous growth. Big bud disease is just what it sounds like. It's easy to spot in mid-winter and remove the buds. It is caused by microscopic pests that also carry viral diseases such as reversion (when the leaves become more nettle like and yields drop).

Blackcurrants keep well once picked as they're firm and tough-skinned. They can be frozen, jammed, jellied and turned into delicious syrups and juices. They need water or other juices such as redcurrant mixed with them, as they are too dry on their own. Jelly is less work than jam as de-sprigging the berries for the latter is tedious work, but adding back in the choicest berries makes the jelly into the best preserve of all.

Blackcurrants can be frozen, jammed, jellied and turned into delicious syrups and juices.

redcurrants

Redcurrants (*Ribes rubrum*) are reliable, productive plants. The fruits are rarely offered for sale commercially yet are useful in the kitchen. Varieties vary little in taste, acidity or season, which may last up to three months. Earliest of Four Lands, Raby Castle and Wilson's Longbunch are good old sorts; Rokul, Junifer and Rovada more modern but still similar.

Whitecurrants such as White Grape and White Versailles are selections without colour and have their own flavour. They crop as extravagantly and are as useful – especially for mint sauce.

These are the easiest of all plants to root from autumn cuttings and it's even safe to do so from old plants. Remove all lower buds from the cutting, leaving just a few near the top. Seedlings come fairly true. Long-lived, redcurrants often survive neglect. Given a little care and bird protection they can soon produce well again. Old bushes can usually be rejuvenated, and even totally replaced, by new shoots from low down.

Redcurrants respond best to a cool, well-mulched soil. They do not need very rich conditions and will grow in partial shade, even quite happily on cold walls – but the berries are sweeter in the sun. These are the most easily trained and forgiving of plants. No matter how you misprune them they

respond with new growth and ample fruit. Redcurrants can be made to take any form – cordon, goblet, fan or espalier– and are quick to form. They fruit best on a permanent framework with spurs; every shoot, bar the leaders, should be cut back in summer and again, harder, in winter.

Redcurrants can be trained to cover large walls. For convenience, grow them as goblet bushes at least a couple of strides apart, but for superb fruits grow them as cordons at a third that distance. They can be cropped in pots and moved to warmth or shade. Do this if you want early or late crops, or pristine berries over a longer season, or have no space for permanent bushes.

The only major threat to the crop is the birds. Minor sawfly caterpillar and mildew attacks sometimes occur but do little damage. The leaves regularly pucker with red and yellow blotches from the leaf-blistering aphis, but surprisingly, this does not affect the yield. These leaves can be removed wholesale, with aphids on board, during summer pruning.

Currants can be picked as soon as they colour for garnishing, adding to compotes and for the most acid jellies. Ripening will continue into late autumn in dry years, when the fruits become less acid and more tasty raw. The berries will hang on pot-grown plants in the cool shade at the back of an orchard house till mid-winter. Being seedy the fruit is best stored juiced and frozen. Similarly currants make better jelly than jam. Redcurrant juice adds tartness and flavour to other juices and can be used in many sweet and savoury dishes.

Whitecurrant juice is a substitute – if not an improvement – for lemon juice and makes even finer jellies.

This page Whitecurrants (above) are better value than redcurrants (left and top) for the basis of many sauces and conserves.
Opposite If you want big blackcurrants, prune hard, feed heavily and water extravagantly.

blueberries

Blueberries (*Vaccinium corymbosum*), one of a range of acid bog lovers, come from North America and are well known for their distinctive taste. The gourmet will be pleased to know there are many varieties, and other related berries, all of which are a pleasure to the palate, easy to grow and impossible to find in the shops.

Most of our garden blueberries are of mixed American origin. The early Earliblue, Goldtraube and Jersey are fairly compact; Berkeley is a spreader; Blue Crop more upright; Top Hat dwarf; and the best flavoured is Herbert.

Many related species have edible berries; the **huckleberry** or box blueberry (*V. ovatum*) is a small attractive evergreen shrub with tasty berries. The **big huckleberry** (*V. membranaceum*) has bigger berries, is fairly drought-resistant and is one of the tastiest.

Bilberries, **blaeberries** or **whortleberries** (*V. myrtillus*) are low-growing native shrubs found on heaths and moors in acid soils.

The gourmet will be pleased to know there are many varieties, and other related berries, all of which are a pleasure to the palate, easy to grow and impossible to find in the shops.

cranberries

Cranberries (*V. oxycoccos*) are essential for the sauce for Christmas turkey and are very similar and closely related, the most noticeable differences being their red berries and that they are evergreen. The American cranberry (*V. macrocarpon*) is much the same but larger in bush and berry. The cowberry, crane or foxberry (*V. vitis idaea*) is also similar, though the berries are more acid and less agreeable than cranberries.

Both blueberries and cranberries come true from seed but the better varieties are best layered in summer; suckers can be detached in winter. Partly self-fertile, they all do better if several varieties are grown together. All of these really must have boggy conditions, in lime-free soil and water. Make beds on the edge of a pool by building up stones covered with a thick layer of peaty, humus-rich acid soil – a substitute of peat and leaf mould will do. The plants must be moist but not drowned – they need to stand above the water. The tall species prefer wetter sites, the dwarfer ones just moist. All prefer sun though will grow in partial shade. The squatter sorts need be only a stride apart each way; bigger bushes need at least double that.

All these berries often have to be grown in containers as they wither in alkaline soils. Ericaceous compost or a mixture of peat, sand and leaf mould is essential – as is regular copious watering with rainwater, not tap. All need little pruning except to remove dead or diseased growth and to rejuvenate some newer stronger growths. However, judicious thinning will result in bigger berries. The dried berries were once beaten to a powder, made into cakes with maize meal and smoke-dried for extra flavour. Better uses for them include as garnishes and in pies, tarts, jams, jellies and syrups.

wilder tastes for the adventurous gourmet

Chokeberries (*Aronia melanocarpa*) are purple-black fruits; very astringent and sour raw, they're fine once cooked and sweetened. The bushes are easy to grow, reliable, self-fertile, highly productive and compact, with a height and spread of about two strides. White hawthorn-like flowers and striking autumn leaf colours make this a most decorative fruit bush and it does well in a large tub. Viking is the variety for fruit production; Brilliant is offered for ornamental plantings.

Kiwi (*Actinidia deliciosa*) is a green gooseberry with an inedible hairy felted brown skin. It is one of a family of delightful edible-fruited climbers which need a very warm wall or to be under cover to fruit. They take up a lot of space but can be trained and hard pruned to form espaliers for superb-quality fruits. They have lovely leaves and attractive bristly stems so you can allow them to ramble over a shed or pergola and if they crop in a hot summer, look on it as a bonus.

Grown this way they don't need pruning and have few pests or diseases. Under cover they are controlled only by being grown in very large tubs. You must have a male as well as (several) females though self-pollinating cultivars such as Jenny are becoming available. Try Hayward with Tomuri, or Oriental Delight, Blake and mini-kiwi *A. arguta Issai*.

Juneberry (*Amelanchier*) fruits are purplish, spherical, about pea size, but can be larger, and are sweet and tasty. *A. canadensis* shrubs are prone to suckering growth and are mainly grown for their masses of white blossoms. This was a favourite fruit of Native Americans. Adopted by the French settlers they became known as *poires* in Canada and sweet or grape pear in the USA. They need plenty of leaf mould, thick mulches and copious water.

Barberry (*Berberis vulgaris*) is a common garden shrub whose berries makes excellent spicy tart preserves. The Magellan barberry (*B. darwinii*) is large and said to be the best raw or cooked. Mahonia is similar in many ways, lacking only the spines, and the blue-black berries of *Mahonia aquifolium* can be made into a delicious preserve once known as Oregon grape jelly.

Autumn olive (*Elaeagnus umbellata*) is a spreading deciduous shrub with small orange to red berries that can be used like redcurrants or dried to 'raisins'. Many species in this genus bear edible fruits: the silver berry (*E. commutata*) has pasty silver berries; oleaster or wild olive (*E. angustifolia*) has sweet berries still popular in southern Europe.

Fuchsias are so well known for their flowers that gourmets will be amazed to discover their berries are usually edible raw – fuchsia clubs make jelly with them for competitions. Like a stoneless cherry (the seeds are minute), the berry is sweet in flavour and I have had berries as big as my thumb. I recommend Californian Dreamer and Malibu Mist for size and Nancy Lou is pretty sweet.

Checkerberry or teaberry (*Gaultheria procumbens*) is a low-growing evergreen with red berries and needs moist acid soil and partial shade. The berries can be cooked to make jellies and tarts. *G. humifusa* and *G. shallon* have purple berries eaten by Native Americans.

Myrtle (*Myrtus communis*) was popular with the Romans and the foliage is aromatic when crushed, making it a good plant for small patios or sunny windows. It has delicious black berries that make wonderful jam. Sadly the plants rarely fruit well unless in a warm sunny spot on a light dry soil. The ornamental forms such as *M. microphylla* and *M. tarentina* are small, barely reaching a couple of feet high, and rarely fruit. *M. ugni* (aka *Ugni molinae*) is the tender Chilean guava myrtle with delicious mahogany red, pleasantly fragrant berries. It fruits well in greenhouses and conservatories.

> The common wild elderberry is a prolific fruiter, and the jelly is exquisite.

Elderberries (*Sambucus nigra*). The common wild bush is a prolific fruiter, and the jelly is exquisite. The plants are tough and easy to propagate from cuttings or seed. Sufficient berries can be had from the wild but the gourmet may wish to try the blue elderberry (*S. nigra* subsp. *cerulea*) from Utah, which produces enormous clusters of fruits popular in California for tarts and jellies. There are several other berry-producing species and some, such as *S. ebulus*, are poisonous, so be careful with identification! Grow elders as a stool and replace a third of the old stems with new every other year.

chapter 5 the gourmet's most tender treats

Long-term treats: citrus, guavas, pineapples, cape gooseberries and others. Quicker treats: tomatoes, chillies and sweet peppers; melons and cucumbers; and also-rans

Living in a temperate climate means a long cold winter when little grows outdoors for the gourmet's delight. Even spring and autumn can be unproductive and summer has its bad days. The cunning gourmet wanting more variety and better quality fare needs an under-cover paradise for their plants – and themselves... Of course, plants can have their own individual cloches but this is nowhere near as congenial as a heated greenhouse.

Any sort of cover improves the microclimate significantly, and so extends the growing season at both ends; it keeps many pests and some diseases away (but encourages others). If big enough to walk in, though, it will be, without doubt, the most enticing part of the garden.

The colour, scent and production all year round in a heated greenhouse is attraction enough, but the freedom from the weather, and the numerous tasks to do inside it, mean once you go under cover you neglect outdoors. Believe me. And no matter how big your greenhouse or conservatory, it will soon be cramped and you'll wish you'd built a bigger one – and one day soon you will.

First of all, cover enables us to start hardy plants off earlier, to then plant out of doors for earlier harvests. Secondly, more tender long-season plants can be started off in time to plant out, mature and ripen while summer lasts and before the autumn frosts. Thirdly, we can bring some crops, such as herbs in pots, under cover at the end of summer to extend their season. Fourthly, growing under cover

The cunning gourmet wanting more variety and better quality fare needs an under-cover paradise for their plants – and themselves...

improves the cleanliness of many crops: the mud and rain don't bother them – crucial for salads and strawberries – not to mention freedom from birds. Fifthly, and probably most importantly, we can grow crops under cover that would otherwise be impossible – especially if we also have heat. With a plastic tent inside a plastic tunnel, soil-warming cables and a couple of bathroom fan heaters, I grow and crop the most amazing plants here in Norfolk, in the UK.

Starting with cloches

To start at the beginning: even cloches are invaluable. Put them in place a week or two before the crop is sown or planted out, to pre-warm the soil. Traditional glass cloches have now been replaced by plastic – either glass-like small units or long tunnels covered with woven or extruded plastic film. Individual cloches can be made from plastic bottles: cut the bottom off and discard the cap. Extra ventilation may be needed on hot days, and extra insulation – a blanket on frosty nights – extends the season further.

Cloches are most useful for getting earlier crops of favourite vegetables but can equally cover flowers and fruits, even bushes if they're supported on boxes! Ingenuity will come up with a way if a crop is really important to you. One of a cloche's most important jobs is protecting tender plants such as tomatoes or courgettes recently moved outdoors. Cloches can be full all summer with melons and watermelons; then in autumn they can protect salad crops through winter.

Permanent cloches – or cold frames

A cold frame is like a more permanent cloche, usually sited in a warm sunny spot. A well-made well-insulated cold frame can cosset even more delicate plants in cold conditions, but may cook them instead on the first sunny day unless the lid is opened. By your opening and closing the lid, covering at night with a blanket and supplying a bit of extra warmth by putting in hot-water bottles each night, a cold frame can protect tender plants against harsh weather.

A cold frame is ideal for growing on tomatoes before planting them out in the open. In summer it is perfect for cropping cucumbers, peppers and melons. A cold frame can also be used like a small greenhouse for propagating plants and for over-wintering nearly hardy plants. Add a soil-warming cable underneath and you can use a cold frame to grow almost anything – even pineapples, honest. The best cold frame I have is made from a dead deep-freezer unit. Basically it's a well-insulated box with a lid for night. A false floor brings the plants up near the light, and two sliding glass sheets sit on top to keep heat in but allow ventilation. It is set into the ground angled towards the sun to let more light in. I have another with the floor filled with sand and an embedded electric soil-warming cable, which keeps it warm enough to function as an enormous propagator.

Left In the UK a watermelon may just succeed if given a cloche.
Below A glass box made up around one vine gives a crop months ahead of other vines that are outdoors, without protection.
Opposite Recycled radiators provide a light-reflecting path.

From cold frame to greenhouse

Commercial alternatives are available, but they're usually too small. The keen gourmet will soon find the average propagator is fine for starting off seeds but not big enough for seedlings, let alone plants. Thus the inevitability of a greenhouse. This is a much better form of shelter and warmth. Its enormous volume creates a more stable environment and the gardener can work in comfort! In a warm wooden-framed greenhouse, staging, potting benches and plant supports can be easily attached to the frame, and it looks relatively pleasing in a garden. Metal-framed greenhouses are colder but have similar advantages. A plastic walk-in tunnel is much cheaper but may be very humid, hard to ventilate and expensive to heat, and the plastic cover needs replacing every few years. This is no more effort than cleaning the glass in the greenhouse but does give the opportunity, where space allows, of moving the tunnel on to fresh soil. It's difficult to fix benches or staging to a tunnel frame but they are convenient for growing directly in the soil.

Whichever you choose, bigger is better and cheaper proportionately. Site your greenhouse near to water and an electricity supply for simple heating and lighting. Put the longest axis east–west to maximise the sunlight. It's always worth having a secure, raised, pest- and weed-proof base.

In winter extra insulation can be fixed inside greenhouses or plastic tents constructed in tunnels. This keeps plants warmer but reduces the available light. You can buy special plant lights but these are as expensive as just adding more heat without the insulation.

You can heat just part of a greenhouse by making internal clear plastic partitions or adding a heated

In a warm wooden-framed greenhouse, staging, potting benches and plant supports can be easily attached to the frame, and it looks relatively pleasing in a garden.

cold frame. Soil-warming cables are cheap to run as most heat is needed at night when you can use off-peak electricity. They heat the sand around them; if you stand plants in pots on top, they keep the roots warm, which is more important than keeping the top growth alive.

To keep the tops warm, the only sensible way is with fan heaters fitted with thermostats. Moving air is much more effective than static heat and you get far fewer moulds. (A paraffin stove is useful for emergencies but causes damp and fumes – no gourmet could stand the taint.) In summer over-heating can be a problem and ventilation needs to be automated unless you are at home all day.

The pros and cons of conservatories

Conservatories are easily heated from a domestic central heating system and are excellent rooms – relatively bright and cheerful compared with most urban caves. But all that glass gets too hot in summer and they become death traps to many plants. What we like and what plants need are very different things. We want it hotter and drier; they want it more humid. The ideal conservatory plant is therefore either a cactus or a succulent or any plant that thrives in dry atmospheres – zonal pelargoniums can become tree size.

The conservatory's unsuitability as a greenhouse does not stop us growing things, but ideally conservatory specimens are those that can go out in summer, such as citrus plants.

Ventilation is important and has an effect on flavour and growth. Plants consume carbon dioxide to grow and if you keep heat in, you also keep fresh air out. More fresh air helps reduce mildews and moulds but wastes heat. Instead you can add carbon dioxide yourself – especially on sunny days in spring. Plastic bottles half-full of water with a cupful of sugar or jam and a sprinkling of live yeast will ferment for about a fortnight or more, giving off copious carbon dioxide. To keep up supplies of this badly needed building block, ferment four bottles in corners of the greenhouse replacing one with a fresh charge each week.

Although plants under cover enjoy fresh air, never chill them by opening up when too cold – or worse, opening up late on a sunny day when they are half-cooked and steaming. I cannot repeat too often: automatic vents, preferably solar-powered, are a good investment. Likewise, automatic watering may be needed if you can't give the immediate attention required.

Automatic humidity control is another good investment: too much encourages moulds and botrytis; too little and you get mildews and red spider mites. In general, during the growing season most plants are happier with higher humidity during the day and lower at night. Misting with water in the morning means they can dry before nightfall.

In a greenhouse the air conditions tend to be too dry; in a polytunnel, too moist – but the ground in both can very quickly become bone-dry unless care is taken. And both can get too dark. All glass and plastic should be cleaned spring and autumn to prevent light from being lost. Overgrown plants should be cut back to let in more light and dark walls can be lightened with white paint. I use old white radiator panels as walkways and they throw much light back up on to the plants.

Although all plants need light, not all need full sunlight or they may get leaf burn, especially if they have been kept cool and shaded till then. (Plants need hardening off to prevent sunburn as well as windburn.) However, for most plants most of the time, the light is insufficient. By adding electric light to weak winter sunlight we can grow earlier and more valuable plants. Ordinary incandescent bulbs don't work as they give out too much heat and the wrong light; special fluorescent tubes and discharge lamps work well, though they're pricey. The idea is to supplement the light for a few hours each day, not to extend the day length, though really advanced gardeners do play with the latter and get all manner of plants to perform at will.

Under cover we also need to attend to the soil or compost we are using with even more care. The very best flavours usually come from plants grown directly in the ground. But rotation is difficult with few crops grown and the watering and feeds may eventually unbalance the soil. Adding copious amounts of garden compost and lime helps, but if yields start to drop, the soil may have become worked out. The answer is simply to swap the top soil with fresh soil dug from another part of the garden or with a good loam made from rotted-down turves. Or you can go over to growing more crops in containers.

It is certainly worth having a small sloped salad bed under cover – it can even go under the staging, as many salad crops do well in low light. It is also worth having small damp trough beds for other more moisture-demanding crops such as celery. Also very effective is to make small hotbeds for some crops under cover. You can use a soil-warming cable but they are usually just compost heaps with soil on top. Traditionally dung, oak bark and leather wastes were used, but I find masses of grass clippings mixed with compost, soil and leaves works well. A big pile between insulating walls heats up a thick layer of soil and compost on top and is the best way I have yet found of growing melons, cucumbers, okra and so on under cover.

Controlling pests under cover

There is little point trying for a 'sterile' environment under cover; instead, encouraging and buying in predators for pest control works efficiently. Common pests such as whitefly, scale insects, red spider mite, aphids and so on all have predators and parasites sold commercially to control them. (We would use them outdoors but it's colder and they can escape!) We can also enlist the help of beetles, spiders, frogs, newts and toads, all of which will eat most 'bugs'. Attract them by leaving out saucers of water with twigs laid in as supports. Also make nooks and crannies with logs and rocks in out-of-the-way corners. Make some damp and some dry nests, and some made of hollow stems rolled up and tied anywhere convenient. I even tie strings to give spiders somewhere to anchor their webs and keep them out of the pathways.

Ground-cover companion plants can be included under staging; I use tender *Lippia dulcis* to keep a host of pests and their predators going. French marigolds are always worth having, especially by doorways where you brush against them; it's the smell that keeps whitefly away. Cover gives protection from the major problems – birds and weather. Protection means not just earlier and tastier crops; the leaves of saladings are simply more succulent once housed out of the bleakest weather, scorching sun and biting wind. The same goes for everything else. Probably most valuable of all, cover allows us to have more green saladings every day of the year.

Salad vegetables are more appreciated in winter than in summer, as there are far fewer fresh foods available. Without heat, even under cover, it is

Several perennial herbs are worth potting up and taking under cover in autumn, such as thyme, mint, tarragon, chives and sage – rosemary and lavender won't take it.

necessary to sow winter salads while the soil is still warm in autumn. Thus they are best if they can be used on a cut-and-come-again basis. With a heated propagator, many can be started off almost any time and planted out under cover to grow slowly. And with heat and light you can grow almost anything (including massive bills). Best value under cover in winter are: rocket, claytonia, parsley, chervil, corn salad, lettuce, spring onions, cress and mustard and, of course, radishes. Several perennial herbs are worth potting up and taking under cover in autumn, such as thyme, mint, tarragon, chives and sage – rosemary and lavender won't take it.

And it's nice to have some winter flowers to cheer you up and for the table (see chapter 7). Almost any bulbs can be forced and are often best for the table in the pots they are grown in rather than as cut flowers. Pineapple sage is a must: its tropical red flowers brighten the drabbest day. For easy cheer, colourful primula and pansy hybrids can be grown from seed and can flower prolifically with no more than a cold frame or cloche. In a warm greenhouse sow *Schizanthus* in mid- to late summer, pot up in autumn, and in late winter they'll become spectacular poor man's orchids. These last ones are somewhat lacking in scent but we'll let them off for the sheer exuberance they bring.

long-term treats

Once you get a greenhouse or conservatory, these are the plants to grow for the most fantastic value. You cannot imagine how fine the flavours and how sweet the fruit until you've tried an English-grown tangerine, pineapple or guava. Better than any I've ever had abroad!

citrus

Citrus trees or bushes are multiple value to any gourmet: their flowers have the most delicious scent and the plants are worth having on their own. The fruits taste fantastic grown slowly in a cool climate, although they crop only lightly. Even the leaves are edible in moderation.

Lemons (*Citrus limon*) are by far the easiest and can be holding worthwhile quantities of fruits almost year round; Meyer's is the most reliable; Lisbon is good as is Eureka. **Tangerines** (*C. reticulata*) and **satsumas** (*C. unshiu*) are also easy and produce the most beautifully perfumed sweet fruits. The **kumquat** (*Fortunella* spp.) is not a true citrus but so similar who cares? It's also good value as the small fruits can be cropped in abundance. **Oranges** (*C. sinensis*) are not difficult but it makes more sense to go for tangerines as you get more; however, with heavy thinning wonderful oranges can be grown. **Grapefruits** (*C. x paradisi*) and **limes** (*C. aurantiifolia*) are also possible but need more warmth than the others.

Buying grafted plants which will fruit while small is wise. Grown from pips citrus plants wait a decade or more before fruiting. I know, I've grown them; they are worth the wait and they can come true.

Citrus need frost-free conditions but not great heat. Their roots need excellent aeration and drainage; their containers should preferably be terracotta or wood slats. If plastic containers are used, drill a host of extra holes in the bottom and lower sides. Fill

with an open, sandy, rich, lime-free potting compost. Citrus need regular nitrogenous feeds: use growth and leaf feeds every week during the growing season, but not those that contain lime or wood ashes.

Citrus should be watered copiously with rainwater, then allowed to drain, but must never dry out even in winter. They do not like being permanently under cover. After the last frosts, harden them off and put them outdoors for the summer months when most pests will disappear and the plants will thrive. Bring them back under cover before hard frosts return, though they can be protected with a fleece through light ones, and enjoy being out as long as

possible. Citrus grow and crop happily but do get attacks of aphids, red spider mite and scale insects. Regular careful inspection is vital; outdoors a good hosing down with a powerful jet works wonders and they love seaweed sprays.

Prune them hard – shear, even, in late winter to keep them compact; the cuttings may be rooted and can fruit more readily than seedlings (though are best grafted on to seedling roots).

Surplus fruits can be made into liqueurs and preserves. Marmalade is a delicious conserve to make, especially from a mix of all sorts of citrus.

guavas

Guavas (*Psidium guajava*) are very similar to citrus in their appearance, hardiness, growth and size. Their fruits are surpassingly well flavoured and luscious to eat – like a fresh fig dipped in syrup and perfume. They are never so good in the heat of their native lands. The supermarkets sell guavas occasionally and those travesties are useful to the gourmet only for supplying the seeds.

Sown in the warmth and grown on, these can fruit in their third year. They need nothing more than a large tub of rich compost in the warm – and more water than you can believe possible. Use growth and leaf feeds while the plants are growing and flowering, but go over to flower, fruit and flavour feeds when the fruits swell. Thin these hard for bigger, more succulent fruits and use nets to support them. Surplus fruit can be used to make jam. The apple-shaped guavas have red flesh and are not quite so luscious as the pear-shaped with yellower flesh. The closely related strawberry guava (*P. littorale*) is even more delightful; resembling the common *Ficus benjamina* house shrub in its glossy evergreen leaves it has purple fruits that are strawberry flavoured and is another easy conservatory plant.

> Guavas are surpassingly well flavoured and luscious to eat – like a fresh fig dipped in syrup and perfume.

pineapples

Pineapples (*Ananas comosus*) from shops are acid, hard and miserable compared with the sweet aromatic vanilla-cream-fleshed home-grown ones. And they are not at all difficult. They just take time and get a bit big if well grown. Admittedly the tips are spiny and sometimes serrated – however, these can be trimmed. Many heirloom varieties are now lost: all you can get are the crowns from commercial fruits, but you can grow them better.

Choose a healthy pineapple with no central rot in the crown; cut off the crown immediately above the fruit and peel away the lower leaves, where you will see vestigial roots already there. Keep the crown warm and dry for several days to dry out the base of the core, then pot into a very free-draining gritty but rich compost.

Give bottom heat, at least to start with, and a hot sunny position. Pot on each spring and summer, spray with seaweed regularly and feed with fish emulsion and soot water, but only in summer.

In autumn let the plant dry off and keep it warm and almost bone-dry till spring. Be patient and after two or three years the plant should be a stride across in a bucket of good compost. Then it will flower like a psychedelic pine cone and this will swell and ripen. Keep watering, if warm and sunny, until the fruit starts to ripen. Pick it just before the last bit of green fades to yellow. The stump will produce side-shoots which will crop in another year or two. These side-shoots can be detached and grown on separately to give really big fruits. Go on, try – it's easier than you imagine!

cape gooseberries

Cape gooseberries (*Physalis peruviana*) are very very tasty and incredibly rich in vitamin A. No different when home-grown but so good they're worth it. Plants are usually promoted as annuals but are far better grown as perennials. Initially, grow them like tomato plants but ideally keep them frost-free over winter and they will produce prolifically the next spring, summer and autumn. From seed the first-year crop comes too late in autumn to ripen well or abundantly, even in a greenhouse. But if the plants are grown on as perennials the flowers and fruits come many months earlier and are sweeter for it. Over-wintered plants can be the originals or small plants rooted from cuttings in late summer. The plants are best ripened until they drop – each comes in its own stay-clean paper case. Even old and dried up they are like wee raisins and still tasty.

The plants can be hard pruned in late winter or early spring, root easily from cuttings and thrive in containers or a warm border. They use a lot of water, need feeding only lightly and suffer from few pests or diseases. The jam is legendary.

also-rans

These are so good they're worth a mention, even though they're nowhere near the value of the last four. However, the adventurous gourmet will find them hard to resist.

swiss cheese plant

The Swiss cheese plant (*Monstera deliciosa*) lives up to its Latin name. Also known as the Ceriman fruit, it resembles a solitary green banana and is delicious once fully ripe (when the skin flakes off in little plates). It's like a cross between a banana and a pineapple on a stick – delicious, but a little suffices. These plants are forest climbers and need a big tub, copious water, light feeding and a frost-free place. Once mature they throw massive arum-like flowers; then the fruit ripens a year or so later.

lemongrass

Lemongrass (*Cymbopogon citratus*) you buy is every bit as good as home-grown, I'll admit, but look at the price for what is a weed where it comes from! An essential for gourmet Eastern dishes, it requires only the same sort of attention you give any house plant – give better and you will have a massive clump. Any fresh bit from the supermarket with a tiny bit of the root crown will root in a glass of water in the warm. Once it's growing away, pot up into rich compost and give growth and leaf feeds, spray with seaweed solution and stand back. The mounds of lemon-scented grass have razor-sharp edges and can be made into a tea, but it's the plumpest young side-shoots you pull off the clump to trim for cooking with.

ginger

Ginger (*Zingiber officinale*) is another expensive spice essential to so many dishes. Yet any bit of fresh root with a healthy bud can be grown up into a whole new 'hand'. Cut off a piece about the size of your thumb with a fat bud on it. Let the cut surface dry for a couple of days. Then pot it just under the surface of a gritty open compost. Stand the pot on bottom heat in a propagator from late winter. Once it's growing away keep really warm and be careful never to over-water – though spray with seaweed solution weekly. Ginger does best on raised beds and – oddly – growing among other plants rather than on its own. I grow ginger in large buckets which I stand amongst other rampant growers. While the stems are green the bulbous bit is

tender and can be candied; once the stem-leaves wither and fall, the root has become ready for lifting and drying. Remember to save some healthy budded bits to start off for the next crop.

passion fruit

Passion fruits (*Passiflora spp.*) come in only a few varieties at the shops but are sold by their dozens from specialist growers. The standard browny purple shrivelled egg is the best flavoured but there are bigger, smaller, sweeter and weirdly shaped ones too. All are easy to start, often easy to flower – staggeringly impressive every time – and easy to crop. You may even have fruits the first winter after an early-spring sowing. But they are hard to keep going in long cold damp winters – even under cover with heat. Grow these climbers up around a tripod of canes in a large tub, water carefully and feed lightly with a flower and fruit feed. If the atmosphere is dry, spray with seaweed weekly.

sugar cane

Sugar cane (*Saccharum officinarum*) – call yourself a gourmet and never chewed it? This delight comes in a multitude of varieties and almost all are sweet; some are just softer or better flavoured. Any piece sold in an ethnic market for chewing can be rooted; lay it on its side in a tray of wet compost and almost cover it with more. Keep warm and wet; once the roots and stems appear, pot up into large pots and grow on. Give as much water, feed, top dressings, liquid feeds and sprays as you like and the plant will romp away. To save your greenhouse you can plant it out after the frosts for the summer; by autumn the clump will be so big all you can do is hack off a small plantlet to over-winter for next year. Eat the cane by cutting off the cuticle and chewing the pith – it's delicious!

eddoes

Eddoes or taro (*Colocasia*) are sold in supermarkets. The tubers or rather the corms, or cormels to be precise, have an irritant fibrous skin covering them; however, once peeled and cooked they are excellent eating and are a West Indian speciality. Easy to grow in a big tub under cover, they make an interesting meal and the most impressive of all house or conservatory plants with enormous healthy arrow-shaped leaves. Pot in a rich, free-draining compost, feed with growth and leaf feed in the water and keep warm and moist. Within a month or so you will need a bucket-size pot!

bananas

Bananas (*Musa* spp.) from the shops are pappy rubbish. They are fantastic when home-grown but I have to put them low down on my list because they are too big a plant for most people to attempt. To guarantee tasty fruits bananas must be grown from an offset, not a seed. The only sensible choice is the dwarf Chinese *M. acuminata* Dwarf Cavendish, which needs nine or ten feet to open its leaves. Young leaves have a distinctive purplish hazing in the middle.

Pot a banana plant up and up, eventually planting it in an enormous tub or the border under cover; feed liberally and keep it warm and watered all growing season and in two years or so it will flower and fruit – honest! On a dry day, nip off the dead flower 'petals' from the ends of the fruits. Once the first start to yellow, cut the whole stem and take into a warm dry place to finish ripening. After fruiting cut down the rest of that 'tree' and allow the biggest replacement shoot to take over. Remove all other shoots as they appear but save one to be a future replacement.

quicker treats

tomatoes

quicker tender treats for those less-than-patient gourmets who want it all really fast

Tomatoes (*Lycopersicum lycopersicum*) are a joy to almost every gardener. Who would ever buy supermarket ones when their own are in season? The gourmet will also appreciate the incredible range of tomatoes: there are white, yellow, orange, red, purple, black, green and striped ones – in all sizes and shapes, with tastes from bland to acid. You just have to try them all – well, several dozen at least.

Tomatoes can be grown outside in sheltered gardens where they develop the most flavour, but under cover they are more reliable. I advocate growing most of them under cover with the outdoor ones as a superb bonus if they ripen. Under cover or not, Gardener's Delight is still the supreme champion bite-size tomato though closely threatened by Sakura and the golden Sungold. Pink Brandywine has a sensational taste but is a poor performer – the peelable Dombito and the old French Marmande beefsteaks give so many more fruits that they're preferable. San Marzano and

Roma-type plum tomatoes are poor eating raw but once cooked become fantastic. The yellows such as Golden Sunrise add colour to salads and make good marmalade with lemons.

Sow tomatoes in individual cells or pots in warmth from late winter for indoor crops and early spring for outdoor. Pot up into a rich compost at least twice, if not three times, never letting the plants get checked. Start training and disbudding early.

Most varieties are best grown as single cordons with all side-shoots removed; this will enable the maximum number to be squeezed in. They need to be tied to strong canes from early on. (Some varieties are indeterminate types which produce sprawling stems and are more trouble than they're worth.)

Keep warm and in the light, and give regular growth and leaf feeds until hardened off and planted out – under cover in spring or early summer outdoors. Do not overfeed!

Once the first truss has set, go over to a flower, fruit and flavour feed but again be moderate. The earliest plants can be sacrificed for an extra-early crop if you remove all side-shoots and cut off the main stem one pair of leaves above the first set truss. Keep these plants in smallish pots, high up on the staging rather than planted in the ground. Any side-shoots removed can be rooted easily to make more plants. These will be squatter and more mature than seedlings of the same size, and are an easy way to have later plants for outdoor cropping. Out of doors tomatoes need wind protection and ideally a plastic flysheet cover until they are well established and summer has warmed up. The flysheet will also keep them drier in wet years and postpone attacks of blight. You may also need to use nets to keep birds from eating the fruits.

Indoors or out, grow tomatoes in the ground if you can, rather than in pots; the watering and feeding regime for pots can never replace a free root run and the fruits never taste as good. Plants in poor soils, pots and containers will need feeding. In fair soil they will tend

Top and bottom Small-fruited varieties, such as Sungold and Gardener's Delight give the most value, and sweet bite-sized flavour, for your efforts.
Opposite Only the enthusiastic gourmet will grow disease prone, greenback (hard, unripe patches as seen here) prone varieties, such as this – the supremely well-flavoured Pink Brandywine.

to make bigger crops of less-tasty fruits that ripen later in the season. If you are after mostly early crops or flavour, do not feed heavily, as this produces growth instead. Remember, it is tomatoes you eat, not lush tropical-looking leaves. Comfrey liquid in moderation is ideal and frequent seaweed sprays are beneficial. Plants in the ground should be watered heavily once a week. In pots or containers it is hard to keep them moist but not drowned. Drying out causes blossom end rot, a brown blotch at the bottom of the fruit. In warm weather twice or thrice daily watering is sensible.

Out of doors pollination happens naturally but early crops under cover need the help of a soft paintbrush. The first green fruits can be helped to redden by an over-ripe banana placed nearby. Tomatoes ripen to their finest on the plant but leaving ripe ones on stops more fruits setting, so pick them as soon as they're ready.

Once the plants start to die back in autumn, cut the roots off and hang the plants upside down in a warm dry place to ripen the remaining fruits. Or pick them and ripen them somewhere warm, such as in a box in the kitchen. Surplus tomatoes can be frozen in bags without blanching for adding to soups and stews; the skins slip off if the frozen fruit is squeezed under hot water.

With extra light and heat some tomatoes can be grown year round. Varieties such as Sub Arctic Plenty are good for this, though not exactly the finest. You can also take slips in autumn from healthy plants and over-winter these in a warm greenhouse for an even earlier crop than from seed-grown plants; this method works with Sakura, Sungold and Gourmet.

peppers

Peppers (*Capsicum* spp.) both sweet and chilli are available in the shops in maybe a half-dozen sorts but the gourmet can cultivate hundreds. They come in every size, shape and colour, and the hot ones in strengths from mild to thermonuclear. Most varieties change from green to orange to red as they ripen. Unripe green peppers may cause indigestion but many people like to eat them. Canapé, Californian Wonder and Gypsy are probably most reliable in the UK; Jumbo Sweet grows bigger and more substantial. For flavour, Sunnybrook is superb as are the smaller Pimento and Cherry types. The chilli varieties seem to get hotter the smaller their fruits. Anaheim and Hungarian Hot Wax are pretty mild; the hottest are the bird's-eye varieties, the Thai sorts and the *habañero*/Scotch bonnet ones from the Caribbean. These all can get surprisingly hot even when grown in the UK.

Peppers are simpler to grow than tomatoes but need just a bit more light and warmth. In very good summers in warm sheltered gardens they may crop out of doors in southern Britain. Under cover they crop sooner, longer and more heavily and – if kept warm over winter – are perennial and crop again even more heavily the next year. To over-winter successfully, plants must be kept warm and nearly bone-dry until spring as they mould easily; however, the earlier, huge crops are worth working for.

Sow peppers individually in pots, preferably in a warm propagator in late winter to early spring; repot monthly and do not let plants get cold or wet. Peppers often do better in big buckets of well-aerated well-drained compost standing up on the staging. Though they can grow bigger in the greenhouse border they are too cold down there. I have found they

do best for me on raised beds under cover; it gets them higher off the floor with a big root run and good aeration and drainage. Never overwater peppers, feed them as for tomatoes and spray with seaweed solution frequently. Hand pollinate the first flowers of the year; later ones usually don't need help. Heavy-cropping plants will need tying to canes for support.

Peppers may suffer from aphid attacks when young; more of a problem is slug damage to ripening fruits of sweet varieties. Surplus peppers dry remarkably easily or can be turned into sauces – especially the hot ones. Chillies will hang fresh on the plants well into the following year if in a dry warm place, even on a sunny kitchen windowsill.

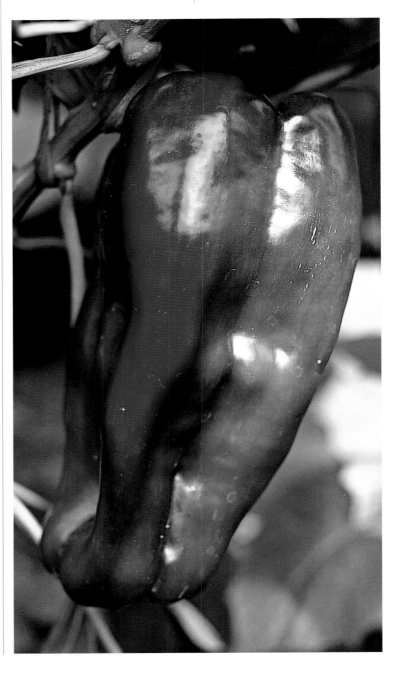

melons

Melons (*Cucumis melo*) are really divine when home-grown. The texture, flavour and perfume can almost overwhelm the senses. A truly ripe melon is eaten either with a spoon or very messily – the juice will ruin your clothes. You can buy good melons in the shops but they're necessarily picked before their prime, so too often they never really match your expectation.

A really well-grown melon may be too much for the novice. Just as with some French cheeses, it takes time to learn to appreciate the depth of flavour. Believe me, you may find your first real melon too sweet and too perfumed, compared with what you are used to. For exquisite fruits grow Jenny Lind, Emerald Gem, Blenheim Orange, also Galia, Charentais and Ogen, but all need warmth. The honeydew types are also excellent if you just want incredible sweetness and, unlike all others, they will store for several weeks. No Name, Sweetheart and Romeo are not quite so divine but more cold tolerant and worth growing under a plastic cloche or in a cold frame.

Melons need heat to keep them growing well and are far happier

A really well-grown melon may be too much for the novice. Just as with some French cheeses, it takes time to learn to appreciate the depth of flavour.

on a hotbed or in big pots up on the staging than down in the cold greenhouse border. Start them off singly in pots of rich limy well-draining compost, sowing the seeds on edge and placing the pots in a warm propagator. When watering take especial care not to let the neck where the stem enters the soil get damaged or wet, as it will rot. Pot up plants so the neck stands proud on a little mound of sterile compost. Pot up fortnightly and tie the stem to a cane.

To produce four medium-sized melons, nip out the tip after four good leaves to produce four side-shoots. Then pollinate one flower on each side-shoot on the same day, using a small brush or cotton wool ball. Or grow a plant as a cordon and allow just one melon to swell at a time and you can have enormous fruits!
Do not let the melons hang but support them in bags or nets – this makes them swell more. If you are growing on the ground,

place the small fruits on a piece of wood to stop them rotting.

Water plants carefully, never giving more than just enough to keep the compost barely moist to start with, and preferably use warm water. Later, as the plants grow, water more heavily and add growth and leaf feeds. Once the compost is seen to be full of fine roots at the surface, top dress with a thin layer of generally enriched compost, and repeat throughout the season. Water very little once the fruits start to ripen.

Melons are prone to red spider mite but do not like heavy syringing with water to control the mites. Occasional misting with seaweed solution helps reduce the problem but you may need to buy in the predators (see page 29). Pick melons when the stalk has started to pull away and you can see it cracking. Eat immediately or gently cool the fruit for a day or so; to rekindle the scent, warm gently just before serving.

watermelons

cucumbers

Watermelons (*Citrullus lanatus/vulgaris*) are a good buy in the shop but I like a challenge. And it is possible to grow far bigger, finer, sweeter, better-textured watermelons in all sorts of colours than those on sale. However, they do need a good summer, even under cover. Try Green Jade, Fun Baby or Golden Crown – there are dozens of heritage varieties too.

Watermelons are started in the same way as melons and need similar conditions, but prefer a less rich, less limy, more open sandy compost and need even more sun and water. They seem to be the most prone of all plants to red spider mite, but you can't syringe or even mist the plants to control them, so make sure you buy the predators early (see page 29). Do not stop the plants or allow more than one fruit to swell; water heavily once growth is strong but do not feed or spray.

Home-grown cucumbers (*Cucumis sativus*) are sweeter and crunchier than the flaccid old green sausages sold in shops. Indoor or frame varieties are finer than the ridge cucumbers grown outdoors. The gourmet can also find many different varieties such as the traditional Telegraph or round white Crystal Apple. Femspot, Tyria and Carmen are excellent long ones; Birgit and Petita are shorter but superb.

Indoor cucumbers need continuous warmth and moisture with a really rich compost, but can be started off during late winter for a spring crop. Sow seed singly, on edge, in pots of rich compost in a heated propagator and pot up regularly. Early crops are best in large containers up on the staging but successional plantings should be in the cooler border soil. Enrich the site well beforehand with compost and grass clippings.

When potting and planting, take care not to let the neck where the stem enters the soil get damaged or wet, as it will rot: raise it on a little mound of sterile compost. Cucumbers trail so need canes, strings or wires to wind around, though the fruits need no supports. It is simpler to train them as cordons, nipping out side-shoots to avoid a tangle. Keep humidity high to discourage red spider mite and mildew; regular syringing with seaweed solution will benefit plants. Top dress and feed regularly, and water copiously. Indoor cucumbers must not be pollinated.

Cucumbers of most old varieties will produce male flowers (no tiny cucumber behind them) and these MUST BE REMOVED before they open or any females will be pollinated and become horribly bitter. Modern varieties are usually all-female but may not always be

so, so be vigilant.

Pick cucumbers early in the morning, before the heat is in them, for maximum crispness. Do not leave any to ripen and yellow as this stops new ones forming. When a plant becomes too old and too long, layer it near the tip by covering the stem at a joint with moist compost in a new pot. Once it has rooted you can detach the tip and grow it on, discarding the old plant. With warmth and extra light cucumbers can be had all year round.

Left Watermelons are ripe if they sound hollow when they are knocked.
Above Indoor grown cucumbers can be used in place of gherkins when small, but real gherkins, such as these, are better – although they are best grown outdoors like marrows and squashes.

Watermelons are a good buy in the shop but I like a challenge.

also-rans

These are crops that the true aficionado will want to try but, to be fair, they will be only a little better than those you can buy in the shop. But, of course, there is still the fun and challenge...

sweet potatoes

Sweet potatoes (*Ipomoea batatas*) are only just becoming available in the UK in different varieties, though some catalogues have just started selling slips in spring. Sweet potatoes sold in the shops as vegetables can be forced in late winter in a propagator – wash them first to remove any chemical preservatives. The orange-fleshed brownish-skinned large varieties are finer but more demanding than the red-skinned yellow- or white-fleshed thinner varieties which are, of course, easier croppers.

The tubers are hard to get to sprout, but once away the sprouts are best detached and grown on separately, rather than left to rot with the tuber. They need a lime-rich, well-drained compost and a lot of water, but feed only very lightly with a flower and fruit type. Sweet potatoes crop far more heavily under cover as they bulk only at the end of a long growing season. The border is usually too cold so they do best on raised beds or in very large containers. Containers are preferable when it comes to digging up the roots, as they often delve too deep in the ground. The foliage is a rambling vine; tie it up so it cannot root anywhere – this also helps give it more sun. The leaves are often eaten like spinach. Some varieties have pretty flowers you can wind up canes in the conservatory in a tub.

Let the compost dry out as the haulm dies off in late autumn, and keep the crop in the pot until needed. Use the tubers as soon as possible: they do not keep well unless heat-treated by oven-curing in a warm dry place. Alternatively, with warmth under cover sweet potatoes can grow on and stay fresh and usable through winter. When you find a good variety, layer young plants in early autumn to over-winter and start them off earlier the next spring.

aubergines

Aubergines or eggplants (*Solanum melongena*) are available to the gourmet in myriad shapes, colours and sizes but sadly all are incredibly similar – even indistinguishable – once peeled and cooked! Commonly available are Long Purple, Black Beauty and Black Enorma; the bigger ones such as the latter are better value because they are less wasteful when peeled. By all means try others: the mini ones are OK barbecued on a kebab stick with loads of nicer things. (That's really damning with faint praise: OK, I admit it, they're poor old stuff.)

Aubergines must have continuous warm moist rich conditions and are definitely greenhouse crops. Sow singly in pots of sowing compost in warmth in early spring. Repot monthly, feed copiously with growth and leaf feeds till flowering, then go over to flower and fruit feeds as for tomatoes. They need tying to canes to support the heavy fruits and, although they can be grown in big pots, they do better on raised beds. For big crops set them a stride apart. Aubergines suffer red spider mite and aphid attacks and do not enjoy being syringed to control them, so use predators (see page 29).

okra

Okra (*Hibiscus esculentus*) is old and tough when shop-bought. It's essential for many great dishes, so is well worth growing. However, you need quite a lot of plants to give you enough pods at once – say a dozen or more, at a foot or two each way, in full sun and warmth on top of a raised bed. Start them off and grow just as for aubergines. Pick the pods while still immature to add their delightful gooiness to sauces; they will stay fresh only a few days.

peanuts

Peanuts (*Arachis hypogaea*) are slightly nicer fresh than dried and really easy to grow, but the yields are not great. Sow freshly shelled nuts individually in small pots under cover in the warm in late winter. The clover-like plants have small flowers which are then 'pushed' into the soil to develop the nuts, so by then they must be planted in the greenhouse border or very wide shallow containers. At the end of the season you dig up new peanuts.

chapter 6 the gourmet's choicest herbs and salads

The gourmet's essential perennial culinary herbs. Choicest saladings: delicious annual herbs and salad leaves. Other succulent crops a gourmet must have

Any gourmet must have a plentiful supply of many different herbs, seasonings and salad leaves, preferably throughout the whole year. You can't grow just one – no matter how superbly! However, the many herbs, salads and actual vegetables all need very different treatments and, though they could be crammed together, each needs to be given more exact conditions to evolve their finest flavours and textures.

Classic culinary herbs such as sage, rosemary, marjoram and thyme are perennials from southern Europe and require sunny dry sheltered spots with well-drained not overly rich soil.

Herbs grown as annuals, such as parsley, dill and chervil, need a moister richer soil and may tolerate light shade. These more succulent herbs and salad leaves are better grown on their own specialised bed than planted with the perennial herbs or among vegetables.

True vegetables require the very best conditions of all: full sun and rich soil – and, as they are grown in bulk, they need their own bed and plot.

A gourmet needs to try most things, and there are many herbs and salads to enjoy with strange and unusual flavours, but the commonplace are always needed. Most gourmets probably do not want to overwhelm their food with excessively heavy use of herbs but some are essential for many famous dishes. A 'bunch of herbs' for soups and savoury sauces contains a sprig each of parsley, thyme and bay – though you may add savory and rosemary as well. A '*bouquet garni*' is just the same herbs tied up in a bit of cloth with some peppercorns. '*Fines herbes*' for egg and cheese dishes and sauces are finely chopped chervil, chives, parsley and French tarragon. 'Mixed herbs' usually contain parsley, thyme, marjoram and summer savory. These few suffice but many others are interesting, if not so widely used, and really must be grown as they are hard to find in the shops – and then only dried, rarely ever fresh.

It seems difficult to consume much of these wonderfully flavoured plants in quantity. Then one day, bored with the blandness of too many standard salads, I experimented by adding some fresh herbs. I discovered that by blending many herbs and salad leaves I could make delicious salads with barely any lettuce or radish at all. The more different herbs I blended, the more pleasing the overall taste – though, of course, very bitter and strong herbs have to be used in minute amounts finely shredded.

Many other and greater gourmets have discovered the same. The basic principle is to combine a multitude of edible plant pieces without letting any one flavour dominate. From each herb take smaller or larger quantities depending on strength of flavour, chop them finely and mix them well together with oil and vinegar. Larger amounts of conventional salading vegetables – shredded cabbage and grated celery and carrot – can be added to dilute the herb portion and add a more crunchy texture.

A gourmet needs to try most things, and there are many herbs and salads to enjoy with strange and unusual flavours.

Here is my recipe for Flowerdew's Super Salad. All ingredients need to be finely chopped. Add, mix and adjust to taste as available.

Small amounts of rosemary, thyme, sage, marjoram, sweet cicely, summer savory, shungiku, coriander, fennel.

Larger amounts of parsley, chervil, dill, French tarragon and basil.

Lots and lots and lots of chives and rocket.

Varying quantities to taste of mint, nasturtium leaves and flowers, purslane, good King Henry, grated horseradish, land cress, citrus leaves, radicchio and alpine strawberries.

Mix up all the above thoroughly and 'dilute' them with background saladings of shredded carrot, grated red and green cabbage, shredded kohl rabi, chopped red and green pepper (and hot ones if you like them), celery, cucumber and gherkin bits, tender curly kale leaves, corn salad, claytonia and even lettuce, chicory, endive – almost any edible greens – and baby peas. Then add pot marigold, day lily (*Hemerocallis*), pelargonium and shungiku petals; borage and rosemary flowers; some violets, pansies, bergamot and loads of rose petals. When ready to serve, top with sliced Gardener's Delight tomatoes and sprinkle with hull-less pumpkin, poppy, celery and sunflower seeds. I rarely use salad dressings on this but prefer to keep it dry and serve it in combination with a well-moistened dish such as taramasalata, hummus, egg mayonnaise and so on. (I have also often eaten, but cannot truly recommend including, very small amounts of clary sage, salad burnet, lovage, hyssop, winter savory, lemon verbena, lemon balm and lavender.)

Left Edible flowers such as this squash make for more colourful cuisine and are especially good for stuffing.

The gourmet's essential perennial culinary herbs

What cuisine is complete without fresh herbs? Most herbs are crammed full of vitamins, minerals and aromatic oils, which makes them such tasty additions to our food. The strong flavours of perennial herbs make them among the easiest plants to cultivate as they are rarely bothered by pests and diseases. Though we may now seldom eat them for medicinal purposes, they are still health giving and help us resist infections and diseases.

Herbs have pleasing odours so grow them where they can be enjoyed – by windows, paths and on patios. Most have good foliage and are attractive anyway. A bed for perennial herbs should not be far from the kitchen if they are to be frequently used. A duplicate planting of your most important herbs could even go right by the kitchen door.

Perennial herbs can be usefully grown in large quantities as low informal hedges around other areas, especially vegetable beds, as most are beneficial companion plants. In the smallest garden we can grow our favourite herbs in containers but the healthiest most long-lived hardy plants are usually grown in the ground. Every effort should be made to ensure the soil is well drained by digging in sharp sand, gravel and fibrous organic material.

Waterlogging will kill many herbs, and the damp conditions and lush growth that go with it ruin the flavour of others. Better they near die of drought! Most perennials come from hot dry regions and require some care to get through our worst winters. It is the combination of damp and cold that kills them. Often the protection of a wall is sufficient; they also benefit from heat coming from other brick or stone nearby, such as paths and drives. In sheltered or town gardens most perennial herbs last for many years.

Perennial herbs grown in pots can be moved under cover to extend their season. Unfortunately most soon expire in hot dry centrally heated rooms but they may do well on a cool light windowsill. The biggest difficulty under cover or indoors is low light

Above Borage flowers add a spot of colour to salads and are edible in moderation.

What cuisine is complete without fresh herbs? Most herbs are crammed full of vitamins, minerals and aromatic oils.

and this causes poor growth and death from moulds. One way round this is to have a sequence of pot-grown specimens ready to bring in from a cold frame; crop them, then compost or revive them. Forcing early and late crops of mint in the same way is also worthwhile. (Pot growing is the only sensible method anyway for mints, which are invasive and prone to take over when grown in a bed with other plants.)

Do not over-enrich, or even bother enriching, the ground or the potting compost for perennial herbs: many then produce rank growth and poor flavour. Likewise, do not fertilise or feed them once they're established, apart from the occasional seaweed spray.

Buy young plants of named varieties rather than grow from seed. Growing from seed is possible for most herbs, but it will cost nearly as much and not give you the full range of gourmet flavours.

You can propagate most herbs by taking cuttings or dividing existing plants, so multiply the ones you enjoy most and dispose of the less favoured. In any case, you should divide and move most perennial herbs systematically every few years. Do this in early spring. Almost all of them are good at preventing weeds from germinating and need little maintenance, apart from trimming off dead or excessive growth. Tender young leaves are best for cooking and eating; cutting back hard each spring removes old withered growths and promotes flushes of new leaves. Always leave pruning till spring so the old growths protect the young from any bad weather. Do not cut back so hard that you're leaving only older wood or most plants will die. Those herbs you need most of should be grown in several places and picked systematically to prevent over-cropping. The earliest and tastiest leaves outdoors come from those in borders next to warm walls.

Most herbs can be dried in the dark and then stored in a dry place till required, but fresh is nearly always better than dried. Freezing chopped fresh herbs in water or oil 'ice-cubes' is a better way to preserve flavours.

choicest perennial herbs

These are the herbs any gourmet simply must have, in my order of preference

thyme

Thyme (*Thymus* spp.) is essential to so many dishes. It smells wonderful and bees love it. Thyme is low growing so goes well beside paths and at the base of sunny walls. Thyme comes in many varied scents and colours and in forms varying from bushy to prostrate. The gourmet will be interested mainly in the grey-leaved bushy forms as these carry the best flavours.

Thymes can be grown from seed but the choicest are multiplied by division in late spring. It thrives in poor dry sunny situations and usually prefers lime-rich soils that are never ever waterlogged. Limestone chippings make an excellent mulch, as does fine gravel, but not sand or leaf mould, which lodges in the leaves. Do not feed or even water much.

Cut back plants just before flowering and dry the trimmings, which also promotes bushier growth and a new flush of tastier leaves.

Thymes are happy in pots or tubs and make nice 'ornaments' on the patio. But they taste best from the ground – I grow a fresh bed every five years or so. It is a good idea to also have several pots of your favourite in a cold frame to extend the season. However, they soon sicken if taken indoors and do better on an outside windowsill.

Thyme can be dried but not frozen and is good used in salads and all meat and cheese dishes. Caraway-flavoured Herba Barona smells divine and is delicious rubbed on the outside of roast beef. I cook rice with coconut milk, bushy grey thyme and a whole uncut *habañero* chilli. I don't add salt or oil and it's unbelievably delicious, believe me.

The gourmet will be interested mainly in the grey-leaved bushy forms as these carry the best flavours.

chives

Chives (*Allium schoenoprasum*) are also essential. They can be easily started from seed or by dividing existing clumps. Several strains and variations exist, including fine-leaved and garlic chives. They are most succulent in rich moist soil, though they survive drier places, but are dismal in shade.

Chives make pretty edgings to paths when they're in flower. If allowed to flower they self-seed and their season is shortened. The solution is to cut back alternate plants hard before flowering and leave the others to bloom, but cut them back immediately after for a later flush. Younger plants produce larger, more succulent leaves so divide every second or third year, and cut back some plants hard every so often as well.

Chives can be grown in pots easily and will force well if taken indoors in winter or merely covered with a cloche. Chives are wonderful in salads, in soft cheeses and egg dishes and in most savoury dishes. They can be dried for use in deepest winter.

marjoram

Marjoram (*Origanum majorana*) and oregano (*Origanum vulgare*) are vital for Italian-style cuisine, though their flavour goes well with most savoury dishes. These herbs are easy to confuse, as they come in many varieties. All of them are similar, but differ widely in hardiness – predictably the more tender varieties are the tastiest. As a rule of thumb, most marjorams are hardy herbs, while any oregano is probably tender. The tougher perennials such as marjoram can be propagated by root division in spring, though the finest-flavoured oreganos must be grown as annuals from seed.

Their soil needs to be open, limy and sandy in full sun; avoid feeding or over-watering for the best flavour, and mulch with limestone chippings. They are low growing so may be planted by paths, and in flower they attract many bees and butterflies.

Hardy marjorams can be easily grown in pots and moved under cover for winter use; tender oreganos are best grown in large squat pots and kept in bright frost-free conditions. Both retain their flavour well when dried or frozen, and fresh leaves can be added to salads.

tarragon

Tarragon (*Artemisia dracunculus*) is relatively little known. Its exquisite flavour – spicy, almost aniseedy – really makes the mouth quicken. Do not confuse the supremely flavoured French species with the miserable rough and coarse Russian one (*A. dracunculoides*). And don't take the vendor's word for it – try it and see! Taste the leaves: the French is sweet, piquant, and most take to it; the Russian is rank and sour.

Unfortunately, Russian tarragon is hardier, easily propagated by either seed or root division, tough, vigorous and sadly far more common. French tarragon needs a warm spot on well-drained gritty leaf-mould rich soil with extra protection from cold damp winters. It can be propagated only by root division – which must be done every third year or it dies away. Do not feed or even water heavily once established. Mulch thinly with leaf mould, sand, grit or fine gravel.

In pots tarragon soon sickens and dies but the roots can still be dug, potted and forced for an earlier crop. Trim back a few plants every so often to promote new growth. Tarragon is no good frozen but can be used to flavour vinegar. Try it with eggs and fish – I like a little in salads. Dried, it is an essential ingredient of *fines herbes*.

mints

Mints (*Mentha* spp.) flavour a range of dishes. There are many many varieties with a vast range of flavours to choose from: pineapple, orange, ginger and apple to plain rank. Cool refreshingly scented mints include eau de cologne and spearmint; then there are golden and silver variegated, yellow, grey and curly forms, which are of little interest to the gourmet but ornamental in the garden. Plain or variegated lemon balm (*Melissa officinalis*) is so similar to a mint it might as well be grouped with them, though does not runner so badly.

Mints' late flowering is useful to bees and beneficial insects but ruins the quality of the leaves, so cut back the majority of plants regularly to prevent flowering and promote more young growths. Unlike most of our herbs, mints enjoy a moist soil and will grow even in shade, but for the best flavour they need some sun and not excessive fertility – apparently they do not like wood ashes.

Mints are one of the few plants that will grow under walnut trees and will even fight it out with stinging nettles – they're then somewhat invasive. Any bit of root grows and takes over the whole area. To keep them in check, grow mints in beds surrounded by concrete or regularly cut grass, or in containers almost buried in the ground or in large pots provided with watering trays. NEVER mix them with other herbs as their roots will choke them out. Decent to eat only when fresh, mints can be potted up for winter use and can be forced by being brought in from the cold to the warm – worth it for a few sprigs to enliven meals, as a garnish or in a cocktail.

rosemary

Rosemary (*Rosmarinus officinalis*) comes in but one flavour, though there are prostrate varieties and variously coloured flowers. Perhaps this is the one herb that could be shop-bought with no loss in flavour, but the price per sprig is high, and one plant – remarkably cheap to buy – provides sprigs for life.

Rosemary is less hardy than many herbs but survives most winters and can be had fresh all year round if given a warm spot against a wall or on a warm patio. It needs exceptionally well-drained soil, preferably limy with a mulch of limestone chips or gravel. Never feed or water once established in the ground.

Rosemary will grow in a pot, but is happier in a cold frame or cold greenhouse than indoors in a hot room. Easily propagated from cuttings in spring, it can be grown as a low hedge and sheared back lightly after flowering. Bees love the blooms. Rosemary adds a spicy warm flavour to almost all meat dishes, especially lamb, and both young leaves and flowers are delicious in salads.

sage

Sage (*Salvia officinalis*) is a traditional flavouring herb that has recently been shown to significantly improve the memory. I'm trying to eat more of it, but keep forgetting to... The red-leafed variant has dark red, almost purple, leaves with a much finer flavour than the grey, and adds a healthier colour to salads. The compact multicoloured sages are rather tender and they have a whole range of very tender relations. I strongly recommend pineapple sage: the leaves are aptly named in scent and the brilliant DayGlo crimson flowers are so cheerful in winter if grown under cover and for adding to salads.

Almost all sage species can be grown from seed but the choicer sorts are grown only from cuttings – easily taken at almost any time. Sages are not difficult as to soil or situation but resent shade; also, never feed nor water them heavily. Sage can be pot-grown but is short lived, especially if brought under cover – though a cold frame may be needed in severe weather, and cover and heat for the tender sorts.

Sage needs cutting back fairly hard each spring and replacing every five years – or once it gets straggly and no longer responds to pruning. Sage does dry or freeze but is hardy enough to pick fresh all year round. It is the traditional stuffing herb and I like it in moderation in salads and with most savoury dishes – oh yes, now I remember, I'm supposed to drink it as a tea...

fennel

Fennel (*Foeniculum vulgare*) has an aniseed-like flavour that goes well with many fish and cheese dishes. The seeds can also be cooked with, which is fortunate as it self-seeds viciously unless you cut it back in time. It can be grown from seed or by division in spring.

Fennel grows very tall and forms an attractive plant; the bronze form is particularly beautiful. It's not fussy about soil but the flavour becomes ranker and the foliage more succulent if it has plentiful moisture and insufficient sun. Grow it in partial or full sun and cut back often to get new softer growths. Fennel is barely worth forcing or pot growing as it pushes up a few leaves almost year round. I use it in most of my salads.

sweet cicely

Sweet cicely (*Myrrhis odorata*) is a gourmet treat, now little known yet surprisingly easy to grow. It has aniseed-tasting leaves that improve salads; the stems, seeds and roots can also be cooked but are scant nibbles. Gourmets relish the foamy flower heads, which can be chewed raw and taste sweet.

Sweet cicely thrives in a moist rich soil and will survive in big containers if kept well watered, but do not over-feed. Be sure you grow the true species: a few similar-looking wild plants are rather poisonous.

horseradish

Horseradish (*Armoracia rusticana*) is a traditional flavouring in both the UK and China. The sauce is best made up fresh and although the purchased root is similar to the home-grown it is not often on sale. The plant is impossible to eradicate once established, as any bit of the root will grow almost anywhere.

Horseradish deserves good culture and its site should be moist rich soil in partial shade. As it is a deep-delving root it is barely worth growing in a tub except from necessity. Horseradish is rich in minerals as well as flavour; I like it combined with *habañero* chillies, garlic, yellow mustard and cider vinegar as a warming sauce. Grate the root to make the traditional sauce for beef and add small amounts to spice up many dishes, especially cheese ones. The root is barely worth storing as it can always be had fresh.

bay

Bay (*Laurus nobilis*) is needed in such small quantities, stores so well (I reckon older leaves taste better) and is available in so few if any varieties that it is hardly worth the gourmet growing a bush – save for adding an aromatic fresh leaf to a rice pudding. Bay plants are not easy to propagate and are expensive to purchase: you could buy a lifetime's supply of leaves for the cost of a small plant.

Bay is a slightly tender shrub that suffers from harsh winds while small and is easily lost. Once established, it becomes tougher and may reach tree size. Small plants are best grown in tubs and taken under cover for the harshest part of winter. They look attractive when trimmed neatly. They are prone to scale insect infestations farmed by ants so stand their containers in saucers of water on blocks to prevent ants from gaining access. I use the leaves in almost all pickles and savoury dishes, especially those containing tomatoes and garlic, and pounded up with pimentos and chilli to 'jerk' barbecue meats.

lavender

Lavender (*Lavandula* spp.) is not often used in cooking nowadays but has such a lovely flavour everyone should try it at least once. There are large and small varieties to suit any garden with a sunny spot. I prefer the white *Lavandula spica* for flavour. The French (*L. stoechas*) and the Spanish (*L. s.* subsp. *pedunculata*) have strong menthol tones and are less suitable for cooking.

Grow lavender in full sun on a chalky soil; do not feed or water once established and shear back each year. A stone or gravel mulch is ideal. One plant in a pot may amply supply sufficient leaves for cooking. I rate very highly lavender rice pudding with lavender shortbread biscuits.

lemon verbena

Lemon verbena (*Aloysia triphylla*) has the truest lemon scent, almost that of a real lemon sherbet, and the dried leaves last for many years. Once you've tried it, you won't want to be without it. It is not very hardy but may survive against a warm wall; protect the roots from damp and cold and they'll sprout again in the spring like fuchsias.

Easily grown from cuttings lemon verbena can be kept in a pot under cover or as a house plant but then is prone to aphids, whitefly and red spider mite! It must be nipped back regularly and kept well watered and lightly fed with mixed feeds. Its exquisite flavour is perfect for fruit salads, sweet dishes, salads and teas, and much better than the coarse lemon balm it is oft confused with.

lovage

Lovage (*Levisticum officinale*) leaves are used in place of salt for giving a 'meaty' flavour to savoury dishes, and for improving vegetable stocks. Easily propagated by root division or seed, lovage is worth growing if you have the space. It must have a moist soil and a good root run or the leaves become too bitter; I grow mine by a pond. Lovage is not at all happy in a small pot but it will just do in a big tub if kept well fed and watered. If blanched like celery (see page 152), the stems can be peeled and eaten raw. The seed is occasionally used to flavour some dishes.

angelica

Angelica (*Angelica archangelica*) is a plant you'd better grow if you like candied angelica stalks, as they're ten times better home-made. This is a tough but usually short-lived herbaceous plant that needs rich moist soil and will grow in partial shade. It is easily grown from seed but takes a lot of space; only the enthusiastic gourmet will grow it. If left to flower angelica is impressive but will self-seed viciously – cut it back well before then and you may get more new young stems. The stems are preserved by candying in sugar syrup. Mixing angelica and sweet cicely leaves with rhubarb improves the latter's flavour and removes the tartness. I add a little of the young leaf to salads but it's bitter unless blanched in the dark for a week first or the greenest outer skin peeled off.

sorrel

Sorrel (*Rumex acetosa*) is a very French gourmet herb – a sort of sour spinach for soups and salads. Sorrel loves moist, lightly shaded soil and can be grown from seed or by division. It revels in a trench, by a pond or on a ditch edge. Water and feed with growth and leaf feeds and foliar sprays for bigger, lusher leaves. Cut the tall stems off to prevent flowering and split and replant every few years to keep up the vigour and to produce young succulent leaves.

winter savory

Summer savory may be superior in flavour but winter savory (*Satureja montana*) is hardier and survives most winters, even in a pot outdoors. Used to improve the flavour of beans and also to mask the smell of cooking brassicas, winter savory can be added to salads in moderation. It grows easily from seed and is happy in most soils or pots. Not indispensable.

bergamot

hyssop

rue

Bergamot (*Monarda didyma*) has aromatic leaves and flowers and makes a calming beverage that was once sold as Oswego tea. It's a compact herbaceous plant with scarlet to purple flowers, the petals of which add vibrant colour to salads. Include a little of the leaf too for flavour. Bergamot is miserable in dry spots and thrives only in moist rich soil. The species can be grown from seed but for named varieties you must root-divide a clump – do this every third year anyway to maintain vigour. Really only for the enthusiastic gourmet in pursuit of exotic tastes.

Hyssop (*Hyssopus officinalis*) is rarely used nowadays, but was traditionally used with rich savoury foods. The flavour is strong, bitter and hot, and it may be toxic in quantity so be careful... This is one for the adventurous gourmet. It is a sun-lover and likes a chalky soil. Hyssop is a superb bee plant and makes a dark heavy honey. Give it a sheltered, warm well-drained site, as you're unlikely to need much, you could grow it in a small tub. You can propagate hyssop from cuttings, root division or seed, but it's easier just to buy a plant. I use small amounts of the young leaves, and the flowers are gay in salads.

Rue (*Ruta graveolens*) is poisonous and reputed to cause madness and liver damage. It is also a skin irritant, especially in hot weather. It was traditionally used in minute amounts to flavour foods, especially cheese. I blithely eat it but I cannot and do not recommend you do so in these litigious times. Rue is easily grown from cuttings or seed and is happy on most soils or in a pot in sun.

Angelica is a plant you'd better grow if you like candied angelica stalks, as they're ten times better home-made.

choicest saladings

delicious annual herbs and salad leaves

The gourmet's skill as a gardener becomes more important with these as they are of finer flavours and textures and nowhere near so robust as the perennial herbs or the vegetables. The delicate flavour of chervil and dill, the delicious scent of basil and the succulence of miner's lettuce are all too easily lost. These, more than most crops, need to be grown extremely well to satisfy the gourmet. Fortunately they are relatively easy, responding to improvements in spacing, airflow, light and water. They also benefit from soil enrichment, and most can be had over much longer seasons with a little extra care.

If space is limited, concentrating on these succulent herbs and salads in their own bed is a good strategy: they are high value, and quick to crop with superior treatment, but deteriorate rapidly once harvested. Although most can be grown on the general vegetable plot, they suffer from competition. Better conditions will promote that rapid lush growth that makes for the sweetest, most succulent salad leaves. A salad bed can fit into a bigger vegetable plot, be worked extra intensively for a few years and then rotated to another area, leaving excellent conditions for following crops.

A dedicated salad bed is worth making well. Obviously the area needs to be weed free, preferably in full sun and not overhung by trees or next to hungry hedges. Grass paths dividing up the plot are a serious error: they look nice initially but are difficult to keep cut and edged; they encourage slugs and other pests, and soon get smeared by wear, mud and compost. Stepping stones are better.

As much organic material as possible needs working into the soil. Heavy soils need mixing with sharp sand and deep digging to ensure drainage. Light soils may benefit from added clay, digging and mixing in thoroughly. Copious quantities of chalk or lime will make the soil sweet, and wood ashes will ensure good disease resistance in the crops. Ground rock dusts and seaweed meal will help raise the fertility. However, the soil should not be given unrotted muck or large amounts of blood, fish and bone meal or similar, as we do not want rank growth. Soil warmth, aeration and texture are crucial, with plentiful moisture and nitrogen added in small amounts.

Ideally the salad bed will never be walked on but tended from the edges, so solid surrounding paths should be constructed. On a permanent site, although it is a great deal of work, it is well worth raising one end (the north in the UK) and grading the whole bed so that it slopes down towards the south. This creates a steep sun-facing slope that warms up significantly as more sun falls on the soil. The result is faster earlier salads in spring, longer cropping in the autumn and some crops can be grown all winter.

The same bed, or another or part of one, may also be sloped in the opposite direction; this gives a cooler, moister, more shady slope which suits many crops, such as lettuce, spinach and so on in the hotter drier weather. It is also excellent for follow-on crops, especially strawberries.

For even more succulent salads all summer, a sunken salad bed, trench or trough will grow some superb crops to a quality usually unachievable on the flat. I dig a shallow trough down the middle of my raised vegetable beds; this gives the cool damp conditions that grow the most succulent leaves. This trench can also be covered with sheets of glass to make a long low cold frame in the soil, which is fantastic for early saladings. In a permanent or temporary trench the bottom soil needs to be replaced with enriched top soil (as for a raised salad bed), as the subsoil in most gardens will not grow much very well. The trench will need copious water though not much feeding. Most annual herbs and salads, or rather those grown as annuals, do not need very rich soil, but warm, moist, friable well-aerated soil.

A good start and constant growing conditions are essential. Some saladings must be sown *in situ*, some are tender and must be sown under cover in the warm. Most can be conveniently sown under cover in pots or multi-celled trays and planted out once the soil has warmed up. Pot them up if necessary, then harden off and plant out after the last frost.

When sowing direct, mark out and station sow thinly. For many annual saladings there is no need to sow or thin to one plant per site – but a few well-spaced plants are better than a lot crowded together. Sow most annuals fairly shallowly; I press a rod into the surface to make a depression; afterwards I cover the seed with sterile compost, not topsoil. This makes the line of seeds easier to see and prevents weeds growing near the seedlings. Finally, I firm down the soil very well and note down what I've sown and when on a card.

With most of these plants, bolting and flowering ruin the flavour. Successional or serial small sowings are sensible, spreading the cropping and reducing the risk. Many saladings can be cut back to get new flushes of leaves, especially if simultaneously heavily watered and fed with a growth and leaf feed.

The earliest sowings must be protected with mini-cloches or a cold frame. The youngest shoots and leaves are the most tender and succulent. You'll get more produced with adequate moisture so water frequently. You can grow saladings in containers, but take even more care to ensure a rich soil and constant moisture. Plenty of compost and superb drainage are necessary. Containers can be isolated from many pests and diseases by standing them on ant- and slug-proof legs and using nets and cover, resulting in very high-quality produce.

Most saladings can be forced for earlier and later crops but only a few can be grown in the middle of winter, even under cover in the warm. Those few, such as miner's lettuce (*Claytonia*), are incredibly valuable and tasty sources of winter salad leaves and a must for every gourmet. The real enthusiast will find that the biggest problem with winter crops is moulds. Increasing the warmth increases the risk of moulds; the solution is more light, which can now be provided with daylight bulbs, which are well worth the expense.

Old-fashioned hotbeds constructed of fermenting materials were difficult to manage. Now we can just put in soil-warming cables with a thermostat. Bottom heat makes it possible to grow many of the salading crops for many more months of the year than just growing under cover alone. For many of the most important saladings, such as rocket, near year-round supplies can be had with successional sowings. You'll need some on a hotbed under cover, some under cover in the border, some outside under a cold frame or cloche and finally outside

unprotected for the summer – reverse the technique as we go into winter again.

Although most of these saladings are easy to grow, they do require continuous attention and resowing – but they also give quick returns, unlike the main-crop vegetables. True vegetables with their longer life also suffer from a lot more

pests and diseases than most of these saladings, so it is more crucial to rotate them. Saladings must also be rotated, but as many of them are grown in small batches, it is likely they will be continuously moving and changing places on the salad bed. Although rotation isn't an immediate concern, over several years the soil will get tired and unbalanced with

all the watering and feeding. For best results the salad bed should be moved or rebuilt with fresh soil every few years. This is especially important where the soil is most intensively cropped: in cold frames, in borders under cover and in hotbeds and containers. And remember, almost all plants benefit from frequent mistings with dilute seaweed solution.

choicest annual herbs and saladings, in my order of preference

rocket

Rocket or Italian cress (*Eruca sativa*) is a gourmet's delight and healthy too, as it's related to the brassicas. The leaves are hot, spicy and peppery and the flowers too can be added to salads. Rocket was once banned from monasteries for provoking lascivious thoughts – should be worth growing lots, then!

It's one of the easiest salad leaves to grow, but old plants get hot and tough unless grown quickly in moist fairly rich conditions. Once plants get leggy, cut them back for a new flush of leaves and feed and water heavily. Sow rocket thinly and often, fortnightly at least, throughout most of the year, in containers and under cover for a longer season. A common but unimportant problem is flea beetle making wee holes in the leaves. There are several strains varying minutely; the 'wild' form is superior.

basil

Basil (*Ocimum basilicum*) is probably the tastiest herb in the garden and there are dozens if not hundreds of distinct varieties. Gourmet aficionados can spend a lifetime studying basils and their various flavours and uses. There are purple, green, ruffled and smooth-leaved, a tiny-leaved and a big-leaved version, lemon-flavoured, cinnamon, minty, orangey and countless other versions, as well as the common sweet basil sold in shops. They are all delicious – well, nearly all – and not difficult to grow, but they do need warmth to start with.

Sow basil shallowly in pots in a warm place, with tomatoes and sweet peppers as they like the same conditions. Plant basil out in the border after the frosts – under a cloche for preference – and feed and water regularly to get lush growth. Once the weather warms up, basil will flourish. It can be kept in pots and moved out for summer and back indoors in autumn, but most die away in winter. Basil may suffer aphid attacks so hose them off. Cut the plants back before they flower and freeze or dry the leaves for winter. Enjoy basil in salads, with cheese, and in pesto, and in huge amounts with garlic in every tomato dish. For the best flavour freeze basil in ice-cubes of oil – the flavour is not as good when it's dried.

chervil

Chervil (*Anthriscus cerefolium*) is a must for the gourmet, though little used in the UK compared with on the Continent. Its subtle parsley-aniseed taste enhances other flavours. Chervil is excellent in quantity in salads and may be used in sauces and recipes in place of parsley. There are few different strains, though the variety with a swollen root (turnip- or bulbous-rooted chervil) can also be cooked as a vegetable.

Chervil will grow in shade, indeed prefers this in full summer; it needs moisture and loathes transplanting. Sow fairly thickly *in situ* from late winter till late autumn; move under cover for winter. It may easily be grown in containers. Chervil will self-seed if left to flower, but if plants are cut down before flowering they may produce new crops of fresh foliage.

parsley

summer savory

miner's lettuce

dill

Parsley (*Petroselinum crispum*): vigorous continental plain-leaved parsley has marginally more flavour than our common curly-leaved form, but both are highly recommended. (The curly-leaved form was originally selected to prevent fools from gathering the poisonous fool's parsley.) Parsley is biennial, flowering in its second year; if left to seed, self-sown plants are always best. Otherwise sow soaked seed on the soil surface, pre-warmed under a cloche; barely cover the seed with sterile compost and firm well. Sow from early spring until autumn and thin plants to a hand's width apart.

Parsley loves rich moist conditions and will stand light shade. It is rich in minerals and its strong flavour is made rank by over-feeding, so water well and often with dilute seaweed solution feeds. The chopped leaves can be frozen or dried; or the plants can be dug up, potted and moved under cover or covered with a cloche for fresh leaves throughout winter. Parsley can be used with every savoury dish as a garnish and added to many; in moderation it is a fresh salading.

Summer savory (*Satureja hortensis*) is less well-known than it ought to be as a wonderful all-round herb for savoury dishes. Gourmets use it in bean dishes and I love the tips in salads. This is a herb definitely best grown in summer; sow shallowly in pots or better still direct, from mid-spring in a sunny site – and again until midsummer. Never allow savory to flower or the flavour will fade. Dry the leaves for use in winter.

corn salad

Corn salad or lamb's lettuce (*Valerianella*) is another tasty gourmet green useful for winter salads. It's well known in France as *machê*, only gourmets are familiar with it here. As with most winter salads, it is sensibly grown under some cover to keep the weather and dirt off the leaves. Given rich moist conditions, these can be large and succulent in deepest winter. Corn salad is best sown direct, or in large pots, from spring till mid-autumn and thinned to a hand's width apart. If left to flower it resembles small forget-me-nots and self-seeds. I find it makes an excellent green manure if incorporated well before this point.

Miner's lettuce or winter purslane (*Claytonia*) is a tasty, succulent weed. It self-seeds prolifically and comes up anywhere moist, even in shade. Fortunately this means it grows staggeringly well in mid-winter under cover. It does on any soil – even under a potting bench will do – and just needs water. It is very tasty in salads and, unusually, every bit of the leaves, stalks and flowers is edible and it's never bitter, even when flowering.

Surface sow claytonia any time, anywhere, and thin to get huge plants up to a foot across. Feed and water heavily for lush growth. Beware 'pinkish' plants – it means slugs are eating the roots. Let it self-seed only if you want perpetual supplies. I find it makes a good green manure, and greens for the chickens, which love it. Even children will eat it! Honest.

Dill (*Anethum graveolens*) deserves wider recognition. Its pleasing fresh clean flavour, somewhat like fennel or chervil, is what gives pickled gherkins (those round green slices in a good burger) their piquant flavour. The leaves or seeds are good in sauces, cheese and fish dishes and in quantity in salads. Sow dill thickly *in situ* or in pots in spring, then successionally until late autumn. It does not respond well to cutting back and winter crops are difficult – they go mouldy. Dill appears to hybridise with fennel, so keep them apart.

lettuce

Lettuces (*Lactuca sativa*) are not difficult to grow well yet are often poorly grown. One reason may be confusion: there is a great number of varieties for sowing at various times of the year and in different soils. Unlike with most salads, the gourmet needs to try all the varieties to find the right ones for his plot and his platter. Greatest value are the salad-bowl, loose-leaf and cut-and-come-again sorts, which are not harvested by uprooting but taken leaf by leaf, and make the best use of the ground. They can be grown in pots, some of them all the year round. Iceberg lettuces have those bland crunchy middles and are easily grown only in summer and autumn; most of the rest are the softer butterheads. Cos lettuces are tall and need tying up to blanch them or they become green and bitter. Over-wintering lettuces need to be grown under cover and are specially selected to prevent them from moulding away.

Never sow a lot of just one seed at once. Instead sow in batches in a seedbed, pots or multi-celled packs. Sow a few seeds each of many suitable varieties every few weeks throughout most of the year. Thin to single plants and set them out, initially protected by a cloche. Later crops can be sown direct if birds are not a problem. In summer, sow lettuce in pots in the shade – they will not germinate if very warm. Ideally grow them on a shady slope or in a trench. Keep birds off with black cotton or netting and practise good slug control. The only real problem is poor growth which makes lettuces taste bitter. So water often, feed lightly with growth and leaf feeds and pray for sun. There is a tremendous range of lettuce varieties, so try many different ones to see which you enjoy most.

chicory

Chicory (*Cichorium intybus*) is like a bitter lettuce and is grown in just the same way. The popular radicchio (Rossa de Verona) is a dark red and adds colour and pleasing bitterness to salads. A few varieties of chicory such as Brussels Witloof are left to grow till late autumn when their substantial roots are lifted and the foliage trimmed off very close. The cleaned roots are stored in a cold dark place until needed. Then they are packed upright in clean sand in a box and 'forced'; that is, kept in a warm dark place where they produce remarkably solid shoots called chicons. Finely sliced, these are a superb addition to winter salads.

If not lifted, chicory roots will over-winter and give a flush of leaves that can be blanched *in situ* by covering with a box part-full of sand. The root can be roasted, dried and ground to make a coffee substitute for those seeking unusual beverage experiences. These robust growers are probably better confined on the main vegetable bed.

Lettuces are not difficult to grow well yet are often poorly grown.

endive

Endives (*Cichorium endivia*) are very similar to and are grown just like lettuce, but most varieties must be blanched or they are bitter – though some can be cropped on the cut-and-come-again basis. Treat them just like lettuce but cover them to exclude the light a fortnight or so before eating.

purslane

Purslane (*Portulaca oleracea sativa*) is a succulent plant with a bland taste that is good in summer salads. It is the most infuriating plant: it is difficult to get bought seed to germinate, but once you have your first plant it self-seeds happily, everywhere, all summer, for ever. Useful for salads, it needs to be grown rapidly and kept cut back hard to produce flushes of young succulent shoots. Sow fresh seed on the surface of a layer of sterile compost on top of the soil, under a cloche or in a border where it is to grow. If you succeed, let it flower and seed and you'll have it everywhere for evermore.

watercress

Watercress (*Nasturtium officinalis*) has an exquisite flavour and a little in salads is so tasty. Its ideal habitat is clean gravel with sparkling, aerated, lime-rich running water passing through. It can be grown in mud but then it is coarser and grittier but still better than none. Watercress as sold in shops can be rooted by simply being stuck in water or wet soil. It bolts and reseeds itself and is best when regularly replaced by cuttings. The keen gourmet should grow watercress, if only for soup.

land cress

Land cress (*Barbarea v. brassicaceae*) resembles watercress and gives a peppery zing to salads. It grows happily in moist soils, even in window boxes. Surface sow *in situ* and keep cutting it back, along with regular feeding and copious watering.

shungiku

Shungiku (*Chrysanthemum coronarium*) is an edible chrysanthemum, rich in vitamin C. It is a good companion plant, keeping pests away from other plants. It is an essential ingredient of Chinese chop suey greens. Very tough and easy to grow, shungiku can be sown direct or in pots from late winter to autumn and under cover. Sow thinly and thin to a hand's width apart. The flavour is very strong and gets bitter near flowering, so it needs frequently cutting back hard as well as regular feeding and watering. The youngest leaves and flower petals are good in salads.

dandelion

Dandelions (*Taraxacum officinale*) are usually seen as weeds – but wait till you try the tender young blanched leaves fried with shallots and bacon, scrummy! You can blanch dandelions where they grow by popping a tin can, pot or box over them. However, bigger, better strains have been developed and these make huge plants near a stride across in rich moist soil. Sow them any time and blanch the heads when they get big enough. Or cut the tops back and blanch the new leaves, which will be even more tender than the blanched older ones. Do not let them flower and seed! The root can be dried and roasted to make an unusual not-quite-coffee-like beverage.

iceplant

Iceplant (*Mesembryanthemum crystallinum*) is the stand-by for barren hot dry sites. The leaves have a peculiar texture and strange taste and can be used in salads or cooked like spinach. It will grow in hot dry conditions when all else fails. Sow in pots and plant out in early summer – it's worth trying, though really more for goats and gerbils than gourmets.

spring onion

Spring onions (*Allium cepa*) can be one of the most disappointing parts of a conventional salad. A good one is crunchy and sweet, not a sad limp old stalk! Spring onions are rarely anything to do with spring: they're onions eaten young and can be had year round. White Lisbon varieties are the standard, with special sorts for winter cropping. The Japanese sorts do not bulb so readily; they include Hikari Bunching, Ishikura and the hybrid Guardsman, which all get quite big without bulbing and have good flavour. Red Bunching and Santa Claus turn red for variety, and are much more succulent. Sow these fairly thinly, and do so successionally, preferably *in situ* but in pots if necessary. Keep them well fed and watered. Seaweed sprays and high potash feeds will improve flavour.

radish

Radishes (*Raphanus sativus*) ought to be tasty and nutritious while still small and tender but are usually miserable fare. They can be sown *in situ* or in pots – anywhere you can pop a few seeds in every week from spring to autumn. Very quick, but not actually very nice unless young and tender – they soon get hot and fibrous. They must have moist rich soil. Some radishes can be allowed to flower for their immature seed pods, which are eaten instead: Munchen Bier is best of these, though Cherry Belle will do instead.

Black Spanish and Japanese radishes are more like turnips than radishes, so treat them as such. Sow them after midsummer for winter use, when they are surprisingly good to eat – grated raw in salads or dipped in salt and nibbled with fresh bread and unsalted French butter.

annual flowers for salads

These add so much colour and so many delightful flavours to salads or can be used as edible garnishes. The flowers should be grown specially for the table. (When you need even more petals you can raid the flower garden but be careful – many garden flowers are poisonous.) You are safe enough with moderate amounts of roses, day lilies (*Hemerocallis*), pinks and carnations, pansies and violets.

pot marigold

The orange petals of pot marigolds (*Calendula officinalis*) (not the French or African Tagetes marigolds) add great colour to salads and do well with seafood and savoury stews. Sow them in pots or *in situ*, any time, anywhere, and thin them to a hand's width apart. Nip or cut back and do not let them self-seed or they'll become weeds.

pansy

Pansies (*Viola* spp.) are usually grown as garden flowers, but the petals of these and the related violas and violets are edible in moderation and add colour to salads. There are pansy varieties to sow and grow almost year round, *in situ* or in pots, and even if you don't eat them they bring good cheer! Add the petal blades alone to salads – remove the bases first.

borage

Borage (*Borago officinalis*) flowers add a splash of colour to alcoholic beverages and can be sprinkled on salads. Sow *in situ* in spring or autumn and thin to a foot or so apart. Keep their soil moist. If you cut back the plants occasionally, you can keep them in flower from late spring to autumn. Cutting back does not stop them self-seeding everywhere.

nasturtium

The flowers of nasturtiums (*Tropaeolum majus*) are delicious and colourful additions to salads, while the young leaves add piquancy. The pickled seeds and pods are better than shop-bought capers. Sow *in situ* or in pots after the last frost. Grow them a stride apart in a warm spot on light soil. Water occasionally but never feed or there will be few flowers.

cucurbit

Cucurbit flowers are mostly edible. The large blooms of squashes, marrows and courgettes make handy cases for filling with tasty stuffings. These plants produce most flowers when growing in hot rich conditions under cover, but may then make mostly male flowers and few females – no problem if all you want is flowers. Otherwise, they are all immensely easy to sow in pots in warmth and plant out later or sow *in situ* in late spring. Keep the soil moist but never waterlogged.

sunflower

Sunflowers (*Helianthus annuus*) are usually grown for their seeds but the petals are edible too, if bittersweet, and the immature heads can be eaten in bud rather like globe artichokes. For heads big enough to eat, sow in early spring and thin plants to at least a stride apart. They rob the soil and need copious watering and feeding to make succulent heads, but are an interesting gourmet treat.

annual herbs grown for their tasty seeds

All of these will give better crops of bigger seeds if each plant is given enough space – say, a foot each way. Sow thinly and space well. These herbs need to be in full sun to ripen their seed well and must be cut and collected promptly to prevent the seed from dropping. Dry under cover, then clean the seed and store in paper bags in a cool dry place.

poppy

Poppies (*Papaver somniferum*) are known for their opium content, but we have all eaten their seed on top of bread and other baked products. Another strain of this same plant is grown in gardens for the flowers alone; however, they become a weed and will self-sow wildly if not picked. For the best seed give plants full sun; sow in spring or autumn, then thin and pick the dead heads before they open and drop their seed. (Growing poppies for opium is, of course, illegal but I believe you may grow poppies for flower or seed in the UK. For home baking a few dozen heads will suffice, whereas for the drug you'd need a small field at least.)

coriander

Coriander (*Coriandrum sativum*) leaves are popular in some Latin and Asian cuisines, as already mentioned. The seeds are often used too: added to bread or baked dishes they give a warm spicy flavour; they go well with tuna and salmon; and they improve almost every dish and salad when added in moderation. Sow coriander *in situ* in late spring and harvest seed in late summer; never feed or water – except in drought.

cumin

Cumin (*Cuminum cyminum*) seeds are the true flavour of a curry. If you acquire a taste for them they can be used like black pepper in almost every savoury dish. Sow cumin in early summer *in situ* and thin to three or four plants to the foot. Support the plants with netting to stop the seed heads falling over into the dirt. Immediately the seed heads are ripe, thresh and dry the seed really well.

Growing poppies for opium is, of course, illegal but I believe you may grow poppies for flower or seed in the UK. For home baking a few dozen heads will suffice, whereas for the drug you'd need a small field at least.

black cumin

Black cumin (*Nigella sativa*) seeds are those of a close relation of love-in-a-mist (*N. damascena*) (above) whose seeds are also edible in moderation. Both have a spicy aromatic tone that is delicious with sweet, spicy, sticky, baked and fried delicacies common in Middle Eastern cuisine. Sow these ancient culinary delights *in situ* in spring and harvest promptly before the seed drops.

anise

Anise (*Pimpinella anisum*) has a flavour that goes well with sweet and savoury foods; the leaves are used fresh and the seed dried. (The smell of the leaves can be rubbed on the skin to discourage biting insects.) Sow in warm soil after the last frost and keep cloched in bad summers until the seeds are ready to harvest.

caraway

Caraway (*Carum carvi*) has feathery leaves that can be used in moderation in salads and savoury dishes; the roots have been boiled as vegetables; but the tiny seed is the real crop. It is excellent in baked products and is an ingredient of gripe water for babies. Caraway is often difficult to germinate and then takes a year to crop. Sow *in situ* in early summer, or autumn if fresh seed is available; cloche it over winter and harvest as soon as the seed ripens the following summer. As the seed won't taste any different from shop-bought, you could always buy a jar.

gourmet vegetables to grow on salad beds

Some vegetables are so demanding, but so rewarding in their produce, that if you are especially keen on them then they are worth growing here on a well-cared-for salad bed or better still in a salad trench. Like most other saladings these vegetables need that same succulent freshness to be gourmet fare and in most cases require almost bog-edge-like conditions to do really well. More fertility is required than for the other more leafy saladings, but again going too far, using too strong a dose, will give rank growth and poor flavour. Water regularly and use seaweed solution sprays and frequent liquid growth and leaf feeds while the plants are small. As they mature, just water often.

celery

Celery (*Apium graveolens*) is a challenge. To grow it just like shop-bought is very difficult! But there are numerous varieties in pink, green and yellow – and, even if you can't achieve perfection, the flavour of the cleaned, tidied, shredded attempts will still enrich all manner of savoury dishes. Celery is prone to bolting and most sorts need careful blanching; self-blanching types are not really such and have poorer textures. Celery must never dry out; it's absolutely crucial to have a constantly moist rich soil. I repeat: celery needs careful tending and a permanently moist, if not boggy, rich soil to grow at all well, so a trench or trough is essential.

Sow seed very thinly on the surface in pots or cells in warmth in early spring; thin and pot on before planting out at about a foot apart in trenches. Surround plants with tubes cut from plastic bottles to keep slugs away. Water and feed often, first with growth and leaf feeds, and then use flower, fruit and flavour feeds as well. Once the plants are nearly full grown, in late autumn, water only – don't feed. As they reach full size, tidy them up and surround each plant with a paper or cardboard collar; then pile earth or similar around them so they will blanch. Cover plants with loose straw and a plastic sheet as well and they will keep for many weeks in the field in winter.

If you want celery flavouring for stocks and soups, sow it *in situ* only and fairly thick and keep cutting it back, using the young leaves and stalks to cook with. This is also the best way for pot culture and can extend the season by months at each end. Let some plants mature, flower and set seed – it's delicious in baked products and stews.

pak choi

Pak choi and Chinese cabbage are Asian brassicas. They are faster growing, and more pest- and disease-resistant than ours, but in dry conditions still suffer from flea beetle – and in wet conditions they are searched out and eaten by slugs more than any other plant I know. Leaf mustards and Chinese greens as they are also known are usually lightly cooked, particularly stir-fried, but can be used raw in salads. They are highly productive and can be cut-and-come-again. Sow them in pots or *in situ* and thin to about a foot apart; keep them incredibly well watered and feed with mixed liquid feeds regularly. They need salad-bed conditions but do not need a trench, only constant moisture. Pak choi is easy but the other relations are often more quirky. Outdoors they crop from summer to autumn; late crops need a cloche or cold frame. They do amazingly well under cover in winter and are welcome fare to the gourmet needing tasty fresh greens.

celeriac

Celeriac (*Apium graveolens v. rapaceum*) is very similar to celery but is a swollen root, not a stem. Start it the same way as celery and give it the same moist rich soil. Celeriac is easier to grow and will produce its swollen root easily – no blanching is needed. The peeled root is grated raw for salads where it is just like celery and it can be cooked where celery flavour is required. The skill in getting celeriac to swell is to strip off the old lower leaves as soon as the root first starts to expand, and to keep adding more water! Celeriac keeps for months in a cool frost-free place.

beetroot

Beetroot (*Beta vulgaris*): in the shops, beets are always either the same poor old things or a plastic bag of pickled balls. At home the gourmet can grow them in a range of colours – red, red and white striped, white, orange and yellow. They can be round, pointed, flattened or cylindrical and come in different flavours too. Especially recommended are the Egyptian Turnip Rooted and the yellow Burpee's Golden. Swiss chard is the same plant but developed to produce swollen stems instead of the root. It comes in the same mix of colours. The leaf of all beets is edible. Beets with more succulent leaves – leaf beet or perpetual spinach – are excellent and easier to grow than spinach. All are closely related to the farm sugar beet, which makes a sweet, mystifying gourmet treat when garden grown, and a base for jam or chutney.

Beets were originally maritime plants and need trace elements: they benefit immensely from seaweed-solution sprays and feeds rather than either growth and leaf or flower, fruit and flavour feeds. They do excellently on a salad bed, especially as the gourmet will probably prefer a succession of mini-beets rather than huge footballs. If space is cramped they can be happy on the main vegetable bed, given those extra minerals and the moisture they crave.

Sow them in pots or cells under cover from early spring; plant out and also sow in the open from late spring to late summer. Beets are sold as seed capsules, not individual seed: put one in a pot and you get a clump of small beet for pickling. Plant out small clumps and they make good-sized beet, given a foot or so between clumps. Likewise *in situ* they can be left unthinned at a foot or so between clumps. Sown direct and thinned to singletons, beets can be grown

larger for winter storage. You can also sow thickly in rows and thin successively, eating the smaller plants in stir fries.

Given a good rich compost they can easily be grown as mini-beets in large tubs or in borders under cover. The most irksome pest at any stage is birds eating the young leaves; wire netting guards, black cotton or plastic bottle rings help.

To prepare beets, twist the stems off, then boil the washed roots and slip the skins and feeding roots off only afterwards, to retain all the juices.

Chards, **leaf beets** and **perpetual spinach** are grown in the same way but must be thinned to about two foot apart. These are unbelievably productive: keep pulling the stems or leaves and they come again all summer and, with cloches, till winter. Then they sprout again in spring. If left to bolt, they reach head height and smell mawkish – cutting back no longer works, so pull and compost them. The leaf is as delicious as spinach and the succulent stems braise well in stock. All have an earthy taste that goes well with cheese and mushrooms.

kohl rabi

Kohl rabi (*Brassica oleracea*) is a delicious crunchy treat, sometimes called the vegetable apple. It is not widely known and looks unusual but is very easy to grow, highly nutritious and immune to most pests and diseases. It's effectively a swollen cabbage stalk and can be cooked, but is best grated raw in salads or cut into crudité dipping sticks. Sow in succession from mid-spring to midsummer in rich moist soil or in small pots and transplant out. As with turnips you must eat kohl rabi before they get big and tough – which for most varieties means tennis-ball size. Superschmelz from Holland is much larger: given a rich moist soil and two foot or so each way, it can get very big yet still remain crisp and tender and good for salads. Kohl rabi can be stored in a cool frost-free place for months – ideal for gourmet winter salads.

florence fennel

Florence fennel (*Foeniculum vulgare* var. *dulce*) is another succulent stem, this time with an aniseed flavour. It is best sown from midsummer *in situ* or in big pots and planted out when very small, a foot or so apart. Never let the plants dry out or they bolt, as will many early sowings. The leaf can be used as the herb fennel though is a bit strong for salads. Pull off the lower leaves when the stem starts to swell and earth up around it. If the swollen bulb is cut off above the root it regrows. Pickle the swollen root or grate it and serve with shredded cabbage. It's even better combined with steamed fish dishes or oiled, marinated and barbecued.

turnips

Turnips (*Brassica rapa*) are often regarded as the humblest of vegetables. They are rarely eaten raw but deserve salad-bed treatment if they are to be real gourmet delights. Variety is crucial: try several till you find one that suits your conditions and tastes. Newer mini-turnips are worth growing as they are quick to harvest. Turnips can be started in cells or pots if planted out while very small but they do better sown direct. Plants sown between early spring and midsummer want to bolt. Sowing after midsummer until mid-autumn is easier: for large turnips thin to a foot apart.

Other than flea beetle, turnips rarely suffer much from pests and diseases, but they need moist, fairly rich soil or they become tough and hot. They grow more succulent in a cool shady bed than in a fiercely hot site and do well in trenches as they need copious watering and fairly light feeding. The smaller varieties can be grown in deep tubs. They respond remarkably in some soils if you incorporate finely powdered bone meal before growing them. The leaves of turnips can be eaten as a spinach. (Swedes are like turnips but sown from late spring for autumn and winter use. They are slower-growing and stand and keep better than turnips, and so need more space and are more sensibly grown with the main vegetable crops.)

spinach

Spinach (*Spinacia oleracea*) is usually cooked rather than eaten as a salad but needs growing like one because it is a succulent leaf. Spinach is often not spinach, as such: many things may be eaten as spinach. Even true spinach comes in two main sorts – round-seeded and prickly-seeded – and countless varieties. You'll have to try them all. Round-seeded spinaches are intended for summer; for winter and early spring, prickly-seeded are better. They are all treated much the same: started in cells or pots and planted out while still very small at about a foot apart, or sown *in situ*, which is invariably more successful. Enrich the soil beforehand with sieved compost or well-rotted manure and maintain continuously moist conditions or spinach will bolt faster than a thief with your wallet. Spinach can grow well in large tubs and pots, resulting in several quick crops for most of the year under cover. Try growing it through a plastic sheet mulch, which keeps the soil off the leaves as well as aiding growth by keeping the soil cooler and moister. Cloches also keep off the weather but may encourage mildew. Deter birds with nets or black cotton, and use slug traps. New Zealand spinach is not true spinach but one of the better alternatives and many people prefer it. It is grown in the same way and is better in hot dry conditions, but needs double the space at two feet each way.

leeks

Leeks (*Allium porrum*) are rarely eaten raw, so how can they be a salad vegetable? Ah, but boil a few plump leeks, preferably in a nice rich stock, then cool and drain and marinade in cider vinegar with a little finely chopped parsley, and you have the most heavenly salad to eat with a crisp baguette and fine butter.

Leeks are a tricky crop; on heavy wet soils they do fairly well with the right spacing and some feeding; in light or dry soils they need copious non-stop watering and feeding. The soil must be well enriched beforehand and although they can be grown on the flat they really do deserve a trench, which improves results immensely. Sow them indoors from mid-winter or in a seedbed from mid-spring, transplanting them out in late spring to at least a foot apart. Make really deep holes, insert the leeks and then twist and align them so their leaves hang out of the way, then water them in. Water copiously and use every feed listed in the last chapter almost to excess, plus seaweed sprays almost daily.

Once the leeks are nearly full grown, surround each with a paper collar and earth up, being careful not to let soil get in the middle. Be selective with your choice of variety: some are early and do not stand but quickly go soft; some are slender and lanky; others more stout and better for stews. As usual, try many varieties to find what suits you.

Leeks are rarely eaten raw, so how can they be a salad vegetable?

chapter 7 the gourmet's finest perfumed flowers

Flowers to visit in the garden and flowers for the house; flowers for evening walks before dinner and flowers in garden design

Who can be without flowers? What table is complete without its garnishing posy? We must have flowers to decorate our lives, and not only with their form and colour but with their perfume as well. Flowers without scent are like meals without wine. Fortunately there are so many wonderful flowers with gorgeous perfumes that you can fill your garden with every form and colour you wish and still not run out of scented flowers. To say little of scented foliage, which is yet another delight.

Luckily for us, flowers are often the easiest of all crops; most plants want to flower – after all, it's their time for sex! Getting plants to flower is easy and we can use the same techniques as with fruit and vegetables to have them a little sooner or later and for a longer season. The most important part is deciding whether the flowers are for visiting and enjoying *in situ* or to cut for the house. If it is the latter then they are best grown as a 'vegetable bed' crop so the cut blooms do not leave a gap in the display. If the flowers are to be enjoyed, say for an evening walk before a meal, then they may be grown and displayed formally in ornamental beds.

For good access to the flowers so we can sniff them, these beds need be narrow or provided with stepping stones so we can reach in to sample those planted further back. It makes sense to have the design as a sinuous walk between long beds so that you progress along, coming across one scented delight after another. Not all are out at the same time of year, and winter-flowering plants have the sweetest and strongest scents so should not be neglected – nor put too far away from the house!

Start with scented evergreens

A backbone of evergreens in a garden is a good starting point: many have scented flowers and they create a structure to fit others around. Evergreen shrubs are never dormant; the best time to plant is in early spring; then keep them watered until well established. Use a growth and leaf type feed for the first spring just to get the plants established. Most do not want further feeding as this promotes soft growth, though a flower, fruit and flavour feed in the water in summer will help many ripen a good flower-bud crop for the next season. Evergreens rarely need pruning but if necessary do this in spring or summer. Many can be grown in large containers but make sure these are well drained and don't let them dry out either.

In my order of pleasure, the **Daphne** genus is superlative. These are mostly evergreens, short-lived, difficult to establish and need well-drained humus-rich soil. But they are very attractive and compact and have the most exquisitely scented flowers from late winter to early summer. My favourites are *Daphne* x *burkwoodii* 'Somerset' and *D. odora* 'Aureomarginata'. Do not prune daphnes or even cut the flowers. And be careful: both the sap and berries are poisonous.

Mahonias have strongly perfumed yellow flowers in late winter with attractive holly-like leaves, edible black berries and the ability to grow almost anywhere. They can be cut back hard when overgrown, make good ground cover in tough areas and have cheerful flowers.

Right Common honeysuckle – so sweetly scented, and not common enough.
Below Mexican orange blossom is double value, with its sweet flowers and weirdly aromatic foliage.

Sarcococca or winter box are compact neat plants with small white flowers full of scent on winter's days. They have attractive berries and tolerate poor soils and shade – real gems, especially as they rarely get huge.

Skimmias are another compact and neat evergreen with well-scented creamy flowers, followed by red berries if a pollinating male is also planted. They loathe hot dry positions and revel in a cool moist humus-rich soil.

Osmanthus resembles privet, but is neater and slower-growing with really sweet-scented white flowers in spring, and it grows almost anywhere.

Elaeagnus species are mostly evergreen shrubs with somewhat nondescript flowers which are nevertheless sweetly scented; some have edible berries. They make excellent specimens for the back of borders.

The **common laurel** (*Prunus laurocerasus*) is another one for the back of the border and makes a good thick screen almost anywhere. The flowers are sweet-scented in late winter, especially those of the compact form Otto Luyken.

Only a few varieties of **rhododendrons** are scented but these make great displays in a lime-free soil and they are surprisingly happy in big pots, especially if well watered. The forms of yellow *Rhododendron luteum* are amongst the best.

Mexican orange blossom (*Choisya ternata*) is excellent value as the scented flowers come in spring and often again in autumn. The foliage is aromatic too. The bush can be cut back hard when straggly and if well fed recovers well.

Growth and leaf feeds will encourage too much growth and not enough flowers.

Most deciduous shrubs grow a bit big but can be pruned back to keep them smaller. Often it is better to remove whole branches in successive years, thus retaining plenty of flowering material, rather than shearing off the surface. Many are happy in big containers which also saves pruning. In the smaller garden this is the best way to have these shrubs, though they will then be somewhat short-lived.

Most shrubs do better if planted small; they benefit from watering well with feeds while establishing, but from then on most need only a little flower, fruit and flavour feed in summer and autumn. Growth and leaf feeds will encourage too much growth and not enough flowers. Here are my recommendations, in order.

Lonicera fragrantissima is a shrubby **honeysuckle** with many small pale-yellow gloriously sweet flowers, blooming on sunny days from mid-winter till spring. It is vigorous enough to cope with some of these being cut for the table. In early summer *L. syringantha* has a magnificent scent. It is less vigorous and has clusters of pinkish flowers rivalling, and named after, lilac.

Lilacs, species of *Syringa*, have powerful perfumes which some people find overwhelming. The common plants get big but there are many choice ones that stay compact, such as the divine Persian (*Syringa* x *persica*), the excellent Preston hybrids and the fabulous *S. meyeri* var. *spontanea* 'Palibin' and *S. pubescens* subsp. *patula*, the Korean lilac. Cut off the flower heads after blooming and give plenty of water and a light liquid feed in spring and summer.

Mock oranges (*Philadelphus* species) are often wrongly called syringas. They have glorious scents but are scruffy shrubs best kept to the back of borders. Their flowers are whitish and powerfully scented with a delightful cloying heaviness especially those of Belle Etoile. They are prolific bloomers; the stems can be cut for the table and bushes will take hard pruning if they get too big. Give flower, fruit and flavour feed in summer and autumn.

Viburnums come in many attractive scented varieties, yet you commonly see the ghastly almost scentless *V. tinus* Eve Price and the miserable guelder rose (*V. opulus*). Look instead for the heavenly scented *V.* x *burkwoodii* Park Farm Hybrid, *V.* x *juddii*, *V. carlesii* and *V. carlcephalum*, all of which have pinky white pompoms of deliciously perfumed blooms in early summer.

Clockwise from top left *Syringa meyeri* var. *spontanea* 'Palibin'; *Philadelphus* Belle Etoile; *Viburnum carlesii* Diana; *Viburnum* x *juddii*; *Viburnum carlcephalum*; *Philadelphus* Belle Etoile.

Roses, especially the shrubbier forms, are wonderfully scented flowers, and although many are not really suited for cutting who can resist them? I love old roses such as Maiden's Blush which is white turning palest pink, the Damasks such as Ispahan (pink) and Madame Hardy (white), the bicoloured Rosa mundi (now officially R. gallica 'Versicolor') and the gorgeously opulent Mme Isaac Pereire (red); Moss roses that have the smell of incense on their hairy buds such as the vigorous William Lobb and Nuits de Young; and the delicate Bourbons such as Boule de Neige and Souvenir de la Malmaison. Most of these are best planted young, in heavy soil. Keep them well fed and watered each spring with growth and leaf feeds, and with flower, fruit and flavour feeds in summer and autumn. Do not prune them hard unless necessary to recover your garden space. For cutting I recommend a dedicated bed of roses grown in the vegetable plot.

Wintersweet (*Chimonanthus* species) is a slow growing nondescript, straggly shrub, but in winter the stems are covered with sweet – almost sickly sweet – pale yellow blooms. As these are so delicious the individual flowers merit detaching and floating in a saucer of water indoors. Witch-hazels (*Hamamelis* species) are almost identical in many ways but need a moister, more humus rich soil to do well – they are really woodland plants.

Buddleias are even more sweetly scented than most shrubs. For maximum flowers they are best pruned hard in late winter, then given regular growth and leaf feeds and in summer flower, fruit and flavour feeds. Cuttings root very easily but bigger plants resent transplanting. The butterfly bush (*Buddleja davidii*), comes in a wide choice of coloured racemes blooming in summer, all with similar rich scents. *Buddleja globosa* is semi-evergreen with orange ball-shaped flowers coming much earlier in spring.

Opposite: top row, from left Great Maiden's Blush; William Lobb; *Rosa gallica* 'Versicolor'
Middle row, from left *Rosa gallica* 'Versicolor'; Madame Hardy; Ispahan.
Bottom row, from left Boule de neige; Mme Isaac Pereire; Nuits de Young.
Right The gloriously spicy wintersweet *Chimonanthus fragrans*.
Below left The orangey flowers of *Buddleja x* 'Weyeriana'.
Below right The gorgeous purple, heavily scented, racemes of *Buddleja davidii*.

As wintersweet blooms are so delicious the individual flowers merit detaching and floating in a saucer of water indoors.

Spanish broom (*Spartium junceum*) has bright yellow sweet-scented pea-like flowers on spindly straggly stems over a long season. It needs a hot dry spot and well-drained soil and no feeding at all. *Cytisus* species are also types of brooms that similarly need hot dry and well-drained positions, and have smaller yellowish scented pea-like flowers. Best of all is *Cytisus battandieri* which has yellow pineapple-like and pineapple-scented flowers and silky semi-evergreen laburnum-like leaves.

Magnolias can have wonderful scented flowers though these fade in your hands once picked and are best enjoyed *in situ*. They mostly prefer a moist, loamy, lime-free soil and resent pruning or being moved or confined in small pots. Water rather than feed them. The evergreen *Magnolia grandiflora* gets enormous and has big sweet scented flowers to match, and I mean big. *M. stellata* is sweet but *M. liliflora* is the real star for scent.

Flowering currants (*Ribes* species) are not usually listed with gloriously scented plants: most are redolent of damp dogs and tom cats. But the white flowering Tydeman's White is a good choice with little of the tom-cat feature. And the hybrid *R. x gordonianum* is a blaze of yellow and red, and smells most pleasing; even better is the yellow-flowered buffalo berry (*R. odoratum*). These are all easy in most places and can be pruned and trained just as for the soft-fruit versions for staggering visual effects.

To connect the house to the garden and to give height in other areas, pergolas and posts festooned with climbers add yet more opportunities for scent. Most 'unimproved' climbers are scented and any with white flowers even more so. Climbers get big and catch the wind so make your supports strong and renewable. Most climbers need pruning only when they outgrow their welcome but then most come back happily. Feed them with flower, fruit and flavour feeds, but never with growth and leaf feeds – except perhaps in the first year. Few are very happy confined in containers.

Clematis are typical climbers and most of the man-made hybrids have lost their scent. Go for the vanilla-ice-cream-scented *Clematis montana* var. *wilsonii* or *C. armandii* and you'll find real pleasure again. Clematis need their roots in cool limy moist soil and their tops in the sun. Prune them hard when they finally grow too big.

Lonicera species, the **honeysuckles**, are nearly all so scented they're almost my first choice; I have over a dozen different ones. They suffer less from aphids when grown in semi-shade and if never fed, only watered. Leave them unpruned as long as possible. Likewise treat *Jasmine officinale*, an old garden favourite needing a warm corner: never feed or prune this, just leave it to go.

Akebia quinata is another must-have. The purple flowers come in late winter for weeks and are strangely perfumed; they are weird to look at closely. The foliage is attractive. Never prune or feed this climber, and grow it in a warm, sheltered spot.

Rambler and **climbing roses** tend to hold their flowers too high up for us to appreciate. Try training them into arches and swags to get at them. Do not feed heavily once established and prune only occasionally; otherwise just twine new shoots back in. The best are legion; I nominate: Madame Alfred Carrière, a white flower scented with musk; the thornless pink Bourbon rose Zéphirine Drouhin; and the reliable golden Gloire de Dijon.

Opposite, clockwise from top left The weird but lovely *Akebia quinata*; *Clematis armandii*; the thornless pink rose Zéphirine Drouhin is one of the best for flowering and for perfume; the white jasmines have the most wonderful scents.

Herbaceous plants are difficult to mix with shrubs and climbers. They can expand only outwards and so suffer from taller-growing plants shading them out. They are better in their own bed or as part of a border and, as they die back in winter, their bed is better placed well away from house, patio and windows – or else directly under them and so out of sight from indoors. These plants are low-maintenance if well mulched. They benefit from watering with a growth and leaf feed in early spring. Cut back the top growths in late autumn but wait till the stems have withered so that the plant has re-absorbed the nutrients. Leave tall stumps when you cut: these old stem bases will support and protect the young shoots as they emerge. Most herbaceous plants can be grown in containers if large enough and well drained; indeed, herbaceous plants often respond by throwing more blooms when confined. However, they must be carefully watered and fed and the roots protected in cold winters.

My favourite of all, **lily of the valley** (*Convallaria majalis*), hates being confined and prefers to ramble under cool stones in humus-rich soil in dappled shade. The scent of the little spires of white bells is simply divine.

Violets are often delightfully scented, especially *Viola odorata*. They all delight in rich moist soil, seaweed sprays and partial shade. The petals give up their perfume to white rum to make a delicious liqueur.

Pinks (*Dianthus* species) are so deliciously clove-scented, you want to eat them – and some do. These need a limy, well-drained soil in full sun; they thrive in pots which is handy as they are so prostrate-growing and are easier to sniff raised up on supports or low walls. Ensure you keep a supply going by propagating new plants each year. Do not feed but spray with seaweed solution.

Paeonies are exquisite, so perfect with the dew on them, and some have subtle perfumes. They need a deep rich moist soil, seaweed sprays, regular watering and growth and leaf feeding. The flowers are superb: Sarah Bernhardt is the classic. They

Opposite, clockwise from top left The regal lily – probably one of the best value flowers in the garden. Violets, violas and pansies are all sweet sisters for our delight. Phlox – a strangely scented flower ushering in the end of summer. Daffodils, indeed most narcissi have light perfumes welcoming spring. Pinks, and their big sisters, carnations, are so wonderfully spicy and sweet to the nose. Lily of the valley is a sublime perfume and for a posy just one stem is enough.

Pinks are so deliciously clove-scented, you want to eat them – and some do.

won't do well in pots though and hate being split or moved.

Phlox are strange flowers: their musty perfume is redolent of empty churches but still fascinating. They need copious water and growth and leaf feeding in spring.

Similar to herbaceous plants are the host of bulbs and corms. These can be planted in beds like herbaceous plants or naturalised in grass around the base of trees and shrubs. Most can also be grown in pots for earlier, and more convenient, flowers. Plant most bulbs and corms deep; in heavy or wet soils bed them in with sharp sand. Feed and water only lightly once established.

Cyclamen are among the most beautiful of all scented flowers, with attractive foliage as well; *Cyclamen europaeum* (aka *C. purpurascens*) is a must. But grow them where you can get at them: beside paths, in low raised walls and containers. The best way to encourage them is with plentiful humus, especially leaf mould.

Lilies too like leaf mould. The regal lily (*Lilium regale*) is so outstanding you need no other. It has enormous white blooms flushed with yellow inside, purple buds outside, and the number of flowers per stem is too great to be believed. It grows in almost any soil and can even be grown from seed to flower in two years. Probably the best plant in the world!

Narcissus or **daffodils**, even the common King Alfred at Easter, have their own fresh scent but the late flowering jonquils and poeticus or pheasant's eye (*Narcissus poeticus* var. *recurvus*) are gloriously scented. They should be bought by the sackload and naturalised everywhere possible. These appreciate a growth and leaf feed every so often and if clumps get congested, they need digging and splitting.

Some of the finest scents come from naturally short-lived plants, the biennials, which we sow this year to grow big enough to flower the next. Many biennials can be left to self-seed. Their main requirement is a good start and most can be grown in large containers, freeing up garden space.

Brompton and **East Lothian stocks** give gorgeous heads of scented flowers; they are sown early summer to flower the next spring. In cold areas many are lost over winter and are best kept under glass in cold frames. *Matthiola incana* is the original from north Africa; it is white, strongly perfumed, tough and semi-perennial.

Wallflowers give more scent than almost any other plant, and flower so early in the year. Although they're really perennial, they're better discarded once straggly. Related to brassicas, wallflowers love similarly rich limy moist conditions. Be careful; bringing in plants may bring in clubroot disease which you don't want spreading to your cabbages. Similar conditions will suit sweet William and sweet Wivelsfield, which are hybrid *Dianthus* and have sweet perfumes as their names suggest. These are happy in pots and love seaweed sprays.

A small pot definitely won't suit **dames** or **sweet rocket** (*Hesperis matronalis*), a tall plant with pale purple stock-like flowers. Closely related is *H. steveniana* with paler flowers; in early evening both species are ethereal to see and smell.

Evening primrose (*Oenothera biennis*) is another evening flower with yellow scented blooms full of pollen for insects that also coats your nose – delicious. This is big and needs space and, be warned, self-sows like a weed.

In any space left we can sow annuals. Most must be sown *in situ* but some can be sown in small pots or cells and planted out earlier or used to fill gaps among other plants. Most may self-seed and the resulting seedlings will over-winter and then flower earlier than spring-sown ones. Use a good compost for sowing in pots and add growth and leaf feed with the water initially. But when growing in the

Opposite Wallflowers give a great deal of pleasure with strong colours and warm scents.
Below Stocks give a lovely, sweet scent.
Bottom Evening primrose has a long flowering period and is full of fresh sweetness every evening.

ground, water the seedlings but never feed – we want flowers, not foliage.

Ten week stocks (*Matthiola* species) are quick-growing, hence their name, as they can flower in as little as ten weeks after sowing. They have well-scented flowers, needing only a moist limy soil to do well. For supreme evening scent sow night-scented stocks (*M. longipetala*) with a few of the scentless Virginian stocks (*Malcolmia maritima*) mixed in to brighten the display.

The **Cape phlox** (*Zaluzianskya capensis*) has small white flowers with the most heavenly evening scent of sweet rich vanilla chocolate and is a must.

Sweet peas, not the varieties for cutting but border ones that are dwarf and long-flowering, are another excellent flower for summer perfume from a spring sowing.

Nicotiana species or sweet tobacco (*N. alata*, *N. affine* and the vigorous *N. silvestris*) have powerful evening scents. They are tender plants that need starting off in the warm or sowing *in situ* in early summer for a late show.

Alyssum is sweetly honey-scented – though some people say it reminds them of cats. The coloured and dwarf forms are more attractive and compact but less well scented than the old-fashioned white. French marigolds (*Tagetes patula*) have a scent few love but they are excellent companion plants so should be grown anyway.

If we are lucky our evening walk might lead via a patio to a greenhouse or conservatory, where yet more delights await. Citrus plants are the best for their long-flowering season as much as their delicious scent. These are easier to grow for flowers rather than fruit; just feed heavily during the growing season with all types of feed. Use only rainwater and spray with water and seaweed solution often. Prune hard in spring and they will flourish. Bring plants under cover before frosts and keep them frost-free over winter, then put them out on the patio for the summer.

Evening primrose is a delightful flower, full of pollen and warm spiciness, opening in early evening.

Above The prima donna, the tuberose.
Opposite What could be more delicious than a bed of paeonies?

Angel's trumpets (*Datura* or *Brugmansia* as we must now call them) are exceptional value. They are tough and need only frost-free conditions like citrus to over-winter and can also go out on the patio all summer. They are very thirsty plants and need regular growth and leaf feeds in early spring and then flower, fruit and flavour feeds to keep them happy all summer. Angel's trumpets can be pruned back really hard each spring and are easy to root more of. The enormous blooms are sensational and beautifully scented – they can hang by the dozen.

Tender jasmines (*Jasminum polyanthum*) are exceptionally well scented and easy to grow in large tubs, with their stems wound around canes. There are many species, all gorgeous and easy to care for. Similar in delight and form but smaller and trickier to keep happy is stephanotis. It is often best grown in a hanging basket so it can be kept up higher in the humid warmth of the greenhouse. It enjoys regular syringing with water.

Hoyas are fantastically well scented when they eventually flower; the little waxy blooms are wonderful and must not be cut off as new ones come from them.

Gardenias are opulently scented greenhouse flowers. They are also tricky, hating full sun but loathing shade. They dislike being moved and dry atmospheres, so in a way are ideal for a bathroom windowsill! They must be kept warm and can't go outdoors even in summer, making them a bit awkward to care for, but the decadent perfume they give off is absolutely irresistible.

The **tuberose** (*Polianthes tuberosa*) is reckoned the sweetest of all flowers. The tender bulbs produce a spike of white flowers carrying perhaps the most delicious perfume of all. Tricky to keep happy, this prima donna needs warmth and water to get it going in spring and copious seaweed sprays from then on. But, wow! If you feel affluent buy bulbs just to force and discard, as they take years to reach flowering size.

The unusual **Cereus** or **Nyctocereus cactus**, a slow-growing straggly succulent, is unimposing for years, then throws enormous dahlia-like blooms that last but one night and knock you down with fragrance. There are several of these with slightly different forms and blooms, and all are tender. They need frequent syringing with tepid water, plus seaweed sprays, and can root in little more than a ball of leaf mould – I grow mine in a wee hanging basket.

Freesias are another tender flower; these are best grown from corms planted in pots in summer and over-wintered with warmth to flower the next spring. It is not difficult to grow on the small new corms that form to crop again but it makes sense to buy in anew each year. Buy in quantity and grow them in large plastic trays rather than pots and cut liberally for the house. The white sorts have more scent than the highly coloured varieties.

Hyacinths have very strong scents and bright colours. Although expensive, they are so easy they should be bought each year and discarded after forcing in pots for the table. They need no more than frost-free conditions to do well. Other hardy bulbs can be forced under cover just for cutting, like the beautiful dwarf narcissus.

Chincherinchees and **ornithogalums** are summer flowers that can be forced weeks earlier. Once cut, the white lightly perfumed bluebell-like flowers can last for a week or more.

It is worth having other gorgeous hardy scented flowers growing under cover just for cutting for the house. **Carnations** are ideal in an unheated greenhouse in big pots. Given a well-drained limy compost and careful watering with a mixed liquid feed, they flower abundantly – though to be fair they are prone to an amazing number of ills, but least said the better...

For more difficult spots under cover there are a host of scented-leaved **pelargoniums** which will thrive anywhere frost-free and fill whole walls with deliciously fragrant leaves.

Find space outdoors in part of the vegetable garden for more scented flowers just for cutting, such as roses and sweet peas. Roses are perennial and need a rich heavy soil, well mulched and watered if you want plenty of blooms. You can make the individual blooms bigger by reducing the bushes in autumn, leaving fewer buds to shoot and flower. Heavy rich soils, heavy mulching and heavy watering, with growth and leaf feeds in spring and flower, fruit and flavour feeds in summer and autumn, will help roses bloom well, as will seaweed sprays whenever they are not flowering. Extra-early blooms can be had by forcing plants in big pots, taking them under cover in late winter and returning them outdoors to recover after forcing. Later flowers can be had by holding smaller pot-grown plants in a refrigerator till late spring or even early summer, before bringing them out and growing them on. Etoile de Hollande, which is dark crimson; Superstar, bright scarlet; and Fragrant Cloud, pinky red, are three gorgeous ones I could never be without. Apricot Buff Beauty is about the most trustworthy and reliable.

Sweet peas are another crop worth growing just for cutting. Indeed, if not cut they go over and stop flowering. Grow them successionally, with the first sowings made in pots under cover in autumn to over-winter. Follow these up with more indoor sowings in late winter and spring, and later still, direct *in situ* sowings once the soil has warmed up. They fit into the vegetable-bed rotation in place of other legumes such as peas and beans, and can even be mixed with runner beans – they don't crossbreed and their flowers help bring in pollinators to the beans. Sweet peas benefit immensely from humus-rich soil, mulches, copious watering when growing strongly and seaweed sprays, but need little feeding. It pays to thin each plant to a single stem tied to a cane and then you get fewer but bigger longer-stemmed blooms. For even bigger blooms, nip out most flower shoots before they swell. Cut off all flowers that do open: if left to ripen seed, they suppress more flowers forming.

chapter 8 the gourmet's pick-your-own farm shop, larder, delicatessen and restaurant

Extending the season by storing and processing

The gourmet can never be satisfied with just the fresh produce from the garden, especially as many delights are available for only part of the year. The table needs more than just the crop of the day. The passionate gourmet must be his or her own greengrocer, delicatessen and cook, as well as running a pick-your-own farm. Rather than self-sufficiency, the idea is more self-provision – to fill the stores and cupboards till they are groaning with every gourmet food in as many forms as cunning can devise. But, remember: store only the best, eat fresh the rest, compost what's left.

The gourmet's pick-your-own farm
Harvesting is a relatively fun task and not confined to just one week of the year. From the first crop to the last, there is always opportunity to salt away a little for later. While you may have a gross surplus today, do remember that soon the garden will be almost bare, with no chance of growing any more for another year. So harvest and put away each delight diligently – do not foolishly give it all away to friends and neighbours. They may not know what to do with some of the produce. But if you invite them round for a meal and share it with them, you all get the benefit while each item is at its peak.

The actual day of harvest for some vegetables, such as carrots, is not often that crucial, nor is a short period of storage. But with vegetables like sweetcorn, asparagus and peas, the time between picking and eating makes all the difference in flavour and sweetness.

Some fruits also can be demanding and at their best only when perfectly ripe – a phase that may last no more than a few hours for melons, for example. These are unusual in that they are improved with a slight chilling before consumption, but most fruits are finest eaten straight off the plant, still warm from the sun.

Others such as pears have to be picked early and brought to perfection, inspecting them daily to catch them at the right moment. For really long storage, apples must be picked carefully and, given perfect conditions, can be put aside for many months.

The best time for harvesting any crop will vary with the weather that year, often being earlier or later than expected – although each fruit cultivar always flowers and ripens in an unalterable sequence with all others. This means you could grow a range of varieties in a row, so that the first to ripen was the first in line, and so on, in order. (Flowering will also be roughly in order but not exactly so, as each variety may take a different number of days to mature.)

On any tree or bush the sunniest part ripens first. In the northern hemisphere this is the south-east facing side, because the morning sun is strongest (in the afternoon the air is full of dust and blocks light). Of course, fruit also ripens sooner in extra-warm areas such as close to a sunny wall, a warm window, chimney or gas vent, or even close to the ground especially if the earth is bare.

For really long storage, apples must be picked carefully and, given perfect conditions, can be put aside for many months.

Left Looks like an apple but in fact is a pear, the deliciously crunchy and perfumed Asian pear Kumoi.

Then, when you think you have picked every last fruit, you may still find some just starting to ripen, hidden away deep in the shade. Watch the sunny side and when the first fruits there are ripe, the rest of the crop will be just becoming so. That's when you need be ready for picking and using, or storing and processing them.

Although many vegetables have a long season and can be picked or dug as required, some – such as peas and beans, courgettes, asparagus, radish and many others – need daily inspection and prompt collection or they're spoilt. Some may keep for another day, but be ready – plan ahead to use them soon. Asparagus, raspberries and petit-pois peas mature and go over so incredibly rapidly that it is important to catch them at their best. Harvest what you need for fresh use on the day, but also pick and process all the others at their peak at the same time.

If you grow many different fruits and vegetables, you're going to have to do a lot of daily processing. If you concentrate on just a few favourites, it's much easier. Many vegetables left in the ground or on the plant till required are best picked at the last moment; however, the crunchy and succulent leaf-salad crops should be picked at dawn with the dew still on them for maximum crispness and then kept in the cool till required. Of course, not everything can be had so fresh from the garden every day, and that's when you fall back on your stores.

The gourmet's farm shop and greengrocer

We store most things to extend their season of use for as long as possible. To be stored for any time, a crop must be absolutely perfect: almost any damage is fatal as that's where rots will start. I repeat: there is no point trying to store anything that has any damage at all, even a bruise! Use up any less-than-perfect produce as soon as possible or turn it into conserves and so on.

It may seem obvious but if you want to store food for months, then choose varieties suitable for storing. Early sorts, huge growers and exhibition varieties are rarely good keepers! And if you want them to stay in gourmet condition, then they need to be harvested carefully and at the right time – and then given ideal storage conditions.

Most fruits (don't forget pumpkins and other vegetable fruits) need to be picked just slightly under-ripe to store or process; they may store even longer if picked younger still but this is at the expense of flavour and sweetness. They must also be dry when picked and are often better 'sweated' for a few days by being rested in a dry airy place to give off a bit of excess water.

You can coat hard fruits with wax though I've never bothered. Certainly, keeping each wrapped separately in clean paper or oiled (vegetable) paper does extend their season further, but is tedious. I find simply layering shredded paper between apples, quinces, squashes and so on helps enough. Basically they must not touch each other or an impermeable surface.

Hard fruits were once dipped in a solution of sodium bicarbonate and dried off for storing, and this worked well, leaving a safe but protective powder on the surface.

The most important element of storage is constant cool conditions with total freedom from vermin. Traditionally spare rooms, sheds, cellars and clamps have all been used, but nothing beats a dead refrigerator or freezer body housed in a shed or garage. Neat, tidy, secure from pests with metal-

coated insulated bodies, they would cost a fortune if purpose-bought for the job. You need several, as different crops must be stored separately. I use one with trays for early pears, with the late keepers stored below in buckets layered with shredded paper. Another, bigger one holds apples, again those for dessert on trays and the bulk in buckets. Another does for roots and yet another for potatoes.

They all sit in a lean-to shed on the shady side of the house. This creates almost constant conditions inside the bodies which are sealed – bar one small vent cut in the door rubbers to allow minimal air movement and prevent condensation. Condensation indicates insufficient ventilation, but too much draught dries out the contents, and risks allowing mice to gain entry.

These recycled units can even stand outdoors if the rain is kept off, as they are not connected to any power, but out of sight in a shed gives better protection against the cold and thieves. Such a unit in a shed keeps out the usual run of hot and cold weather, but extra frost protection for extremely cold periods is simply achieved by popping a sealed bottle of warm water inside each unit night and morning. Likewise, to delay potatoes and apples going over as the weather warms in spring, I add plastic bottles of frozen water each day.

Fruits taken from any closed store need to be aired for a day before use to remove mustiness, though this is not so important with vegetables. Many

These recycled units can even stand outdoors if the rain is kept off.

vegetables store better and for longer than fruits, as they wither rather than rot. You can prevent this by packing them in slightly damp sand in a box kept in the cool and dark.

When filling your store it is usually best to leave the new crops to chill overnight, under cover in their trays or buckets. Load them into the store in the morning when the dew has dried off, but before they've warmed up. It also helps them keep longer if you cool them off further by leaving the stores open on chill dry nights and closing them down during the day – do this for a week or so once full. Some crops are hardy and are actually better left in the ground; this includes most roots and leeks. Cover with a layer of straw or other dry insulation and a plastic sheet to keep out the hardest frosts and you can dig them fresh for months after they stop growing.

Onions and pumpkins need careful drying before storing in a very airy frost-free place, ideally spread out on nets – not hung in twee ropes or bunches. Of course, you can just keep fruits and veg in boxes in the garage but that's not going to give gourmet quality; they will go off quickly and pick up taints from any smells in the air. It is never a good idea to store your crops in the same place as strong-smelling paint or fuel, but even vegetables, especially onions, need to be kept away from fruits! Standing fruit on treated wood can taint it too, and shredded paper is much better for packing than straw or hay – though stinging nettles are reputedly best.

Inspect your stores often, first to ensure no rodent has got in and secondly to remove any rotters. Even perfect crops start to rot after a certain time and can go off very quickly – use them as soon as they show the first signs! To allow for losses to rotting, if you want to have one tray's worth for six months, then you have to start off with two trays – even if only one in ten fruits goes off each month. So the sooner you use up your stores, the fresher they are, and the less you waste. Processing surplus produce prevents waste during storage and the processed fare is available for even longer.

Lemon

The gourmet's own larder and delicatessen

A gourmet is not content with a diet of superb fruits and vegetables, plus fine flowers on the table. He or she wants the things that go with them to make the feast complete. Pickles and sauces to spice up the fare; dried fruits and herbs for flavour; frozen foods for year-round use. Then there are all the home-made juices, squashes, conserves and preserves. But I must introduce a note of caution. Preserved fruits that have gone mouldy or rotted are not often as immediately or completely hazardous as rotten vegetables or meat – which are extremely risky. If you are not good at following instructions and find details such as hygiene troublesome, then you'd best concentrate on processing fruits! But do not fear, people have long made safer and better-quality fare at home than perfidious manufacturers supply to gullible fools.

Pickles and relishes of various sorts are easily made and liven up a meal. What gourmet can conceive of buying mint or horseradish sauce when the real thing is to hand. Most pickles are simply vegetables with spices and herbs, all preserved in acid vinegar; many are salted first to remove some water and bring out their flavour. Pickled onions are just clean onions in spiced vinegar – couldn't be simpler. Nasturtium seeds can be salted in brine for a day then dropped in vinegar to make a delight you cannot buy (similar to capers, but just better).

By the addition of lots of sugar as well, even better preservation is achieved and flavours are strengthened. For example, pears poached and pickled in sweet vinegar with spices are excellent with cold savoury dishes. Tomatoes can be bottled on their own with care. Their sauce or ketchup is basically a ripe tomato jam made with sugar, vinegar and spices to stop it going off easily. Many other sauces are based on this method with added chillies or pepper to give them warmth. Relishes are pickled bits of vegetable in various fruity sauces or sauces with vegetable bits, if you prefer. Chutneys are much the same as pickles and relishes but with a curry or tamarind overtone added – peach chutney is divine. My favourite pickle, piccalilli, is salted pickled bits of gherkin, onion,

Opposite, clockwise from top left Dried red peppers, sweet and hot, are useful all year round; home-grown bananas in rum for winter treats; lemon slices in white rum to add zest to drinks and compotes; nasturtium seeds make the most delicious of pickles in sweet spiced vinegar.
Right The Asian pear, Kumoi, dries to make the tastiest rings you've ever chewed.

It is amazingly easy to dry apples, pears, apricots and so on, and just as easy to dry grapes and have your own exquisite raisins and sultanas.

courgette and cauliflower in a sweet mustard sauce. Heavenly and healthy. Whatever your favourite condiment or accompaniment, you can make it better and more varied yourself with ease.

Dried foods are so handy and delicious – good for gourmet snacks and adding to dishes. It is amazingly easy to dry apples, pears, apricots and so on, and just as easy to dry grapes and have your own exquisite raisins and sultanas. It even works with vegetables. Fruits are safer than vegetables, as stated, though onion rings and chilli peppers dry quite safely. Once dried and sealed in dark containers, many fruits and vegetables can keep for years in a cool dry place, to be eaten dried or reconstituted when required.

In many homes the air is too humid and cool and simple drying methods do not work unaided. Commercially-sold dryers work really well: ingenious gourmets can construct bigger versions or use a good airing cupboard or, with care, use their oven.

Oven drying is risky: if you cook the food it won't keep, and, worse, the flavour will be caramelised or burnt. If the temperature is low and the door kept partly open, an oven will do. By slicing the fruit or veg very thinly and laying it on stainless-steel wire trays you can pack it in while allowing for good airflow. With regular inspection and rotation of the trays, a good result can be produced.

Grapes need halving and pipping first; the black ones make raisins and the white sultanas – Muscat grapes dry to the most delicious of all. Apricots and plums dry easily, but do them coolly and slowly; the longer you store them the more like prunes they become, so enjoy them while still plump. Under-ripe gages dry best. Apple rings and pear halves are easy and a delight and dried Asian pear rings are the best of all dried fruits.

Most vegetables are barely worth the trouble as they can easily be stored in other ways. Onion rings are easy and useful, as are mushrooms. Peppers are excellent dried; chillies even more so. Then, of course, there are tomatoes.

Herbs are easiest. Gather them once the dew has dried and hang them in small bunches, pegged on lines in a dry airy place out of the full sun. Once the bunches are completely dry, seal them in paper bags in a tin or glass container. Do not pass the herbs through a sieve first to save space as this destroys some of the flavour. Store containers of dried herbs in the cool and dark.

Leathering is akin to drying and makes a confection that is hard to find in the shops yet is one of the most delicious old-fashioned gourmet treats. A fruit leather is fruit cleaned of its skins and pips, reduced to a thick paste and then dried to a piece of 'leather', which can be chewed as a snack or

Herbs are easiest. Gather them once the dew has dried and hang them in small bunches, pegged on lines in a dry airy place out of the full sun.

chopped and used in cakes and biscuits and so on. The concentration increases the acid and sugar content, making the leather keep well, and enhances the flavour. Some acidic fruits such as strawberry, blueberry and cherry are too much on their own but excellent when bulked out with apple or pear. Blackberry and blackcurrant also go well with apple.

Boil the washed chopped fruits with a little water until sievable. Heat the sieved purée gently to reduce it. Once thick, pour in thin layers on oiled trays. Dry these sheets of purée slowly in a just-warm oven; peel off as soon as handleable and dry further on wire trays in the oven. Dust the finished leather sheets with icing sugar and cornflour to stop them sticking together; pack them in jars and keep somewhere cool. Scrumptious. It even makes it possible to make, wear and eat your hat, which will indeed look and feel just like real leather – till it rains.

Freezing is a way of storing many foods that cannot be kept easily any other way without loss of flavour. Only the very best quality is worth freezing as space is limited – there is no point freezing potatoes, for example. Freezing is especially good for herbs; parsley and basil can simply be chopped and frozen as portion-controlled cubes in water or oil. Drop these directly into soups and stews, or thaw for other purposes.

Almost every fruit freezes easily, with no preparation other than a wipe clean, but defrosted turns into a flaccid replica sitting in juice. However unappealing this looks, the fruit is still tasty and packed full of flavour, making it ideal for cooking with, especially in sauces, compotes, tarts, trifles and pies.

Below Fruit leather is ecological to make, easy, long lasting and best of all, scrumptious to chew. **Opposite** Summer savory being dried in a shady shed.

Stone fruits need de-stoning before freezing or the stone will give an almond taint. Fruits may also need cutting up to remove any damage; dredge cut surfaces in sugar, which helps absorbs juice, then freeze loose on wire trays or greased dishes and pack into bags when frozen. Tough skins of tomatoes and plums can be removed if you carefully squeeze the frozen fruit under hot water – the skin will slip off easily.

Vegetables do not have the natural acidity of fruits and deteriorate rapidly once frozen unless blanched first. This involves chopping the vegetables into a uniform small size and immersing them in boiling water for a minute or three, and then rapidly chilling them again, before freezing them on wire trays and eventually packing in bags.

Blanching is extra work and effort but then you can have your own home-grown gourmet vegetables every month of the year. I reckon you cannot freeze too much asparagus. Globe artichoke hearts are wonderful for pâtés; peas, beans and sweetcorn are useful – a handful can be added to so many dishes. Tomatoes are probably best of all for least effort – just pop them in plastic bags and freeze whole. A mixture of all the soft fruits is also handy: a handful turns a simple bowl of yoghurt or breakfast cereal into a gourmet feast.

Juices concentrate the goodness and flavour of a crop and take up less space in the freezer. Using fruit and vegetable juices, the gourmet can mix and blend cocktails, smoothies, squashes and drinks beyond compare. Freezing juices with sugar or honey and then partially defrosting, mixing and re-freezing them makes water ices and sorbets so delicious there is never enough.

Most of us can squeeze some juice out of fruits like grapes and gooseberries by hand. However, not all crops can be juiced without equipment. Harder fruits and vegetables such as apples and carrots need a specialised electric juicer or food processor to express the juice. If your harvest is too large for a kitchen juicer, look at the hire or purchase of presses and crushers made for small-scale wine production.

You can use heating and/or freezing to break down fruit solids so the juice can be strained off. Then if you add sugar or salt to taste, these also increase the flavour and colour and improve the keeping qualities. It is possible to sterilise juices and bottle them, but freezing is so much easier, and safer. Commercially juices are passed through micro-fine filters or flash pasteurised – not practical in the average kitchen. Juices rapidly ferment in the warm, and still go off even in the refrigerator, though they keep for years once frozen. Freeze juices in plastic bags or bottles, never glass! Always leave an expansion space when filling, and screw the lids on only after the contents have frozen solid. Freeze juice in small containers that you can use up quickly after thawing, and be especially careful with vegetable juices.

Grapes, gooseberries and redcurrants are very easy to juice and you can still ferment the pips and skins afterwards to make thin wines. Solid fruits such as blackcurrants, apples, pears and plums can be simmered with a little water till the juice can be strained off. Fruits with really delicate flavours cannot be heated. Raspberries and strawberries are best frozen whole, then strained once they've defrosted; the juice collected is superb and while the pulp that's left over has less flavour, the fact that it's less moist than fresh fruits is useful for tarts and pies, and good for sauces.

Apples are without doubt the fruit to juice in quantity. These are often available free for the picking if you don't grow your own, and almost all apples make a tasty juice. Mixtures tend to taste better than single-variety juices, and cooking varieties are excellent to include as they have a clean, more acid taste. Apples need to be washed well and any bruises or rotten bits removed before juicing; but then the amber liquid expressed is a nectar for the gods.

Opposite Apples today, juice for tomorrow and cider for winter!
Right Fresh, home-squeezed fruit juice is the best in the world.

Preserves and conserves, jams and jellies are all more wonderful ways of catching summer's flavours and enjoying them throughout the year. If nothing else, the gourmet must learn to make these. A cupboard of newly filled jars is your treasure chest of delights that taste far better than preserves from the shop. The taste of your own raspberry or cherry jam is not just good food – it's also memories of it growing in the sun and being picked and savoured while the jam was a-making. Double value. The truest flavours are captured in freezer jams, made by blending the fresh fruit with sugar and then freezing until required. These are fantastic but go mouldy once defrosted, even if kept refrigerated, so must be consumed rapidly. So, that's not a problem then.

True preserves and jams work by preserving the fruit pieces in a sugary gel; in jellies the coarse bits are strained out. In a true preserve the fruits are barely cooked and gelled in a sugary gel of juice. A jam preserve is where the fruits are still distinguishable in bits gelled in a sugary gel of juicy pulp and sugar. (The sugar content needs to be at least half, as even if well made, these go mouldy easily.) In a conserve the fruit is reduced down a bit more and keeps more reliably. Any commercial jam tends to have more water and sugar but less real fruit. And although common garden jams can be bought in better brands of higher quality, no manufacturer I know sells yellow alpine strawberry jam or Coe's Golden Drop preserve.

Almost any fruit can be jammed or jellied, and many vegetables if you so desire. I joke not: beetroot jam is good tucker and sugar-beet jam made with lemon and ginger is amazing. Some acid or tough fruits such as rowans and aronias are palatable only if made into sweet preserves, but then their tart flavours make excellent accompaniments to cold meat and savoury dishes.

Most fruits need to have about their own weight of sugar added to them to make them set. This also effectively doubles your produce, which is handy with scarce crops. For example, a small harvest of cherries makes twice as much jam, and even more if you bulk them out with a lightly-flavoured juice of apples or whitecurrants. Other economies are bad; do not add water just to add weight. Some recipes for jellies recommend the expressed juice be mixed with the second squeezings of the fruit pulp after reheating with water. This thinner solution then requires proportionately more sugar to set and ruins the flavour of the whole batch. Good jellies are made from the strained juice and not washings: then they set clear and bright and are more worth your trouble.

Picking fruit for jellies can be less work as the odd twig or bit of leaf is not a major problem after straining, but do not let mouldy fruit or many such bits of detritus spoil the quality. On the other hand, there is a lot to be said for having pieces of fruit in

Some fruits are difficult to set, especially strawberries in a wet year, so mixing them with a better 'setter' such as apples or redcurrants helps the jams gel.

jam. Where the fruit is better suited to jam (as say with blackcurrants or half-ripe raspberries) you can make a much finer product if you carefully pick out the very finest berries and put them aside. Use the bulk of the fruit to make into jelly. The bulk is strained to produce a juice that is brought nearly to the boil when the pre-selected fruits are added back in and cooked quickly until just breaking down. Then the weighed measure of pre-warmed sugar is dissolved in. The lot is brought quickly to the boil and finished by careful pouring into heated jars fitted immediately with good lids.

The ideal method for most fruits is to simmer down the cleaned and chopped fruit with the most minimal amount of water; strain if it is for jelly; weigh and add the same weight of sugar. Then bring up to the boil, skim off any scum, pour into hot jars and put the lids on immediately. It is much quicker and easier – and results in a better product – to make several small batches rather than one large one. Large batches take much longer to cook and the flavour then degrades more or, worse, the jam caramelises and burns. And with several small batches you can vary each to give a range of gourmet treats. For example, you can make a dozen jars of plum jam, but if you peel half and add their skins to the other half, you now have two very different jams. You can go further and de-stone them first, then adding the kernels to some of the jars (take care, too many kernels could be toxic).

And, of course, there are your own personalised mixtures, such as apple and apricot or raspberry and blackcurrant. Some fruits are difficult to set, especially strawberries in a wet year, so mixing them with a better 'setter' such as apples or redcurrants helps the jams gel. The extra acidity of redcurrant juice is good for bringing out flavours of other fruits, not only in jams but in juices as well.

Liqueurs and alcoholic preserves are an intoxicating way to preserve fruits. Nothing could be simpler. Buy bottles of a good clean alcohol: traditionally brandy was used, but I find white rum to be far better for the purpose, and gin and vodka rather nasty. Empty half a bottle, then refill with your favourite fruit: strawberries, raspberries, blackcurrants, plums or sloes – or mixtures. Put in a cool place and once a week gently invert the bottle a couple of times. After a few weeks, strain off the fruit and add sugar syrup

to the extract to make a fruit liqueur. Or add the sugar syrup to the fruit and the extract together. You can also make liqueurs with edible flower petals – violet liqueur is heavenly.

Cider is a connoisseur's drink if well made and doesn't need to be rough and cloudy and knock you over – unless, of course, you like it like that. You can turn good clean apple juice into a clean bright strong cider by simply adding some already fermenting white-wine yeast and keeping it warm enough to ferment – but not too warm or the flavour is poor. This is easy, and if you don't preserve apple juice, it turns into a rough cider anyway. With extra sugar you can increase the strength from tasty to quite mind-blowing; however, the flavour becomes poorer once you pass white wine strength. With simple hygiene it is easy to make both still and sparkling ciders; for the latter you must use champagne bottles or similarly robust ones.

Grape wines are nearly as easy: for reds the grapes are simply crushed and fermented with their skins, while for whites they're pressed and fermented as juice like cider. Wine can be excellent made from gooseberries and white or redcurrants; strawberry and raspberry need an acid fruit such as gooseberry added or the wine is insipid.

Smoking foods is another way to preserve them but also to turn them into the most amazingly delicious fare. And you don't need a proper smoker: a house chimney is ideal especially if there is no fire in any adjoining chimney. Simply hang the items in the top and then smoulder a pile of good sawdust underneath for a half-day or so. The skill lies in keeping a small smoky smouldering pile and not letting it turn into a hot fire. Once smoked, most foods need to be wrapped in paper and kept cool for the smoke to permeate and mingle through. It is crucial to use clean sawdust from untreated wood, ideally from fruit trees or hardwoods. (I cut up my heavier hardwood prunings for firewood with a chainsaw. This is normally lubricated with chain oil, but I replace it with cooking oil so as not to contaminate my sawdust which I catch on the

Top Simple equipment helps press more juice more quickly.
Above Eggs – the best fruits of the garden.
Opposite top Sorry Eric, you're not needed, hens lay anyway.
Opposite below None sweeter than your own.

carpet I work on, but don't try this or blame me if it ruins your saw.) I use nut shells and successfully smoke peppers, tomatoes, sliced courgettes, garlic, onions and eggs as well as sausages, chicken and cheese.

Admittedly the meat and dairy section of the gourmet's own delicatessen is not fully stocked unless you are truly fanatical. Hens for eggs and one for the pot is simple enough, but four-legged fare is a risky business in many ways and likely to prove fatal to your garden if any escape – and they always do! Eggs are the most useful fruit in the garden and available nearly year round if you have young fowls. Hens go well in a garden as they improve the fertility, control the grass and turn many pest problems into more eggs. Marans, Black Rock and Rhode Island Reds are good egg breeds for most households. Bantam breeds lay as many slightly smaller eggs, are better mothers, but also escape more often and do more damage.

A couple of hens are no more difficult than a dog or cat and can be kept in a small shed and a run. Ideally house them in a mobile ark on a lawn and move it each day. For more birds you must make a (fox-proof) hut, also preferably mobile and arranged so the hens can have access to different garden areas at different times of year. The more you move them to different sites, the better the egg quality and production will be and the fewer the problems. By the way, you don't need a cockerel if you just want eggs; hens lay anyway.

Hens need more than fresh air. Household scraps and garden wastes are not enough, so buy in organic feed or grain plus some grit and oyster shell. To make your girls happy, make some secure perches in their hut, and give them nest boxes full of straw, and fresh water. In return they will give you eggs from late winter to late autumn, on and off, for about five years. In winter you can get eggs by always having young birds hatched early that year and by giving them extra light and hot mashes. Hens try to hide their eggs; if you let them run free they will succeed. Keeping them locked in till late morning ensures most eggs are laid in their hut where you can find them. Where foxes may be a problem, shutting them in at night is also the solution.

Chickens appreciate all sorts of foods, and neighbours may be happy to give you their scraps. They love greens, so grow extra cauliflower, broccoli, lettuce, beetroot and chard leaves – then if you eat their eggs you get much of the benefit without chomping through all that fodder.

And of course if you – or rather, if they – hatch a set of eggs, for sure half will be cocks. Then you are going to have to choose between killing and eating them or letting them do the same to each other. The first choice is neater and tastier; I starve them all day then give them bread soaked in rum; before they know it they're marinated and in the freezer!

Duck eggs are bigger than hen's and superb for cooking, but, to be fair, most people prefer the latter. Ducks are more garden-friendly than chickens as they waddle about but do not scratch. However, they destroy any water feature like a pool or pond. Ducks do not need a hut like hens but will often join them, and may use their nest boxes – or you can provide for them or go hunt. They eat a lot more grass than hens and search out slugs and snails.

Muscovy ducks are the ones for pest control, but for the table White Aylesburys are by far the best eating, and for eggs Khaki Campbells or Indian Runners are prolific layers.

Goose eggs are huge and make the most wonderful egg custards. Geese are nature's lawnmowers; they convert grass to eggs and the odd bit of grain or slice of bread is just a treat if they have enough grass. Unfortunately they also like many garden plants and even debark young trees and low branches. They must have clean water for their eyes and are fastidious cleaners, but do not need a pond to swim in, though they love it. Geese are very winter-hardy but will enjoy a small hut to nest in. Honey is another gourmet product that is a million times better home-grown. Bees do not take much

A couple of hens are no more difficult than a dog or cat and can be kept in a small shed and a run.

looking after and the upfront investment is small; often the equipment can be found second-hand, with bees, for a nominal price. They are an ideal occupation for someone who is methodical, has time on their hands, and is good at slow gentle movements. Bee care is not difficult but must be done at the right time of the right day so mostly suits retired people. Beekeepers in town often get better honey yields than those in the country and the hives are ideal situated on low flat roofs. A hive can give a couple of dozen jars of honey each year, but nothing can describe the joy of sinking your teeth into fresh warm comb, straight from the hive and heavily perfumed with the fragrance of the wax and the sweet honey oozing everywhere...

The gourmet's own restaurant

If you want gourmet foods then your kitchen must be as carefully stocked as the garden. Having grown produce with the finest fresh flavours and quality, you hardly want to spoil it by using anything that may let the side down. Be careful to eliminate regularly anything old and past its best, especially oil, which goes rancid, and spices that are stale, and be especially vigilant with frozen foods, as these linger on ridiculously long. Always buy organic or similarly high-grade items if you can find them; they give by far the best flavours and will keep fresher for longer.

And be careful how you store food; keep anything with a strong smell away from unwrapped foods that may become tainted. Do not carefully keep your onions and your apples in separate stores outside, only to have them sitting together on the kitchen vegetable rack! In your refrigerator, seal foods off from each other; it's unreasonable to expect your lettuce, melon or soft fruit to remain unsullied if next to an open curry!

It is sensible to stop using aluminium, copper and brass pots as these may taint the cooking or even be poisonous. Stainless steel or enamelled castiron are preferable and give cleaner flavours. Avoid plastic containers that smell and don't use strong-smelling cleaning products. Always rinse off detergents after washing pans; the perfumes used in these easily detract from fine flavours.

Final words of culinary advice from a gardening gourmet (from *Bob Flowerdew's Organic Bible*)

1 Never cook with less than the best. If you are using something only to save waste, give it to the hens instead or put it on the compost heap.

2 Food is far too important to spoil by using inferior ingredients; and if it can't be made with love, it is probably better just to pass it up and have some fruit to be going on with.

3 Always keep guests waiting and get their appetites whetted with delicious smells. Then serve crudités, then soup, and never, ever serve up all of a dish at once – give them small portions so they must come back for more!

4 Do not overkill the flavour. If you have fresh organic home-grown produce, you have the real flavour already. Cook delicately and sparingly, and add herbs and spices in extreme moderation, so as not to overwhelm the true glory of your food.

So, go plunder your plot and, as I said at the beginning, *bon appétit.*

If you want gourmet foods then your kitchen must be as carefully stocked as the garden.

other publications by the same loveable author

The Companion Garden (**Good Companions** in the USA) (Kyle Cathie) My first published book soon joined by the expanded investigation, **Bob Flowerdew's Complete Book of Companion Gardening** (Kyle Cathie). I explore the many ways plants interact with each other and the garden fauna and how we can use these to our great advantage.

The Organic Gardener (Hamlyn-Reed Octopus) My organic methods in detail. Full of luscious photos of my flowers and produce taken by Jerry Harpur, this came out in soft back as **Bob Flowerdew's Organic Garden** and also in French and Spanish. It was recently reworked, updated and reissued as **Go Organic** (Hamlyns).

Bob Flowerdew's Complete Fruit Book (Kyle Cathie) is an encyclopaedic testimonial to the delights that fruits and nuts offer to the gardener, the gourmet and to us all. Much travelled with editions in the USA, Canada, Australia and in Dutch, French, German, Hungarian, Polish, Greek and Czech translations.

Bob Flowerdew's Organic Bible Hard-core information on being organic. Every beautiful photograph (204) in this book was taken in my garden and these are in themselves lasting testimonials to the methods, and to the exquisite quality of organic flowers, fruits and vegetables.

the no work garden (Kyle Cathie) In this comic diatribe of vitriol poured enthusiastically on 'instant garden makeovers' and 'experts' I explain easier ways of getting more pleasure and production from your garden for much less effort or expense. Ideal for all non-expert gardeners.

Also co-author of **Gardeners' Question Time All your gardening problems solved** (Orion), **Gardeners' Question Time Plant Chooser** (Kyle Cathie), **The Complete Manual of Organic Gardening** (Headline) and **Gardeners' Question Time Techniques and Tips for Gardeners** (Kyle Cathie).

book list
All of these have interest for the enthusuastic searcher

The Physiology of Taste. J. A. Brillat-Savarin, translated from the French by M. F. K. Fisher. Pub. Alfred A. Knopf, 1972. ISBN 0-394-47343-4.
Gardening for Maximum Nutrition. Jerry Minnich. Pub. Rodale, 1983. ISBN 0-87857-475-1.
Quality of Horticultural Products. V. D. Arthey. Pub. Butterworths, 1975. ISBN 0 408 70645 7.

Nutritional Values in Crops and Plants. Werner Schuphan. Pub. Museum Press, 1965.
The Good Fruit Guide. L. D. Hills. Pub. HDRA, regular editions. ISBN 0 905 343 123.
The Veg. Finder. Ed J. Cherfas. Pub. HDRA, regular editions, ISBN 0-905 343-19-0.
Fruit, Berry and Nut Inventory. Pub. Seed Saver Pub, 1993. regular editions, ISBN 0-882424-51-4.
The Oxford Book of Food Plants. Pub. Peerage Books, 1969. ISBN 1 85052 017 8.
Roy Gender's Scented Flora of the World. Pub. Granada, 1977. ISBN 0 583 12891.
Food for Free. Richard Mabey. Pub. Fontana/Collins, 1972/75.
Treatise on Gardening. William Cobbett, 1821.
The Vegetable Garden. Vilmorin-Andrieux. Pub. John Murray, 1885.
Tropical Planting and Gardening. Pub. Macmillan, 1949.
Plant Physiological Disorders. Pub. ADAS, HMSO, 1985.
The Diagnosis of Mineral Deficiencies in Plants. HMSO, 1943. **Soil Conditions and Plant Growth**. Sir John Russell. Pub. Longmans. regular editions.
Science and Fruit. Long Ashton Research Station. Pub. University of Bristol, 1953.
Organic Plant Protection. Ed. R.B.Yepsen. Pub. Rodale. ISBN 0 87857 110 8.
Food Adulteration, London Food Commission. Pub. Unwin, 1988. ISBN 004 440212 0.

some interesting addresses and sources
Organisations with facilities for visitors are marked *

The Henry Doubleday Research Association. National Centre for Organic Gardening, Ryton Gardens,* Ryton on Dunsmore, Coventry CV8 3LG, and at Yalding*, Benover Road, Kent, ME18 6EX. Also for heritage seeds: **Association Kokopelli,** www.kokopelli.asso.fr
Brogdale Horticultural Trust. Brogdale Farm, Faversham, Kent, ME13 8XZ (for heritage fruits).
The Soil Association. 86/88 Colston Street. Bristol, Avon BS1 5BB. At same address: British Organic Farmers. Organic Growers Association. Book Shop.*
The Royal Horticultural Society. Vincent Square, London. SW1P 2PE and at Wisley* , Woking, Surrey. GU23 6QB
The Centre for Alternative Technology. The Quarry, Machynlleth, Powys.*
The Northern Horticultural Society. Harlow Car Gardens, Crag Lane, Otley Road, Harrogate, W. Yorks.*
The Bio-Dynamic Agricultural Association. Woodman Lane, Clent, Stourbridge, West Midlands DY9 9PX.
Permaculture Association. 4 Red Lake, Dartington, Totnes, Devon. TQ9 6HF

photographic acknowledgements

All photography by Pete Cassidy except:

AL – Andrew Lawson
GPL – Garden Picture Library
PH – Photos Horticultural
JG – John Glover
BF – Bob Flowerdew
GH – Geoff Hayes
HS – Holt Studio

36 AL
39 top, GPL; bottom, PH
41 both AL
42 PH
43 PH
50 BF
51 BF
55 top left, PH
58 all PH
60 top left JG; top centre PH; centre left, BF; centre right, JG; bottom left, PH; bottom right, PH
62 top right, BF; bottom, PH
64 BF
65 top and bottom left, BF
69 left and bottom right, PH
70 PH
74 AL
77 top centre and bottom right, GPL; bottom left, PH
78 bottom left, PH; top right PH; bottom right JG
80 top centre,top right, left centre, centre, bottom left JG; bottom centre, PH
83 top right, PH; bottom right AL
84 PH
85 bottom left, PH; bottom right, AL
88 top left, JG; top right, AL
89 top left, HS; bottom right, GPL
90 top left and bottom right, AL
91 top left, HS; bottom right, AL
92 top and bottom right, HS
93 left and right, GPL; middle left and middle right, HS
96 BF
98 JG
99 bottom left, BF; bottom right, PH
100 top left, JG; bottom right, PH
101 JG
106 AL

107 PH
108 BF
109 top and middle right, GPL
110 top left and right, PH; bottom right, AL
114 top left and bottom right, PH
115 top left AL; middle left, Michelle Garrett; middle right, PH; right, GH
124 top right, PH; bottom right, AL
125 top and bottom left, HS; middle left, PH; middle right, BF, right, AL
129 bottom left, JG; top right, PH
131 top centre and right, PH
136 left bottom and top centre, GH; top right, JG
137 top left, JG; top centre, GH; bottom right, AL
138 left, AL; left and right centre, GH; right, AL
139 left centre, top and bottom right centre, GH
140 left, GPL, left and right centre, GH; right, HS
141 left, GPL; centre, GH; right, HS
143 PH
144 left, PH; right, HS
145 left, AL; left and right centre, PH
146 left, AL; right, GH
147 left, GPL; left centre, HS; top right centre and right, PH; bottom right centre, BF
148 left. PH; left centre, HS; right centre, Sally Maltby; right, JG
149 top centre, PH; bottom left and right, GPL
150 centre, GH; right, HS
151 left and centre, HS; right, GH
152 bottom left and top centre, JG
154 bottom left, PH; top centre and right, HS
155 bottom left, PH; bottom right, GPL
157 JG
158 GH
159 top left and bottom right, PH; top right, centre right and bottom left, AL; centre left, JG
160 top left, top right, bottom left and bottom centre, JG; top centre, centre and right centre, AL; left centre and bottom right, PH
161 top, PH; bottom left, JG; bottom right, AL
163 top left, AL; top right and bottom left, JG; bottom right, PH
165 top left and top centre, AL; top right, bottom left and bottom right, JG; bottom centre, Torie Chugg at AL
166 PH
167 top, PH; bottom, AL
168 AL
169 AL

index